First published 2004
by Merrell Publishers Limited

Head office
42 Southwark Street
London SE1 1UN

New York office
49 West 24th Street, 8th floor
New York, NY 10010

www.merrellpublishers.com

Publisher Hugh Merrell
Editorial Director Julian Honer
US Director Joan Brookbank
Sales and Marketing Director Emilie Amos
Sales and Marketing Executive Emily Sanders
Managing Editor Anthea Snow
Editor Sam Wythe
Design Manager Nicola Bailey
Production Manager Michelle Draycott
Design and Production Assistant Matt Packer

Text © Neil Parkyn 2004
Design and layout © Merrell Publishers Limited 2004
Photographs © the copyright holders; see opposite

British Library Cataloguing-in-Publication Data:
Parkyn, Neil, 1943–
SuperStructures : the world's greatest modern structures
1.Architecture, Modern – 20th century 2.Buildings 3.Civil engineering
4.Structural engineering 5.Curiosities and wonders
I.Title
724.6

A catalog record for this book is available from the Library of Congress

ISBN 1 85894 238 1

Produced by Merrell Publishers Limited
Designer Helen Taylor
Project Manager Iona Baird
Editor Kirsty Seymour-Ure
Picture Researchers Mariana Sonnenberg, Helen Stallion, Jo Walton
Indexer Vicki Robinson

Printed and bound in China

FRONT COVER: MAIN PICTURE Pont de Normandie; DETAILS, FROM TOP Hubble Space Telescope; Dutch Sea Barrier; Solar Furnace; Eden Project.

FRONT FLAP: DETAILS, FROM TOP Alamillo Bridge; Tidal Surge Barrier; Channel Tunnel; Munich Olympic Stadium.

BACK COVER: DETAILS, FROM TOP Oriente Station; Thames Barrier; NASA Sixteen Foot Transonic Wind Tunnel; Telstra Stadium.

PAGES 4–5: Falkirk Wheel

PAGE 15: Yokohama Port Terminal

PAGE 101: Solar Furnace

PAGE 137: Vehicle Assembly Building

PAGE 159: Top Thrill Dragster

ACKNOWLEDGEMENTS

Thanks to all those engineers, architects, friends and colleagues who have helped to shape this book. They were so supportive, generous with their advice and enthusiastic about the project.

Thanks also to the team at Merrell Publishers – professional, patient and good-humoured throughout – especially Iona, Nicola, Julian and Matt. And to my family, Carol, Adam and Rosie, for living with the book. Without you all there would be no SuperStructures.
Neil Parkyn

PICTURE CREDITS

Jacket front (top): NASA; 4–5: View Pictures; 8–9t: Alison Wright/Corbis; c: Roger Ressmeyer/Corbis; b: Courtesy HOK Sport + Venue + Event; 10–11t: Corbis; c: Hulton Deutsch Collection/Corbis; 10b: Corbis Hulton Archive; 11b: Bettman/Corbis; 12–13t: Arup; b: Frank O. Gehry and Partners; 12c: Corbis/Bettman; 13c: Foreign Office Architects; 15: Foreign Office Architects; 16t: Hashimoto Noboru/Corbis Sygma; b: Angelo Hornak/Corbis; 17t: Dallas and John Heaton/Corbis; b: Patrick Robert/Corbis Sygma; 18t: Dennis Gilbert/View Pictures; 19t: Peter Cook/View Pictures; 18–19: Nicholas Grimshaw & Partners; 20–23 and jacket back (top): Santiago Calatrava SA; 24–27: GMP Architects; 28: Peter Durant/Arcblue.com; 29t: Hopkins Architects; b: Dennis Gilbert/View Pictures; 30t: Foster and Partners; b: Nigel Young/Foster and Partners; 31: Nigel Young/Foster and Partners; 32–33: View Pictures; 34l: China Photo/Reuters; r: Associated Press; 35: China Photo/Reuters; 36–37t: David Gallagher; 37b: Ezra Stoller/Esto; 38–39: Nathan Willock/View Pictures; 40–41: Jay Langlois/Experience Thread; 42–43: Dennis Gilbert/View Pictures; 43t: Foster and Partners; 44–45: Dennis Gilbert/View Pictures; 46–49: Richard Rogers Partnership; 50t: Hulton Archive; b: Dennis Wheatley/Architectural Association Picture Library; 51: Hulton Archive; 52–53: Palladium Photodesign; 54–55: Freek Van Arkel; 56–60: Foreign Office Architects; 60–62: Hufton & Crow/View Pictures; 63t: RMJM; 63b: Hufton & Crow/View Pictures; 64–67 and jacket flap (second from bottom): QA Photos; 68: Norwegian Public Roads Administration/Olav Handeland; 69: Camera Press/Scanpix; 70tl/tc: Teeside Archives; b: Freefoto.com/Ian Britton; 71: NPS Visual Communications; 72b: Yann Arthus-Bertrand/Corbis; 72t/73: Rex Features/Roger Viollet; 74: E.O. Hoppe/Corbis; 75: Paul A. Souders/Corbis; 76t/76b/77r: Image Archive ETH-Bibliothek, Zurich; 77l: Architectural Association Photo library; 78: Imperial War Museum; 79: Hulton Archive; 80l: Image Archive ETH-Bibliothek, Zurich; 80r: Construction Photography; 81: Image Archive ETH-Bibliothek, Zurich; 82–83: View Pictures; 84: Yann Arthus-Bertrand/Corbis; 85tl: Bruno de Hogues/Corbis Sygma; tr: Science Video Service/Corbis Sygma; b: Yves Forestier/Corbis Sygma; 86–87 and jacket front (main image): Massimo Mostrorillo/Corbis; 88–89 and jacket flap (top): Freek van Arkel; 90–93: ARUP; 94t: Foster and Partners; 94c: Nigel Young/Foster Visualisation; 95: Nigel Young/Foster Visualisation; 96t: Photos12; 97r: Reproduced with kind permission of BAE systems plc; cl/bl: Hulton Deutsch Collection/Corbis; 98t: Foster and Partners; 98b: Foster and Partners/Ben Johnson; 99: Foster and Partners/Xavier Basianas; 101: Corbis; 102t: Bettmann/Corbis; b: Kevin Schafer/Corbis; 103t: Gabriel Moulin/Corbis; b: Otto Rogge/Corbis; 104–105: Library of Congress Prints & Photographs Division Washington, DC; 105–106: Tennessee Valley Authority; 108: Coyne et Bellier; 109: La Médiatheque EDF/Pierre Berenger; 110–111: Lloyd Cluff/Corbis; 110tr: Bettman/Corbis; tl: Hulton Deutsch Collection/Corbis; 112–113: Carol and Ann Purcell/Corbis; 113tr: Adam Woolfit/Corbis; 114t: Associated Press; b: Reuters/Corbis; 115: Dung Vo Trung/Corbis Sygma; 116–117: Reuters/Corbis; 116br: Keren Su/Corbis; 118–119: Verbund 1999; 120/121t: Paul Almasy/Corbis;121b and jacket front (second from bottom): Adam Woofit/Corbis; 122–123: Consorzio Venezia Nuova; 124–125: Corbis; 124t/125r: Patrick Ward/Corbis; 126–127 and jacket front (second from top): Corbis; 128tr: London Aerial Photo Library/Corbis; 129: Tim Hawkins/Eye Ubiquitous/Corbis; 130–131 and jacket back (second from top): Macduff Everton/Corbis; 132–133 and jacket flap (second from top): Environmental Agency; 134t: Michael St. Maur Sheil/Corbis; 134c/b: Imperial War Museum; 135: Corbis; 137: NASA; 138–139: NASA; 140tr: London Aerial Photo Library/Corbis; 140tl: Annie Griffiths Belt/Corbis; 141–142: Jonathan Blair/Corbis; 143: Robert Estall/Corbis; 144–145: Isaac Newton Group of Telescopes; 146–149: NASA; 152tl/153t: Ecliptique/Laurent Thion; 150–151 and jacket back (second from bottom): NASA; 153b: 2002©Inter Atlas – Cities Revealed; 152tr: ONERA Aerospace Research; 154–155: CERN; 156–157: NASA; 159: Courtesy of Cedar Point Resort; 160–161: Corbis; 162–163: Brigitte Kernmeyer; 164–165: Courtesy of Cedar Point Resort; 166: Peter Cook/View Pictures; 167 and jacket front (bottom): Jason Hawkes/Corbis; 168: Dennis Gilbert/View Pictures; 168t: Andrew Southall Photography; b: Grimshaw Architects; 170tl: Buro Happold; 170tr: Dennis Gilbert/View Pictures; 170b: Weald and Downland Open Air Museum; 171: Buro Happold; 172–173: Index; 174–177 and jacket flap (bottom): View Pictures; 178–179 and jacket back (bottom): Courtesy HOK Sport + Venue + Event; 180–181: Foster Visualisation; 182–183: NASA; 184l: EnviroMission Ltd; 184–185t: Arup; r: T.R Hamzah & Yeang Sdn. Bhd.; 186–187t: The Palm, Dubai; c: Santiago Calatrava SA; b: European Southern Observatory.

LIST OF ADVISORS

Malcolm Buchanan, Chairman, Colin Buchanan & Partners; Nick Derbyshire, Managing Director, Nick Derbyshire Architects; George Ferguson, President, RIBA; John Glover, Transport Consultant; Richard Haryout, Director, Arup; Anthony Hunt, former Chairman, Anthony Hunt Associates; Farahmand Jahanpour, Director, Special Structures Division, Building Design Partnership; Bert McClure, architect and course director, Ecole des Ponts et Chausées, Paris; Prof. Lawrence Nield, Director, Bligh Voller Nield; Rod Rhys-Jones, former Director of Development, Imperial College, London; Barry Shaw, Director, Kent Architecture Centre; David Walton, former Managing Director, Llewelyn-Davies Planning; Jane Wernick, Managing Director, Jane Wernick Associates, Engineers; Mark Whitby, Chairman, Whitby & Bird Engineers; Prof. Ken Yeang, Director, T.R Hamzah & Yeang; John Zukowsky, John H. Bryan Curator of Architecture, Art Institute of Chicago.

Neil Parkyn

SuperStructures

The World's Greatest Modern Structures

MERRELL
LONDON • NEW YORK

Contents

Introduction

A world without structures is difficult to contemplate, since the activities of our daily lives are underpinned by the work of the structural engineer. Whenever we travel, attend a sports event or simply switch on a light, for example, we are relying on infrastructures and services that we take for granted and that we assume will do their jobs well. Occasionally we might be struck by the power and elegance of a particular structure – an airport terminal, perhaps, appreciated when we pass through it as a space of unusual beauty or calm – but much else of equal merit, such as many of the greatest dams or river bridges, remains relatively obscure – hence the guiding principle of this book.

In presenting this selection of superstructures we celebrate not only the work of designers across the world, but also the way in which such projects exemplify the art and the science of engineering. While any selection of projects from the many thousands completed during the twentieth and twenty-first centuries is bound to appear almost arbitrary, those included here all have qualities that merit being described with superlatives. They have proved themselves to be special in a number of ways – by their size and

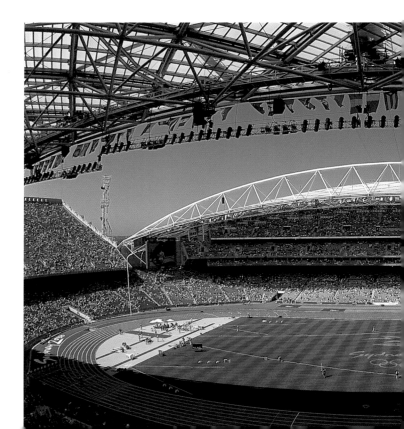

scale, by the technical innovations they embody, by the ingenuity and boldness of their construction, or by the fact that they represent the finest work of an important designer. These criteria are broad enough to include acknowledged masterpieces, such as the dams built by the Tennessee Valley Authority (TVA) in the 1930s, alongside temporary structures, such as the Mulberry harbours and Bailey bridges of World War II, and the more recent Telstra Stadium in Sydney.

There are, of course, notable omissions. For example, among the bridges that could be classified as superstructures, suspension bridges are not represented here, although clearly there are a number of significant designs with a claim for inclusion. San Francisco's Golden Gate, the Humber, Severn and Forth road bridges in Britain, Istanbul's Bosphorus Bridge and Japan's record-breaking Akashi Kaikyo Bridge, among many others, have advanced the genre and could have been included in our review. That they have not been included does not diminish their importance.

A further excluded category is that of high-rise towers. These are, of course, significant

TOP The traditional architecture of Istanbul forms the backdrop to the elegant span of the Bosphorus Bridge, one of a famous family of long-span suspension bridges.

CENTRE An undisputed icon of twentieth-century engineering, San Francisco's Golden Gate Bridge combines daring in the construction process – its piers are founded in the treacherous currents of the bay – with great aesthetic refinement, as seen in the design of the piers themselves.

BOTTOM Built for the 2000 Olympic Games held in Sydney, the Telstra Stadium exemplifies the ongoing evolution of the giant stadium that can host a variety of events and provide all-weather protection for spectators.

structures, having evolved into a unique genus all their own (they even boast an exclusive organization, the World Federation of Great Towers); but this book aims to celebrate notable structures rather than tall buildings, which are discussed at length elsewhere. Moreover, the most significant era for the evolution of the tower may well lie ahead (see pages 185–87).

Continuity and Progress

Although the exhibits before them offered various glimpses of the future, visitors to the many world's fairs during the nineteenth century would probably have assumed that the typology of public buildings with which they were familiar – railway termini, great exhibition and assembly halls, galleries and so on – would remain constant. In many respects they would have been right, since the century that followed – in which the structures presented in this book were developed – saw a direct line of evolution in such public buildings. In the case of railway stations in London, where there is a particularly strong sense of continuity between, for example, the grand sweep of glazed vaults above the platforms of Isambard Kingdom Brunel's Paddington station and those of the new Waterloo International Terminal (pages 18–19) by architect Nicholas Grimshaw and engineer Tony Hunt, no less stunning a work. There is a parallel, too, with Berlin's new Lehrter Station (pages 24–27) by architects Von Gerkan, Marg & Partner and engineer Jörg Schlaich, in which the roof over the platforms for the intercontinental express trains promises to achieve a comparable elegance and transparency.

Pushing the Limits

Such parallels aside, it takes only a brief review of one field of design – that of bridges – to appreciate that structural engineers in the twentieth century were able to push the distances spanned and the efficiency with which materials were used to new limits while creating structures of great refinement. The first advances were made in the design of concrete bridge structures by such pioneers as the French

TOP Uncluttered by ornament, the Galerie des Machines (Paris, 1889) provided a powerful demonstration of the way in which a steel structure could create a huge enclosure.

CENTRE The great vaults of Isambard Kingdom Brunel's Paddington station in London (1854) have inspired the designers of modern stations to emulate their boldness and clarity.

BOTTOM LEFT With its ingenious 'kit of parts' to throw across such obstacles as rivers, the Bailey bridge system speeded the Allies' advance across Europe during World War II.

BOTTOM RIGHT Research and experimentation led by Frei Otto in Germany heralded a whole generation of lightweight tensile structures able to provide shelter on the largest scale.

designer–contractor Eugène Freyssinet and the Swiss engineer Robert Maillart; the latter built a series of bridges during the 1920s and 1930s that are regarded as designs of lasting significance (pages 76–77).

Bridges that capture attention tend to be singular in form and dramatic in profile. The Pont de Normandie (pages 84–87), for instance, is a fine example of a long-span, cable-stayed bridge, but it also serves as a gateway and a landmark, much as does the central High Bridge of the Øresund Link (Øresundsbron) between Denmark and Sweden (pages 90–93). In such cases, the design transcends functionality, construction feasibility and the efficient use of materials to result in structures of elegance, balance and great presence.

New Forms, New Possibilities

Advances in structural engineering have usually been made through innovations in design, use of materials and construction techniques, with each significant project leapfrogging well-established typologies to present new possibilities. Yet the history of twentieth-century structures is also marked by the introduction of families of forms for which there were no precedents in the previous century. Tensile structures, taking the form of tent-like nets, membranes and other space-enclosure frameworks, were pioneered in the early 1960s by the Institute for Lightweight Structures in Stuttgart, led by Frei Otto. This form of structure offered the promise of creating a shelter that could extend over a whole 'landscape', a notable example being that of the 1972 Munich Olympic Games (pages 174–77).

A second significant group of space-enclosing structures has flowed from the work of American inventor Richard Buckminster Fuller. His geodesic domes, capable of enveloping hitherto unprecedented volumes, are epitomized by the one built in 1958 to shelter the workshops of the Union Tank Car Company in Baton Rouge, Louisiana. At 116 m (375 ft.) clear span, this was a record-holder of its day. Built forty years later, a sequence of interlocking geodesic domes, or 'biomes', encloses the plant habitats of the Eden

Project (pages 166–69) in south-west England.

The third, well-established strand of innovation has centred on shell structures, especially those with extremely thin shells that are very strong and capable of forming flowing but stable shapes, thereby offering attractive sculptural possibilities while making efficient use of material. Pioneered in concrete by Eduardo Torroja, Félix Candela and others, shells have become emblematic forms of the twentieth century.

From Cardboard to Computers

In reviewing the story of twentieth- and twenty-first-century engineering, it is interesting to speculate to what extent advances in computing have shaped what it is possible to build. Certainly the construction of the Sydney Opera House could not have been achieved without computing, but the real breakthrough in what initially appeared to be an unbuildable design occurred when Arup, the project's structural engineers, realized that all of the vaults could be shaped as segments of the same sphere, thus simplifying the calculations at one stroke. Neither did the limits of computing power prevent American architect Eero Saarinen and his team from devising the complex vault structure and roof form of his TWA Flight Center at John F. Kennedy Airport, New York (pages 36–39) through the use of cardboard models, or the engineers from teasing out the deformations in the cable-net roofs for the 1972 Munich Olympics by building 1:125 scale models and photographing the results. In all cases, the concept was developed without the use of the computer. Yet other fields of structural design, such as that of cable-stayed bridges, have advanced rapidly with computing support.

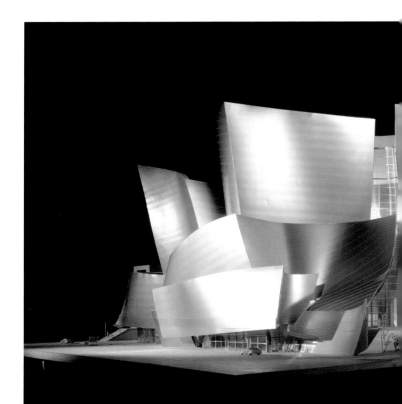

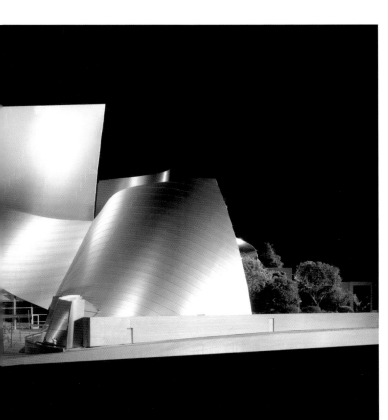

About the Book

Our presentation of superstructures groups them into four broad categories according to their function:

Communications

Structures that provide for the movement of people and goods – the railway stations, airports, bridges, tunnels, ports and waterways that are the components of transport networks, and including electronic telecommunications. Many of these were developed to allow the crossing of natural barriers and obstacles.

Energy and Natural Forces

Structures built to control natural forces or to generate power.

Discovery and Exploration

Structures built as platforms for equipment that advances scientific knowledge, notably telescopes on earth and in space, or that tests designs, such as wind tunnels.

Leisure

Structures built as venues for public events or as visitor destinations.

What these superstructures have in common is that they are the outcome of teamwork and creative collaboration in both their design and their construction. Although all design teams need leadership and direction to move forward, it is often the chance remark or the sketch on an envelope that actually prompts the next break-through, whether in the overall construction strategy for a great bridge or in the detailing of a structural frame. It is this spirit of creative interplay that has led to the best of these superstructures. They satisfy because they are designs that are fully resolved and that appear inevitable.

Observation, judgement and imagination mark the work of those who designed these superstructures and those who built them. There is perhaps no better description of the design process than the words of Sir Ove Arup, a great engineer of singular humanity, who wrote: "Engineering is a creative activity involving imagination, intuition and deliberate choice."

TOP Structural engineering of the highest order was needed to translate the architect's competition-winning sketches into the soaring vaults of the Sydney Opera House (1973).

CENTRE LEFT Often with the simplest of means, Félix Candela designed and built a series of remarkable thin shell structures in concrete that were economical, robust and elegant.

CENTRE RIGHT In the Yokohama Ferry Terminal, a whole 'landscape' of passenger concourses and external terraces has been created with a structure of folded steel beams.

BOTTOM The realization of the dynamic forms of Frank O. Gehry & Partners' Walt Disney Concert Hall in Los Angeles (1998–2003) required computer programs that were first developed for the aerospace industry.

14 Communications

Despite the growth of electronic traffic along the information superhighway, the physical aspect of communication remains what it always has been: a matter of moving people and goods between destinations in safety and at an acceptable cost. In this respect the process of present-day travel and the structures needed to make it possible are not so different in purpose or form from those that have evolved through recent history. The great railway networks built across Europe in the nineteenth century have a parallel in their modern motorway equivalents; concourses built to receive passengers from ocean liners have much in common with the public spaces in an international airport. Underlying these structures, of whatever pedigree, is a celebration of travel: the point of departure, the route travelled and the destination – an enthusiasm for movement and change that has inspired the exceptional examples presented here.

As points of arrival and departure, railway stations have always held an important place as gateways to the life of a city. Today this role has been extended, with the station frequently becoming a catalyst for urban regeneration, as witness Berlin's new Lehrter Station at the crux of intercontinental routes (pages 24–27), or the Oriente Station in Lisbon (pages 20–23), which unites previously fragmented districts. Many recent stations have assumed the confidence and panache that shaped those built a century earlier. Great glazed platform halls benefit from the 'airline' approach of those running the high-speed trains

passing through them, and lead on to generous concourses for ease of interchange to new metro lines that further reinforce the notion of quality.

A traveller's well-being is even more important an issue in airport design, where sheer size and the logistics of passenger handling can be tamed only by a design that smooths and calms his or her passage to the departure gate. From the 1960s onwards, various configurations of passenger concourse, piers and satellites were built at new international airports worldwide. Very few achieved the clarity, calm and, above all, the expectation of flying as a pleasurable experience that informed the design of London's Stansted Airport and the best of Scandinavian terminals. The most recent – and the largest – airports built or currently on site promise to re-create these qualities. The passenger areas of Japan's

Kansai Airport, Hong Kong International Airport at Chek Lap Kok (pages 42–45) and Madrid's New Area Terminal (pages 46–49) are each unified by grand, oversailing roofs composed of repeated vaults, with views outside and daylight used to calm and orient travellers. Supporting these roofs are elegant structures that are allowed pride of place.

Communications would be unthinkable without bridges to span inconvenient obstacles and to create essential links. Bridge design has continued to prove as fertile a field for the ingenuity of the structural engineer and constructor as it did in the era of the Brooklyn Bridge, New York (1869–83), or the Forth Bridge, Scotland (1890); advances are being made not only in materials and construction techniques but also in methods of calculation. Yet some of the most remarkable bridges ever designed, such as those of the Swiss engineer Robert Maillart, were the products of intuition and observation, supported by calculation.

Great bridges of distinctive profile have always carried the inherent potential to become landmarks or icons, especially as crossings. This fact has not been lost on client authorities seeking to create either a gateway into a region, as exemplified by the Pont de Normandie (pages 84–87), or a highly visible link to a new regeneration area, as formed by Rotterdam's Erasmus Bridge (pages 88–89), or by Seville's Alamillo Bridge (pages 82–83), which served as access to that city's Expo site. Elsewhere, the challenge for the bridge designer has been to devise a form that can complement or even enhance the existing landscape of a valley. Successful examples include the work of Christian Menn in Switzerland, and the Millau Viaduct that will carry the A75 Motorway across the River Tarn in France (pages 94–95).

Invisible communications too have created their own, highly visible family of superstructures. Telecommunications towers are a familiar urban landmark, often the objects of curiosity and even affection. Whether boasting the record-breaking height of Toronto's 'skypricking' CN Tower or the filigree structure of Barcelona's Torre de Collserola (pages 98–99), these towers are remarkable demonstrations of structural engineering, besides offering visitors the chance to gaze down on cities or countryside from their observation decks or sky lobbies.

Because they are highly visible, in public service and in daily use, these structures that serve communications have assumed an importance in our lives that makes the best of them artefacts to be appreciated and savoured. Whether a passenger passing through the Channel Tunnel (pages 64–67) on a Eurostar train to Paris, a driver crossing the Øresund Link between Sweden and Denmark (pages 90–93), or a commuter riding the escalator up from the grand concourse at London's Canary Wharf (pages 28–31), a traveller is in the realm of great structures.

Key Facts

Architects: Nicholas Grimshaw & Partners

Engineers: Anthony Hunt Associates

Internal floor area: 60,000 m² (645,000 sq. ft.)

Length of terminal: 400 m (1320 ft.)

Span of terminal: 35–50 m (115–165 ft.)

Design life: 125 years

Cost: UK£130,000,000

Anthony Hunt

One of the most respected and best-loved personalities among British structural engineers, Tony Hunt (born 1932) began his career in the office of Felix Samuely, gaining experience in designing light steel-framed structures. His subsequent career flourished, owing to a highly imaginative and creative approach to design, which produced structures in a variety of materials that impress by their sinewy elegance.

The international reputation of Anthony Hunt Associates, the practice he founded in 1962, is based on fruitful relationships with such leading architects as Norman Foster, Richard Rogers and Michael Hopkins on landmark buildings including the Sainsbury Centre for the Visual Arts, Norwich, England (1990), the Inmos Plant, Newport, Wales (1982), and the Schlumberger Research Building, Cambridge, England (1985).

Recent works of the practice, such as the Waterloo International Terminal and the Eden Project, both with Nicholas Grimshaw & Partners as architects, continue to demonstrate the ability of Hunt and his colleagues to devise structures of great elegance and lightness that also celebrate their means of construction down to the smallest detail.

Waterloo International Terminal
London, England, 1989–93

ABOVE The roof-glazing panels are arranged in a series of overlapping layers for simplicity of construction and to accommodate movement.

Those old rivals for our travel patronage, airlines and railways, are becoming more evenly matched. While airports seemingly become ever more mundane in character, recent railway terminals re-create something of the sense of occasion historically associated with air travel, or indeed with the great railway stations of Europe a century ago. With the advent of branded high-speed trains, such as the Thalys network and Eurostar linking European capitals, the rail terminal has become an important means of promoting these new services.

Successful solutions to international rail terminal design might seem to call for large, unconstrained sites, yet with ingenuity, experience and a great deal of development work, impressive results have been achieved even where there are adverse external factors. Such is the case with London's Waterloo International Terminal, built on a tapering site cleared of the old Waterloo–Windsor lines and just wide enough to accommodate the five new tracks that take

the Eurostar services through the Channel Tunnel to France, and make Waterloo Britain's literal gateway to Europe. On the east side lie the pre-existing platforms, serving suburban electric rail services, and not far below the building are located the tunnels of the London Underground. In this context vertical layering of the building was necessary to achieve a streamlined movement of international passengers and the precise alignment of the building, at 400 m (1320 ft.) twice the length of the Eurostar trains, to encompass the curving tracks.

The vertical layering of the terminal begins at its base with a concrete box that straddles the Underground tracks and provides on-site parking. This is topped by a double-height concrete viaduct supporting the Eurostar tracks and housing the passenger concourse and other facilities. For clarity of orientation, departures and arrivals have each been allocated their own levels. Frequent links between levels are essential to facilitate the boarding

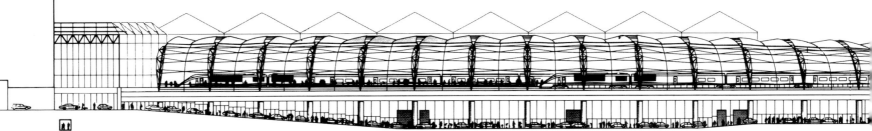

of what are among the longest passenger trains in the world.

Although it accounted for a mere tenth of the total cost, the glazed roof is the most memorable element of the terminal and the most direct homage to Victorian engineering achievements. The roof had to accommodate the sinuous plan of the terminal, which narrows from 50 m (165 ft.) in width at the concourse end to 35 m (115 ft.) over the Eurostar platforms, and had to be higher on its western side to provide headroom for trains on a single track on this side. The optimal structural solution proved to be thirty-seven prismatic, three-pinned bow-string arches, varying in span, and with the position of the centre pin-joints moving across to accommodate the required changes in roof height from west to east. At each pin-joint the roof structure changes from an external inverted truss with a pair of tie rods on its outer face to an internal bow-string truss with a single lower tie rod. In effect, these trusses are a direct expression of the

stress diagram for the roof structure and are designed to allow movement in their supports.

Cladding design for this complex, undulating roof was dramatically simplified by the bold decision to adopt a loose-fit approach to the 2500 panels of glass that form the western face of the terminal roof and that provide passengers with views out towards Westminster and passers-by with a glimpse of the 400-tonne Eurostar trains. Rather than opting for a cladding system that required each panel of glass to be custom-cut to size, the engineers developed a limited range of shapes and sizes. The panels were then overlapped to fit the changing roof profile and weatherproofed with concertina-shaped neoprene gaskets to produce a glittering carapace.

At Waterloo International the design team has succeeded in creating a contemporary version of the grand historical station, where the sense of departure or arrival is further heightened by the luminosity and presence of the remarkable roof.

ABOVE The roof structure consists of thirty-seven prismatic, three-pinned bow-string arches, which vary in span along the length of the curving platforms.

BELOW Long elevation from the south, showing how the length of the platform hall is twice that of the Eurostar trains.

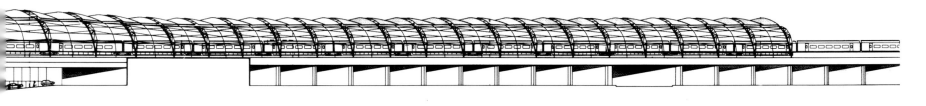

Key Facts

Architect/Engineer: Santiago Calatrava

Terminal building area: 175,000 m² (1,885,000 sq. ft.)

Length of terminal: 313 m (1033 ft.)

Width of terminal: 68 m (223 ft.)

Trains per day: 320

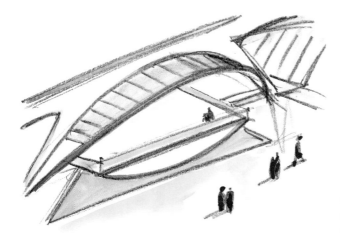

LEFT Concept sketch
showing the main entry
level under its grand arch.

Santiago Calatrava

Most notably among his generation, the Spanish architect-engineer Santiago Calatrava (born 1951) has broken away from narrow definitions of building-type to create works that have strong echoes of natural, living forms, an approach that has attracted controversy because it does not fit neatly within the discipline of either architecture or engineering. He first demonstrated his highly personal approach to expressive structure in the complex sectional planning of Zurich's Stadelhofen Railway Station (1984), and later in a series of bridges in Spain, including Seville's Alamillo Bridge (1992).

Calatrava and his team have designed a large portfolio of structures that fully exploit the dynamic possibilities of steel and concrete, many of which enclose grand public spaces, such as the Lyon–Satolas TGV Station, France (1989), Bilbao's Sondica Airport, Spain (1999) and the City of Science/Palace of the Arts Complex for his native Valencia (2001). Besides these stand-alone complexes, he has also designed interventions in the existing urban fabric, such as his gallery within a commercial centre in Toronto, Canada (1993), in which the steel roof structures resemble an avenue of giant trees.

Oriente Station
Lisbon, Portugal, 1993–98

As points of change and departure, new railway termini, when conceived on a grand scale and cleverly located, have often served as catalysts for urban regeneration. Such was the intention behind Lisbon's newest station. Though originally conceived to transport visitors to Expo '98, it was designed also with an eye to its future role as the main terminal of the city, as urban expansion is channelled to the east bank of the Tagus River. The 60-hectare (148-acre) site chosen for Expo '98 was located on former industrial wasteland between railway tracks and the river embankment in Lisbon's Olivais district, some 5 km (3.1 miles) north-east of the city centre. Its western edge was defined by a 9 m (30 ft.) high railway embankment, which formed historically the division between industrial and residential areas. From its conception as an entry in an international design competition held in 1993, Oriente Station was intended to play a central role in the restructuring and upgrading of this whole urban district. As part of the infrastructure supporting Expo '98, the site is linked to the other bank of the Tagus by the striking Vasco da Gama Bridge, one of the longest bridges in Europe.

Oriente Station was always intended to be a major transport hub, allowing passengers easy interchange between modes of transport. It is used largely by rail passengers, with 75,000 of them per day (more than twenty-five million per year and rising) passing through the station to board the more than 300 suburban, regional and international services, but it is also served by the city's metro, tram and bus networks, and taxis. Motorists can avail themselves of the 2000-space underground park-and-ride facility, while air travellers are offered a dedicated check-in and airport shuttle.

Yet the station's organization is a model of clarity, being composed of three distinct elements arranged on three levels. The upper level, corresponding to the pre-existing railway embankment, is reserved for the platforms of the national and international rail network. Below that lies the breathtaking station concourse incorporating the ticket hall and other passenger services. At ground level are located a shopping mall, the entrances to the former Expo '98 site and, directly to the west, the portal of the bus terminal, while to the east a plaza is defined by new commercial floorspace. These elements are linked by a continuous glazed 'backbone' or gallery at concourse level, which also receives bus passengers moving up from the stands at ground level.

Much of the drama of the building derives from the vertical transition that rail passengers make from other modes of transport accessed at ground level

BELOW Passengers from the bus interchange pass upwards to a bridge leading to the central concourse level below the rail platforms.

and below − as well as from the Expo site and the eastern plaza − upwards through the concourse to the railway platforms. The entrance at ground level is an epic, cavernous space, shaped by *in situ* concrete arches of complex, changing profile that support the station concourse above. Little of this structure is conventionally orthogonal: columns rake or merge into the arches to compose a framework that echoes skeletal forms in nature. Hanging bridges, ramps and passages, and lifts and escalators criss-cross the space and connect it with other operational levels.

Directly above the station concourse, the four island platforms, accessed by ramps and glass-sided lifts, serve eight lines of the rail network. The whole platform area is covered by a 238 m x 78 m (780 ft. x 255 ft.) glazed roof, open at the sides on the model of great stations of the past, and formed of ten rows of steel pillars 25 m (80 ft.) high, arranged on a 17 m x 17 m (55 ft. x 55 ft.) square grid. Each unit takes the form of a 'tree', the trunk of which divides into four curved branches linked by inverted triangles formed of purlins on the diagonal.

This steel structure, painted white, extends upwards to support a folded glass roof that shimmers and appears to dissolve in the Lisbon sun. Efficiently repetitive, robust and elegant, the roof structure recalls in its lightness and grace certain works of late Gothic architecture, or the filigree creations of France's *grands constructeurs*. From this high elevation, passengers can enjoy the prospect of the River Tagus as they wait for their trains.

Steel makes a further dramatic appearance in the bus terminal, where canopies in the form of giant palm leaves shelter the staircases that lead down from the gallery to the buses at ground level. These canopies are part-supported by outrigger struts, which enable the use of long cantilevered sections. Together with the huge canopy signalling the main entrance to Expo '98, they complete a bravura display of structural steelwork. For all the visible dynamism and modernity of the Oriente Station complex, there are also intentional notes of homage to the particular heritage of Lisbon. The station is paved with the same stone as used habitually for the city streets.

BELOW A slightly off-centre view of the dramatic main entrance with its canopy of white-painted steel. The undulating glass-and-steel structure that roofs the train platforms adds to the drama.

RIGHT Eight high-speed tracks were built at the level of the former embankment, the highest in the station complex. The roof is supported by branching, tree-like pillars.

Cantilevered steel-and-glass canopies shelter the stairways that take passengers between the bus terminal and the station concourse.

RIGHT Ground-level view of the passenger bridge link into the main concourse. 'Palm-leaf' canopies shade the passengers on the bus station platforms.

Key facts

Architects: Von Gerkan, Marg & Partner

Structural Engineers: Schlaich, Bergermann & Partner

Total floor area: 164,000 m² (1,765,000 sq. ft.)

Length of terminal: 320 m (1050 ft.)

Trains per day: approx. 2300

RIGHT Close-up detail of the glazing over the roof vault.

Jörg Schlaich

Jörg Schlaich (born 1934) is one of Germany's most notable and distinguished engineers. Following studies in Stuttgart and Berlin and in the United States, he gained much experience in designing river bridges, as well as tensile roof structures, such as the Munich Olympic Stadium, with the pioneering practice led by Professor Fritz Leonhardt and Wolfhardt Andrä. With his own consultancy, Schlaich, Bergermann & Partner (established 1980), Schlaich has been responsible for a number of stations in Helsinki, Finland, and in Berlin and Hanover, Germany, as well as for work on the design of stadium roof structures, including that in Montreal, Canada.

Apart from buildings, with his partners he has been responsible for advances in the design of cable-stayed and box-girder bridges as well as for innovations in environmental design; his pioneering work in this field includes research into solar power and the design of solar chimneys (see pages 184 and 187). He has always been involved in teaching and in 2000 was appointed Professor Emeritus at the University of Stuttgart.

Lehrter Station
Berlin, Germany, 1992–2006

Re-establishing the city of Berlin as Germany's capital after the fall of the Wall in 1989 is proving an undertaking of daunting and much-criticized expense as well as one of logistical complexity, but critics are left in no doubt that it is one driven by vision, and even passion. Evidence of commitment at the highest level is everywhere to be seen in Berlin's skyline filled with tower cranes, from the new Reichstag, the Chancellery and the Government Centre, via the huge, glossy Potsdamer Platz complex, through to the once-prosperous quarters of Mitte and Moabit, now being rapidly refurbished. International design teams have been at work on some of the largest and most prominent building sites in Europe.

Reunification has brought about the need for dramatic changes across the whole spectrum of life in Berlin. In particular, a new transport infrastructure is required to service a nation in which the city is now less marginalized geographically than before and in which it can contemplate a central role in the expanded European Union as a pre-eminent transportation hub. The cities of Prague and Frankfurt are within three hours' travel time by high-speed train, and Warsaw can be reached in just under five. Two intercontinental express (ICE) rail axes cross here: the high-speed section through Germany of the north–south axis from Scandinavia to Sicily, and the east–west route from Moscow to London. The

forecasts for Berlin's rail traffic are highly confident: an estimated fifty million long-distance passengers a year by 2010, with eighty-five million on regional rail services. Add to these figures a million passengers using the S-Bahn suburban commuter services and those travelling on the U-Bahn city routes, and the scae of operations becomes self-evident. Radical plans are called for to accommodate both the trains and their passengers.

For all the routes mentioned there is one natural point of intersection: the site of the old Lehrter Station – former terminus for the railway lines to Hamburg, Bremen and Bremerhaven – located immediately west of the Humboldthafen (Humboldt harbour). A magnificent building in its time, in its later life the station fared less well. Following war damage in 1943 and subsequent neglect, the-then ruined building was eventually demolished in 1959, but its strategic location was safeguarded from development and has become the site of the new station. This was planned on the grandest scale to receive, on completion in 2006, up to thirty million passengers a year, or upwards of 250,000 a day, half of whom will be interchanging between long-distance and regional express trains. A train will leave the new Lehrter Station every 90 seconds. Some 500 long-distance express and regional express services, 800 S-Bahn and nearly 1000 U-Bahn trains, will run daily.

LEFT Passengers will move up through the station levels to the main platform hall where high-speed services arrive and depart.

ABOVE Visualization of the entrance to the station.

BELOW The main platform hall under construction. Its roof incorporates solar-powered photovoltaic panels for generating electricity.

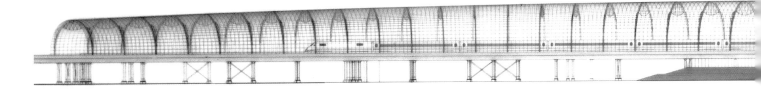

ABOVE East–west sectional view through the main platform hall, showing the crossing platforms for local and regional services below.

Despite these myriad movements of passengers and trains, the plan of the station is notably clear and direct, aiming to provide the shortest possible routes for passengers changing trains and ensuring that all station users can easily orient themselves at any point within the 164,000 square metre (1,765,000 sq. ft.) complex. In this they are aided by high levels of natural light reaching the lowest platform levels. Clarity of purpose is also evident in the fact that, from the outset, the new Lehrter Station did not have to function foremost as a shopping centre, with the provision of rail services becoming incidental. It has been conceived instead as an important catalyst for the urban regeneration of its hinterland through making an uncompromising visual statement of its purpose as the most important transport interchange in Germany.

Uncluttered by nonessential floorspace, the new Lehrter Station building will achieve a degree of lightness and transparency that recalls the qualities of the great station roofs of the past, including that of Berlin's own Anhalt Station (1880), a 170 m (560 ft.) long, clear-span structure. Elevated 10 m (33 ft.) above street level, the main platform hall hosting the east–west ICE high-speed trains extends more than 320 m (1050 ft.) in length. It is covered by a barrel-vaulted glazed roof of elliptical cross-section, which is supported by composite steel arches that are cable-hung from the primary structure. The roof is formed by glazing units, each 1.2 m x 1.2m (4 ft. x 4 ft.), which are stiffened by edge members and bow braces; because the station hall curves to follow the tracks, each glazing unit is a slightly different shape, with the cable tensile structure being carefully calculated to ensure that each unit settles into place. Fifteen metres (50 ft.) below street level lie the platforms for the north–south ICE high-speed trains.

Construction on this epic scale would be unthinkable without impeccable logistics. A fleet of barges from the nearby Humboldthafen removed the 1,500,000 cubic metres (2,000,000 cubic yards) of spoil excavated from the site. Had this quantity of material been transported by road, a convoy of heavy dump trucks more than 1300 km (800 miles) long would have been the unpalatable alternative.

OPPOSITE An impression of the main platform hall, with its elliptical roof hung from the external primary structure.

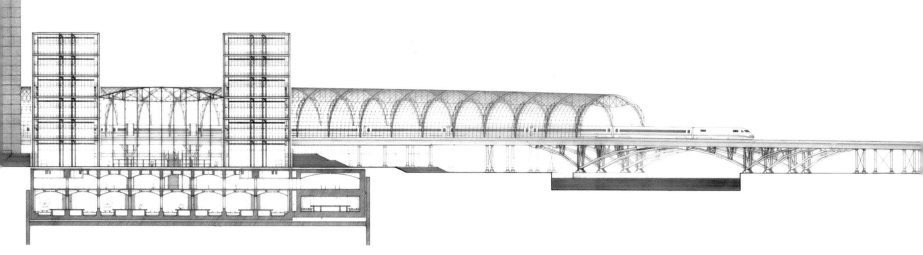

Key Facts

Architects: MacCormac Jamieson Prichard (Southwark); Michael Hopkins & Partners (Westminster); Foster & Partners (Canary Wharf)

Client: Roland Paoletti/London Underground

Number of stations: 11 (6 new, 5 enlarged or rebuilt)

Length of extension: 16 km (10 miles)

Capacity: 27 trains per hour, 2,500,000 passengers per weekday

Cost: UK£3.5 billion

RIGHT The top-lit drum of Southwark station recalls the elegance of the 1930s Piccadilly line stations of Charles Holden.

BELOW Southwark's dramatic intermediate concourse with the deep-blue fritted-glass wall designed by glass artist Alexander Beleschenko.

Roland Paoletti

A great deal of the credit for the outstanding quality of the Jubilee line stations as public architecture can be ascribed to the Italian-born architect Roland Paoletti (born 1931).

Already distinguished for his leadership in the design of the Hong Kong metro, Paoletti was able, as architect-in-chief for the Jubilee Line Extension, to select a group of exceptional architectural practices to work with him at a time when signature architects were not heavily involved in transport design, or was this field seen as promising for leading designers. His persistence and personal leadership in the face of complex engineering constraints and possible compromise have given London a number of new stations that are in every way equal to the pioneering Piccadilly line designs of architect Charles Holden in the 1930s.

Paoletti was appointed CBE in the Millennium honours list in recognition of his achievements in masterminding this outstanding programme of public architecture.

Jubilee Line Extension
London, England, 1991–2000

"This is a station, not a room. There's a railway running through it." No more direct advice could be imagined than that given to the eleven independent architectural teams hand-picked by Roland Paoletti, architect-in-chief for London's Jubilee Line Extension (JLE) and the impresario behind this remarkable programme of new stations to serve Britain's capital. Such a project had not been undertaken since that in the 1930s by London Underground's managing director Frank Pick and his architect Charles Holden for the Piccadilly line stations.

Southwark

A distinguished example of Paoletti's vision in action can be found in the new JLE station at Southwark, located on an important, if previously run-down, street corner close to the South Bank and Tate Modern. On this underused site the station could serve as a catalyst for the regeneration of its hinterland. Southwark guides the passenger by the architecture alone, through a carefully stage-managed sequence of experiences that could be regarded as subtly civilizing in their overall effect. From the street-corner entrance on The Cut and Blackfriars Road passengers descend a short flight of generous, concentric steps into the circular booking hall, which, in its architectural spirit, recalls the work of Holden, but with its flattish dome and careful control of natural light seems also to pay homage to the sublime interiors of the English architect Sir John Soane (1753–1837).

Leaving the booking hall, the passenger descends by escalator to the soaring space of the intermediate concourse level, which also incorporates a pedestrian link to Waterloo East suburban rail station. From here, passengers pass through an opening in the full-height wall clad in polished concrete blocks laid in masonry courses, and take the down escalator to a linear, vaulted space that is also an interchange between platforms. This is a volume of considerable presence, generously proportioned, and animated by travellers crossing at its mezzanine level and moving on to the platforms. In the other direction, the glimpses of daylight are intended to draw travellers up the escalator and onwards.

The unchallenged centrepiece of the station is a work of public art: an inward-sloping, glass-clad wall rising 16 m (53 ft.) and extending 40 m (130 ft.) in length to sheath one side of the elliptical cone through which daylight is funnelled down to the inter-mediate concourse level. On examining the computer modelling of the cone in three dimensions, the station's architects decided to clad it in triangular panels of glass. In developing the pattern of triangular tessellation with the noted glass artist Alexander Beleschenko, the design team used a specially written computer program that, in conjunction with the architects' own modelling software, determined the precise format of each of the 630 panels forming the curved surface. This information was then transferred to the glass fabricator. The surface of the panels was treated with a pattern of graduated enamel fritting involving thirty-six variants of colour, to Beleschenko's design: a deep blue for the lower courses of panels at eye level, with the colour lightening towards the top of the wall, creating by night an elegant counterpart to the 'sky' vault as seen by day.

Westminster

London Underground's brief to the design team for Westminster was to build a new station to link the existing District and Circle lines with a set of platforms for the new JLE, which was to run east-wards to the Greenwich peninsula. The JLE tracks are located far deeper than those of the District and Circle lines, the tunnels of which were constructed using the historical cut-and-cover method on a curved 45-degree alignment turning northwards from the Thames Embankment. At Westminster, as well as the normal concerns involved in upgrading a busy transport interchange in the heart of a city, there was an additional factor to take into account: that of the siting of the project a few metres from both a world-famous landmark (Big Ben and the Houses

of Parliament) and a great river. Furthermore, London Underground had undertaken to build the station below a new Parliamentary office building, Portcullis House, planned for the corner site opposite Big Ben.

Planning of the project was, unsurprisingly, complex, as it was necessary to design Portcullis House and the station in tandem. Rather than a conventionally scaled column grid, a tied-arch transfer structure was used, so that the building's weight could be transferred to foundation level on a limited number of bearing points, which would not unduly compromise the planning of the station below. At the same time, the architects of Portcullis House were intent on retaining its entry floor at street level rather than raising it on a podium. By lowering the District and Circle line tracks by 30 cm (12 in.), it proved feasible to insert both the new ticket hall and the platforms in the space between track level and the ground floor of Portcullis House. The eastbound Jubilee line track was positioned directly above the westbound track to ensure that no damage was caused to the delicate foundations of Big Ben's tower, which has a long-standing tendency to incline towards the north-west. Direct underground connections between the old and new parliamentary buildings were also built into the complex.

An enormous and very rigid concrete box 72 m (235 ft.) long, 22 m (70 ft.) wide and 30 m (100 ft.)

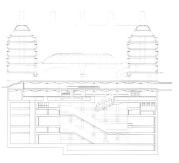

ABOVE Section through the new parliamentary building and Underground station at Westminster. The station is enclosed in a deep concrete box, with central supporting columns taking the loads from the building above.

BELOW At Westminster the escalators are enclosed in finned metal tubes slung from flying beams supported by the central columns.

ABOVE Long section through Canary Wharf Station showing the progression upwards from platform level to the plaza and park above.

OPPOSITE Canary Wharf's entrance canopy was fabricated in Italy from bespoke double-curved panels of glass.

BELOW Passengers travel up Canary Wharf's bank of escalators from the cavernous concourse, to emerge under the glass canopy in the new plaza beyond.

below ground encloses the volume of the Underground interchange. Besides serving as a retaining structure, the box picks up loads from the perimeter of the building above and from the six columns that support its internal courtyard, allowing the new station to be supported by a structure that is relatively light in comparison. The space is criss-crossed by solid steel flying buttresses, each 60 cm (2 ft.) in diameter, which connect the outer diaphragm walls to a central row of concrete columns. Further animated by intersections of escalators and stairs giving access down to the Jubilee line platforms, this single volume is unashamedly theatrical in spirit, an effect enhanced by dramatic lighting produced by spotlights and wallwashers. References to the engraved visions of classical architecture by the architect Giovanni Battista Piranesi (1720–1778) are somehow unavoidable.

In keeping with the designers' concept of a huge box traversed by 'incidents' yet retaining its character as a single open volume, the escalators are treated as independent tubes sheathed in finned metal casings and slung from the flying beams. Above the box and immediately beneath the new parliamentary building lies the ticket hall, which is a more conventional space of standard headroom, and is enhanced by a ceiling displaying rectangular and lozenge-shaped coffers carried on columns with cruciform capitals.

Canary Wharf

The setting for the final JLE station of the three explored here, Canary Wharf, or 'Gotham City' as a leading architectural commentator dubbed it, has emerged triumphantly as a potent rival to the Square Mile (London's financial district). Its facilities attract major corporate tenants, and in the process what were, by the 1980s, abandoned dock basins and wharfsides have been transformed into a totally new urban environment, a complete city in its own right.

Boasting the largest passenger capacity of any JLE station – upwards of 40,000 people an hour during the morning peak – Canary Wharf station extends horizontally the same length as Cesar Pelli's tower, One Canada Square, does in the vertical dimension. Built by the cut-and-cover method within the former West India Dock, the station takes the form of a rectangular box 280 m (920 ft.) long, 32 m (105 ft.) wide and 24 m (80 ft.) deep. It was created by driving 150 coffer dams into the dock basin, which was then drained of water, leaving the concrete outer diaphragm walls exposed at the platform level. This process could take place only after a series of wells had been sunk into the underlying layer of chalk and a continuous pumping operation had begun to prevent flooding of the dock from infiltration of groundwater.

The construction of a large box makes it possible for natural light to reach right down to platform level, allowing passengers to orient themselves easily and offering them a welcome sense of arrival up into the plaza and park created above the station. Passengers emerge under one of three glazed canopies protecting the station entrances, the only outwardly visible signs of the huge construction lying below. Linking the vault of fair-faced concrete forming the undercroft of the park with the platform level, a central full-length row of elliptical *in situ* concrete columns emphasizes the grand scale of the station interior.

Unlike many other JLE stations, Canary Wharf is unconstrained by those accidents of urban geography and existing development that have, nonetheless, stimulated the most imaginative responses from other architectural and engineering teams working on the line. Yet on any other site it would have been impossible to create the single, dramatic volume of Canary Wharf, which instills calm on those who traverse it, almost as some ancient underground basilica might engender devotional sentiments in its visitors.

Key Facts

Entrepreneur: Carl Eugen Langen

Length of transit: 13.3 km (8.3 miles)

Capacity: 178 passengers (2-car train)

Average speed: 27 km/h (17 mph)

Passenger capacity: 80,000 passengers per day

Monorails

Whether in the form of a suspended or central beam track, monorails have been prevented from achieving wide popularity as an urban mass-transit mode by their long association with world fairs. Nonetheless, they are capable of carrying large numbers of passengers: the monorail at Walt Disney World at Orlando, Florida, transports a creditable 200,000 visitors a day.

During the 1960s, various monorail links were built to serve short, high-intensity routes such as that between New Jersey's Newark Airport and its parking facilities, or the loop around the central district of Sydney. In 1964 a proposal was advanced by the American Machine and Foundry Corporation to extend the route from Newark out to New York's JFK (previously Idlewild) International Airport, but it got no further than a promotional concept.

The planning of a more promising and viable monorail is well advanced in Seattle, following on from the system the city built to serve the 1967 World's Fair. The Green Line will follow a 22 km (14 mile) north–south route, carrying initially 3000 passengers an hour, though this figure is expected to double. Understandably, despite all their promoted advantages, this and other urban monorails are subject to intense environmental scrutiny.

Suspension Railway
Wuppertal, Germany, 1898–1903

ABOVE Suspended cars of the more traditional design, with curved frames supporting the suspension track.

BELOW Later structural systems involve raking trellis supports.

Along a busy route it makes obvious sense to double up on modes of transport to make the best use of precious right-of-way width; examples include the stacking of rail tracks and road carriageways to form a multi-level bridge crossing, or the aligning of underground metro lines with existing streets above. At a smaller level, there have been numerous attempts to insert dedicated light-transit routes serving exhibition sites or other visitor destinations into the existing urban fabric, with notable examples in Seattle and Sydney. But these are hardly mass transportation modes. Perhaps the most striking instance of a radical approach to alignment of routes is to be found in Wuppertal, Germany, 20 km (12 miles) east of Düsseldorf. The towns of Eberfeld and Barmen were amalgamated in 1928 to form the present city in the Wupper Valley. Yet Wuppertal's claim to innovation in public transport is now more than a century old.

The Wuppertal *Schwebebahn* (suspension railway) began as a personal initiative of the sugar manufacturer and inventor Carl Eugen Langen from Cologne. Having devised a method of transporting flour sacks by suspending them from a horizontal track, Langen realized that a similar system might work just as well for the transport of people. The more remarkable part of his scheme for Wuppertal's new urban railway was to follow: why not avoid the considerable problems of forging a suitable right of way through dense urban areas, by building the new route to follow as far as possible the alignment of the River Wupper, which remained reassuringly unobstructed? It transpired that about 10 km (6 miles) of the railway, a large part of the route, could be run above the river. A trial trip by Kaiser Wilhelm II in the autumn of 1900 was followed by phased opening for public service from 1901 to

1903. The passenger car in which he rode has survived and is available for private hire.

As befits a major project from the age of the Eiffel Tower, the supporting structure for the suspension rail was fabricated in steel: more than 19,000 tonnes of it were used to form 472 individual frames. Wuppertal's *Schwebebahn* is a true urban metro. It runs on a four- to six-minute frequency, at an average speed of 27 km/h (17 mph), operating with two-car trains that can carry 48 seated and 130 standing passengers. It takes around half an hour to complete its 13.3 km (8.3 mile) route through 20 stations, between Vohwinkel in the west and Oberbarmen at the eastern end. Trains pass round a turning loop beyond each of these termini. As the city's main form of public transport, the system carries up to 80,000 passengers a day, a sizeable number for a city of 375,000 inhabitants.

The Wuppertal *Schwebebahn*, in general, ranks as one of the safest public transport systems in the world, for good reason: it is equipped with safety devices to safeguard against rear-end shunts, or cars parting company with the overhead suspension rail; the track forms a large, continuous oval loop without crossings; there are no interchanges to negotiate and no competition for the airspace above the River Wupper. However, accidents have occurred during its century of operation. The most notorious misadventure happened in July 1950, when the director of the Circus Althoff decided that public relations would be well served by taking Tuffi the elephant for a ride on the railway. This prospect proved less than attractive to the animal, which promptly jumped from the railway car into the river below, but injuries suffered by the elephant, journalists and spectators were only minor.

The same cannot be said of events on 12 April 1999, when the first train of the day, at 5.45 am, was derailed and crashed near Robert-Daum-Platz station, which was at that time being rebuilt, and plunged into the river with the loss of five lives and with nearly fifty other passengers suffering severe injuries. Official investigations subsequently revealed that the derailment had been caused by a workman's tool from the station reconstruction being left attached to the suspension rail. Human error, rather than any fundamental flaw in the design or operation of this essentially very simple transportation system, proved to be the explanation.

Errors apart, the bold concept of the Wuppertal *Schwebebahn* continues to impress. While there have been various similar proposals, none has been developed commercially: for example, the pre-World War II Bennie Aerotrain was a British prototype using a streamlined, propeller-driven railcar hung below a suspension rail on the Wuppertal model, but it ran on only a short test track.

Key Facts

Length of railway:	30 km (20 miles)
Highest recorded speed:	501 km/h (311 mph)
Average operating speed:	430 km/h (270 mph)
Estimated passenger capacity:	10,000,000 per year
Cost:	US$1.2 billion

Maglev Train
Shanghai, China, 2001–04

ABOVE LEFT On its high-level track, a train emerges from a station.

ABOVE RIGHT Assembly and testing of the car units.

Is maglev (magnetically levitated) transportation an idea whose time has finally come ... again? First mooted seriously more than a century ago, and first patented in Germany before World War II, the technology of frictionless electromagnetic propulsion by means of linear induction certainly retains an attraction for designers and engineers. Over the years, numerous test tracks and pilot projects based on maglev technology have surfaced, notably in Germany and Japan, with the advantages of travel speeds of up to 500 km/h (300 mph), very rapid acceleration in the order of 0–300 km/h (0–185 mph) within the space of 5 km (3 miles) and, theoretically, no components that wear out, since the vehicles do not actually touch the guidance track. There are, additionally, the more subjective benefits of quiet running and a futuristic image of the train slicing through urban areas on its dedicated, elevated track.

Much of the allure of the maglev system lies in its simplicity. It is a means of transportation without rails or wheels, in which the usual functions of support, guidance, propulsion and braking are replaced by a non-contact magnetic elevation-and-propulsion system, based on the forces between electromagnets located on both sides of the vehicle and below the guideway. The levitation magnets lock the vehicle to the guideway while the guidance magnets propel it in the right direction. An electronic regulating system

ensures that the vehicle hovers above the guideway at a constant height of 10 mm (0.4 in.). Additional flexibility can be built into the system by generating more power in the guideway along uphill or acceleration sections.

The acknowledged downsides are that all maglev trains require dedicated double-track guideway of steel or concrete beams, around which the bottom of the train wraps and above which it levitates by electromagnetism. The transit vehicle can, therefore, never move on to conventional railway track, as can the French TGV or the Spanish AVE trains that travel on special high-speed sections, representing only a small part of the total railway network. In addition, a maglev transport link is undeniably costly, with the US price tag for a full system estimated at $10,000,000–$30,000,000 per mile (0.6 km), although recent advances in the technology of the superconducting electromagnets required may see a breakthrough reduction in that section of the bill.

So, maglev makes best economic sense when used to provide a very fast, high-capacity link between two related destinations, typically a city downtown and its airport, with a 30 km (20 mile) journey taking only ten minutes. On this basis, maglev systems are currently under consideration for high-speed links between Washington and Baltimore, and Amsterdam and Groningen; and from Munich, Pittsburgh and

Melbourne to their airports. In all these cases, there is likely to be sufficient revenue from potential passengers to go some way towards underwriting the heavy capital costs of system construction, chiefly in the overhead structures involved; but there can be no denying the additional attraction and political capital of having a brand new maglev, speaking eloquently of progress, as an advertisement for a city or region.

With European maglev projects stalling under environmental and financial concerns, China seized the initiative. The city of Shanghai signed a contract in 2001 with a German consortium, comprising Transrapid International, Siemens and Thyssenkrupp, to build a 30 km (20 mile) rapid-transit link between Long Yang metro station in the city centre and Pudong International Airport. In economic terms, this relatively short route is unlikely to prove remotely viable against its reputed $1.2 billion cost, even if it carries its estimated ten million passengers in 2005, rising to twenty million in 2010. Current frequency of operation, since Shanghai's maglev route began its public trials in 2003 and entered full operation in January 2004, is twenty minutes, with three trains making the eight-minute trip to the airport at a maximum speed of 430 km/h (270 mph).

The real future and logical application of maglev systems must surely lie in transport corridors far longer than the Shanghai airport link, in which the speeds attainable could offer a significant premium in terms of time saved and passenger comfort. While the once-mooted Berlin–Hamburg maglev link remained impractical and raised environmental concerns, it would have been an impressive demonstration of a land-based system reaching speeds that could rival those of cruising aircraft with none of the familiar airport delays. More promising as a bankable future project would seem to be the proposed 80 km (50 mile) maglev route linking the cities of the Ruhr, Europe's most populous region. This route, from Düsseldorf to Dortmund via Duisburg, Mülheim, Essen and Bochum, could be run in less than forty minutes, with the train reaching a maximum speed of 300 km/h (185 mph).

In the absence of any credible commercial viability, the main factor behind Shanghai's maglev would appear to be purely political prestige, perhaps an acceptable motive at government level; it is undoubtedly valuable as an image-raising project that can, at a stroke, add a neat and perfectly formed icon to Shanghai's claim to world-class city status.

BELOW A three-car unit leaves Pudong International Airport; approximately eight minutes later it will be in the centre of Shanghai, 30 km (20 miles) away.

Key Facts

Architect: Eero Saarinen	
Structural engineers: Ammann & Whitby	
Area of vaults: 5000 m² (54,000 sq. ft.)	
Cantilever of roof: 24 m (80 ft.)	
Length of vault: 96 m (315 ft.)	
Vault (shell) thickness: 15–91 cm (6–36 in.)	

Eero Saarinen

Eero Saarinen (1910–1961) was undoubtedly one of America's greatest modern architects, with a highly distinctive approach to creating the appropriate form for each commission – the so-called 'style for the job'. The son of the Finnish–American architect Eliel Saarinen, after an early training in sculpture at Yale University he succeeded in developing an architecture that was a direct reflection of the corporate ethos of the 1960s, whether expressing the sheen of a huge corporation, such as in the John Deere Headquarters at Moline, Illinois (1963), or the prestige of the Ivy League in the Ezra Stiles residential college complex at Yale (1962).

His versatility included a range of structures that fully exploited the expressive possibilities of steel and concrete, notably the Gateway Arch at St Louis, Missouri (1966), and Dulles International Airport, near Washington, DC, (1958–62), which presaged the dynamism of his TWA Flight Center.

As well as being a celebrated architect, Saarinen is renowned as a furniture designer, producing among other twentieth-century design icons the 'Womb' Chair (1947) and the 'Tulip' Chair (1956).

TWA Flight Center

JFK International Airport, New York, USA, 1956–63

ABOVE The complex forms of the terminal were developed by the architects using cardboard models.

Without undue recourse to nostalgia for the flying boats of Imperial Airways touching down for black-tie dinners at Port Said in Egypt en route to India, or the Clippers of Pan American Airlines flying down to Rio, an undeniable matter-of-factness has overtaken the day-to-day business of international air travel. Crowded check-ins, long, grim corridors and a general ethos hardly conducive to the passenger's peace of mind have together engendered low expectations of the typical airport environment. Yet it does not have to be so. At the end of the 1950s, the great Finnish-born American architect and designer Eero Saarinen proved that, for his client TransWorld Airlines (TWA) at least, a far more imaginative interpretation of the air terminal was possible, one that embodied in its architecture the romance and allure of flight.

With its form often compared to that of a bird in flight, or one about to take off, the TWA Flight Center (Terminal 5 at New York's JFK International Airport) is entirely at home within the proud pedigree of Expressionist architecture. In this tradition, a building is conceived down to the smallest detail as an embodiment of a central, generative idea, in this case a celebration of air travel. Elsewhere, Saarinen, with

his pluralistic philosophy of 'style for the job', succeeded in devising an appropriate architecture for a giant corporation, in his campus for the General Motors Technical and Research Center at Warren, Michigan, and for an Ivy League residential college complex, at Yale University. Both buildings are remarkably suitable for the function yet entirely different from one another in style. At TWA, the imagery of flight pervades every corner of the building – except that there are no corners in the conventional sense. Walls slope, the roof vaults soar upwards and curving balconies sail into the central volume, a complex space that is comprehended from a sequence of viewpoints as departing passengers change level to reach their departure gate. Nothing is static yet everything is an uplifting surprise.

To achieve the soaring, complex curves of the four segments of vault required a compound structure composed of a web of reinforcing steel bracing the concrete, on the lines of the steel 'hammock' that covers the concourse of Saarinen's 1962 terminal building at Dulles International Airport, Washington, DC. At TWA, the concrete vaults are entirely supported on four massive bearing points – Y-shaped, stumpy columns that each resemble the base of a

ABOVE Every element of the building follows the same sculptural aesthetic, including the flight indicator boards.

BELOW Seen from a distance, the terminal building takes on the form of a swooping eagle.

tree; clear glazing between the segments of vault allows daylight to penetrate inside and play on the soaring upward curves of the soffit. The window walls provide no support for the vaults and are designed to appear as unobtrusive as possible to preserve the visual pre-eminence of the oversailing roof.

To achieve such visual dynamism and uplift required state-of-the-art engineering design, especially in the placement of steel reinforcement. Reputedly, the structural engineers on the job resorted to experimenting with bent paper clips in their efforts to find ways of placing all the necessary reinforcement within the thin shell sections proposed by the architect. In any event, the terminal as built represented a remarkably faithful interpretation of Saarinen's original design concept, right down to the 'family' of building details – the streamlined staircases, the free-standing information pod, the sweeping curvaceous seating and an elegant signage system. As Saarinen himself explained, "We wanted passengers passing through the building to experience a fully-designed environment, in which each part arises from another and everything belongs to the same formal world."

Yet aviation – or commerce – inconveniently never stands still. Despite its status a great work of architecture – critics equate it with New York's Grand Central Station (1903–13, Warren and Wetmore/Reed and Stem, architects) – the TWA Flight Center has proved vulnerable to recent redevelopment plans by its owners, the Port Authority of New York and New Jersey. The initial intention was to demolish the terminal's satellite concourses and to interpose a lumpish new building airside that would effectively block views to the tarmac, while the authority's decision to bypass the terminal with a proposed light-rail system precludes any future role the building might have played.

However, in the wake of passionate protests and effective local lobbying, there appears to be a distinct prospect that the new airline operators (successors to the now defunct TWA) will succeed with their plans to utilize the terminal as an entrance to a new passenger building, with other parts of the landmark structure finding fresh purpose as flight exhibition and visitor facilities. Whatever the outcome, it is rare to encounter a building that so directly embodies the optimistic spirit of air travel and the sheer thrill of flight.

RIGHT The principal concourse, showing its fluidity of circulation. Passengers move upwards to the departures level at the intersection of the four curved vaults.

Key Facts

Architects and engineers: Skidmore Owings & Merrill (SOM)

Area of terminal: more than 40 ha (100 acres)

Total area of roof fabric: 510,000 m² (5,500,000 sq. ft.)

Weight of steel for support pylons: 30,000 tonnes

Area of each tent unit: 2400 m² (26,000 sq. ft.)

Passenger capacity: 80,000 per day (peak)/1,000,000 per annum

Haj Terminal

Jeddah, Saudi Arabia, 1978–81

ABOVE The Haj Terminal at King Abdul Aziz International Airport is at its busiest during the pilgrimage to Mecca, when more than 50,000 passengers use its facilities.

ABOVE RIGHT Erection of one of the 210 tent units that make up the vast structure.

OPPOSITE TOP The distinctive profile of the tent modules suspended from the steel pylons, modern yet not out of keeping with the desert setting.

OPPOSITE BOTTOM Simple repetitive bays shelter pilgrim facilities, the whole forming a small town in itself.

The tighter the better, it sometimes seems, might describe the ideal client's brief. In the case of a building to cater for the movement into and out of Jeddah of Muslims making the pilgrimage to Mecca, known as the *haj*, the logistics of dealing with huge numbers of people were absolute requisites of design from the outset. In addition, a major factor was that vast numbers pass through within the single month (Dhu al-Hijjah) in the Islamic year favoured for the journey, quite apart from the fact that many of these pilgrims need to spend up to twenty-four hours after their arrival at King Abdul Aziz International Airport making their onward travel arrangements to Mecca. While some groups continue to follow the traditional overland routes, many more take to the air, with annual numbers of pilgrims approaching one million, and a peak of 50,000 extra arrivals per day occurs at Jeddah during the month of Dhu al-Hijjah.

Obvious logistical problems arising from the need to cater to the pilgrim numbers arriving during the very narrow peak period were compounded by the fact that many are old, infirm, unused to travelling, and disoriented. More than half will not understand Arabic. In planning a structure to shelter, service and succour these visitors, the design team was challenged by the basic imperative to provide a building that could, first, process the pilgrims as international travellers, and then accommodate up to 50,000 of

them at any one time, most probably overnight, pending their onward journey to Mecca. The Haj Terminal was designed with a capacity of 80,000 people for thirty-six hours, and up to one million pilgrims a year.

Yet any such building, if planned as a conventional enclosed structure, would be enormous – and exceedingly expensive to build and maintain. The breakthrough decision proved to be the notion of dividing the Haj Terminal into two distinct elements – one a set of air-conditioned, enclosed spaces to house disembarkation, immigration and customs, and the other a huge separate waiting area, including space to sleep, wash and cook, open but shaded from the desert sun. Here, the *hajjis*, pilgrims making the *haj*, would benefit from all the facilities of a modern terminal building while, in effect, 'camping out'. The final plan of the terminal building takes the form of two huge identical rectangles of roofed space with a mall between them, from which buses to Mecca depart. At either end is an aircraft apron, capable of housing ten Boeing 747s. The total covered area is more than 40 hectares (100 acres).

Roofing a space on this scale was unprecedented. The pressured schedule meant that any construction system proposed needed to be absolutely straightforward and foolproof, since errors would very soon be compounded. Initial structural concepts

involving concrete 'mushrooms' or metal fabrications were disregarded once the need for huge quantities of material became clear. The solution as built turned out to be one that, while highly efficient in terms of delivering shaded space for minimum material outlay, also resonated with the traditions of the overland pilgrimage and of the desert itself. Tents in various forms were a valued life-support system in Saudi Arabia and the Persian Gulf, and their reinvention as a means of covering the 45 m x 45 m (150 ft. x 150 ft.) bays of the Haj Terminal made good sense, especially once the design team became aware of a new fibreglass fabric, developed by the American firm Owings Corning, that was reputedly six times finer than silk but, weight for weight, stronger than steel. When coated with Teflon to reflect the sun and chemically treated to protect it from the harsh salty atmosphere of the Red Sea, this relatively inexpensive substance proved ideal for roofing the terminal. More than 500,000 m² (5,500,000 sq. ft.) was installed over the 440 support pylons made from 30,000 tonnes of rolled steel in Japan, carried to Jeddah by ocean-going barge. Each of the 210 tent units was raised on site, much in the same way as a circus tent would be erected.

The giant roof canopies thus formed are intention-ally translucent: dappled light filters down into the building through the fabric and making artificial light

unnecessary during daytime; an element of natural air-conditioning is provided by the welcome Red Sea breezes that enter the terminal through its open sides and exit though a central circular opening at the top of each tent, with some further assistance to air movement provided by low-level fans.

'Modern' tents, if not on the heroic scale of the Haj Terminal, are now a well-established element in the architectural language, often used to liven up an otherwise nondescript building, yet very few have the logic and conviction of the real father of them all — still, after twenty years, faithfully serving the pilgrims.

Key Facts

Consortium: Foster Hong Kong, Mott Connell, Arup, British Airports Authority

Length of terminal: 1.27 km (0.8 mile)

Internal floor area: 516,000 m² (5,554,000 sq. ft.)

Passenger gates: 75

Passenger capacity: 35,000,000 per annum

Cost: UK£39,400,000

Hong Kong International Airport
Chek Lap Kok, Hong Kong, China, 1992–98

Few commentators on the Asian–Pacific scene would doubt that the Chinese government always operated on a long-term strategy as regards the return of the former British Crown Colony of Hong Kong to Chinese control. In retrospect the evidence for such a strategy is conclusive and offers an explanation for such decisions as the one to build an enormous new international airport, as a replacement for congested Kai Tak, on the remote islet of Chek Lap Kok (CLK). Hitherto the islet was two hours by boat from central Hong Kong, but it is now served by a high-capacity road/rail corridor 32 km (20 miles) long. Kai Tak included, there were already four international airports within the Pearl River economic region, so the decision to promote the new airport ahead of existing sites was a purely geopolitical one, mindful of the fact that half the world's population lies within five hours' flying time of Hong Kong. This

decision also explains the enhanced passenger and cargo capacity of the new airport to fit it for service as a global – not merely a regional – transport hub.

On the one hand, CLK can be described in terms of its gargantuan statistics – with an internal floor area of approximately 516,000 square metres (5,554,000 sq. ft.), it is the largest enclosed public space ever built, equalling the size of ten London Wembley Arenas; eighty million passengers a year are predicted with the completion of its second phase, equivalent to more than the combined capacity of London's Heathrow and New York's JFK airports; and the whole building is 1.27 km (0.8 mile) long. On the other hand, it can be read as a case study in highly successful design and project management, with clear and robust principles established at the outset and maintained to completion, despite the fact that upwards of 200 subgroups were working within the multidisciplinary project team.

The designers were certainly helped by being offered a genuine *tabula rasa*, a flat, featureless site of 1250 hectares (3100 acres), 6 m (20 ft.) above the level of the South China Sea. The site had been prepared in thirty-one months by levelling the existing mountainous terrain using three times its volume in sand, which was scooped up by the largest fleet of dredgers ever assembled. On that score, comparisons will inevitably be made between the site of CLK and the artificial island in Osaka Bay on which Japan's Kansai Airport was built. At 1125 hectares (2780 acres) Kansai is slightly smaller than CLK but its terminal building, albeit far thinner than CLK, extends 1.8 km (1.1 miles). The plan of the Hong Kong International Airport terminal has been likened to a cartoon drawing of a stick-man, with a large 'hat' – the terminal building itself, offering no fewer than 288 check-in desks – joined to a narrow 'body' formed by the 75 aircraft gates accessed by travelators. Both

CLK and Kansai exemplify the emerging genus of major international airports that, evoking the many 'Atlantis'-type projects found in 1920s science fiction, are located on their own man-made or artificially flattened island sites and joined to the metropolis by a corridor of fast, high-capacity public transport links.

Moving on from the overall site strategy, CLK has provided the architects with an opportunity to further develop, on the largest possible scale, the concepts they first demonstrated at London's Stansted Airport. In both structures, the basic premise is clarity, an apparently simple and overarching roof form admitting a controlled level of daylight and formed of repeating modular bays extending over the concourse area required to accommodate the various processes of departure and arrival, as well as the inevitable quantum of retail floorspace. The scale at CLK, however, has been jacked up several notches from that at Stansted. The standard structural bay size is 36 m x 36 m (120 ft. x 120 ft.), far larger than that at Stansted, but retains the feature of diffused daylight filtering down through a central slot within each of the shallow vaults. These are placed side by side over the main concourse area, decreasing in height from the high entry level of the central spine and the public transport interchange towards the departure gates.

Moving forward under these naturally lit parallel vaults, passengers progressively approach their departure gates, encountering facilities and formalities on the way, housed in free-standing binnacles. The process begins at upper level as they enter from the elevated expressway or the railway station, and are then led down ramps through a double-height space to the departure desks; from here they descend a further level, out along the concourse, to the departure gates. Arriving passengers proceed straight through at lower level to emerge landside into the same double-height space that fronts the terminal.

Despite the enormous dimensions of the terminal, the architects' use of a roof structure with a strong, calm and unifying presence, coupled with views outwards from the core of the building, successfully engenders a much-needed feeling of comfort and reassurance, as well as conveying something of the sense of excitement and anticipation once evoked by the prospect of flight.

OPPOSITE An aerial view of the overall complex, with train and road access in the foreground, and the passenger concourse leading to the Y-shaped terminal gates beyond.

Key Facts

Architects:	Richard Rogers Partnership/Estudio Lamela
Structural engineers:	Initec/TPS/Anthony Hunt Associates
Length of terminal:	1.25 km (0.8 mile)
Internal floor area:	700,000 m² (7,500,000 sq. ft.)
Aircraft gates:	36 (Terminal), 24 (Satellite)
Cost:	UK£760,000,000

RIGHT Computer-rendered view down into one of the 'canyons' that bring daylight into the public areas.

BELOW Computer-rendered view of the check-in area, showing the floating quality of the roof and the slenderness of the V-shaped steel supports.

Richard Rogers Partnership

Many projects by the Richard Rogers Partnership have become landmarks in their own right. Such examples as the Centre Georges Pompidou in Paris (1971–77, as Piano & Rogers), the Lloyd's of London building (1978–86) and the European Court of Human Rights, Strasbourg (1989–95), all testify to the practice's ability to design uncompromisingly modern buildings that contribute to their urban context.

Its work is characterized by the assured use of technology to create buildings of great elegance and confidence, for example the Channel 4 Headquarters (1991–94) and 88 Wood Street (1994–99) in London. Other designs outside the UK include offices for DaimlerChrysler in Berlin (1993–99) and research facilities for Amano Pharmaceuticals in Gifu, Japan (1997–99). As well as the new terminal at Barajas International Airport, the Richard Rogers Partnership has designed the new Terminal 5 at London's Heathrow Airport.

The practice has a strong involvement in urbanism and has prepared a number of masterplans and design concepts for key urban sites in Europe.

New Area Terminal
Barajas International Airport, Madrid,

RIGHT Terminal plan, with parking modules at the top leading through to the terminal and thence to the aircraft gates.

BELOW Cross-section of the terminal at the competition stage. The built design has changed very little from this concept.

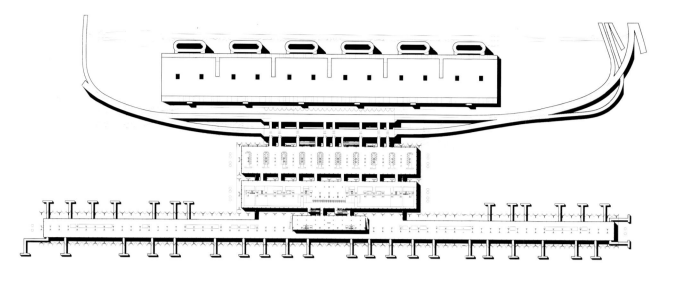

Spain, 2000–04

Reputedly the current largest construction site in Europe, the extension to Madrid's Barajas International Airport (1977), known as the New Area Terminal (NAT), is certainly no minor add-on. Together with its satellite, the new building will encompass upwards of 700,000 square metres (7,500,000 sq. ft.) – the existing terminal covers a still daunting 200,000 square metres (2,000,000 sq. ft.) – and is capable of handling thirty-five million extra passengers a year, setting it firmly in the league of such major hub airports as Paris, Frankfurt and London Heathrow. Observers see this bold expansion as a reassertion of Madrid's role as capital city after playing second fiddle to high-profile Barcelona, in terms of international perception, during the past decade or so. Whether or not driven by political motives, progress on the project has been remarkably swift, considering its scale and impact: completion is due in 2004, following an architectural competition in 1996 and a start on site in 2000. Such speediness contrasts with the slower, more bureaucratic progress on London Heathrow's new Terminal 5 building, designed by the same architects.

Unlike all too many international airports, the Madrid terminal exhibits a strong sense of place. The terminal complex is visually anchored against a backdrop of rising land, which has made it possible to integrate the roads, ramps and service structures into a coherent whole. Particularly careful attention has been paid to the architectural treatment of the airport's 9000 on-site parking spaces, which are housed in six modules arranged in line; pedestrian circulation has been brought forward to the front of the parking decks, facing the new terminal, to animate what might otherwise – or, indeed, elsewhere – be an overimposing wall of building. Further softening of its impact is promoted through its integral 'green roof' of low-maintenance planting, irrigated by the recycled rainwater system that supplies the whole complex.

Both the main terminal building and its satellite share the same architectural concept: that of a series of parallel blocks or bars separated by 'canyons' – multi-storey spaces through which daylight streams down to the lower levels, and across which passengers pass on bridges to or from the departure gates on the 1.25 km (0.8 mile) pier. These canyons are indeed grand; they aid passenger orientation and at the same time provide a welcome alternative to the familiar low-ceilinged circulation areas found in airports worldwide.

Oversailing the blocks and canyons is a dramatic undulating roof the form of which recalls waves or wings. It is supported by central rows of 'trees' and extends far beyond the façades to provide shade from the sun, the cantilevers being supported by V-shaped elliptical props. The façades are hung from

the roof structure on 'kipper' trusses – simple cable trusses at 9 m (30 ft.) centres – both to avoid the need for vertical supports or mullions between the panels of 36 mm (1.4 in.) thick high-performance glass, separated by silicone joints, and to preserve the visual primacy of the roof overhang on elevation.

Fabrication of the steel framework of this impressive roof drew directly upon techniques and skills perfected by the still vibrant Spanish shipbuilding industry. From each corner of the concrete 'tree' a tapered steel strut projects outwards, which, with its neighbour from the next 'tree', provides support for the S-form roof trusses. A triangular arrangement of struts and roof purlins provide the necessary rigidity for the roof structure, which celebrates the fact that it is very evidently made up of a set of 'stick' components, each directly expressing its structural role. This design strategy ensures that there are many points at which any

inaccuracies in construction can easily be rectified. The modular, repetitive design of the roof, with its S-form trusses spanning 72 m (236 ft.), the unobstructed, rectangular floorplate and the regular spacing of the canyons also make for convenient reorganization of functional areas in the future without compromising the building envelope.

The speed of construction on this scale has required a very robust architectural concept and a regular structural grid, in this case 18 m x 9 m (60 ft. x 30 ft.), corresponding to a 1.8 m (6 ft.) planning grid. The building's lower floors, including a basement level that descends up to 20 m (65 ft.) below grade, are built of *in situ* reinforced concrete with some masonry walls, although precast components are showcased in locations visible to the public. Despite the concrete installation being allocated between no less than five contractors, consistency and quality have proved beyond reproach.

ABOVE The terminal pier under construction, showing the near-complete kipper-truss structure holding the glazing. External shading has yet to be installed.

OPPOSITE Computer-rendered view of one of the multi-level 'canyons' that slice through the terminal, admitting natural light. The baggage reclaim area can be seen at its base.

Key Facts

Contractors:	A.J. Main & Co/Cleveland Bridge & Engineering Company
Shed length:	245 m (805 ft.)
Shed width:	85 m (280 ft.)
Shed height:	55 m (180 ft.)
Length of largest airship housed:	235 m (770 ft.) (R101 airship)

Cardington Hangars
Bedfordshire, England, 1917–28

ABOVE Number 1 shed, the first of the identical pair to be built, showing the enormous doors opening to admit the airship.

BELOW The hangars at Cardington loom over the Bedfordshire plain, their combined floor area the equivalent of six-and-a-half soccer pitches.

"**B**rooding they stand." These words were used by the Finnish composer Jean Sibelius as a programme note to his music, but are equally applicable to the twin hangars at Cardington, rising unchallenged from the brick-fields and potato farms south of the English county town of Bedford. Although individually surpassed in size by Germany's CargoLifter Hangar (pages 52–53) and by several of the Zeppelin hangars of the 1930s, these structures retain their awesome presence, as impressive in their own way as the spires of cathedrals in the Fens or the giant grain elevators of the American Midwest.

In its heyday, at the end of the 1920s, Cardington was able to host the two great British airships the R100 and the R101, stabled in its hangars or moored, by turn, to its tower mast. The airships were the product of British concerns over Germany's emerging technical supremacy in the building of intercontinental airships. Britain embarked on a twin-track strategy, with manufacture of the R100 being entrusted to private enterprise (Vickers) and that of the R101 to an Air Ministry team. The projects had the same overall specification, as a somewhat simplistic and ultimately tragic test of capitalist against state enterprise. When completed, the R100 was intended to fly a round-trip from Britain to Montreal in Canada and back, while the R101 was to be despatched to India, then a cornerstone of the British empire. The intention was thus to prove air travel around the empire could be a reality, and to make plain the relative merits of each design. Cardington had become one of the world's premier airship hubs and the centre of Imperial Airships' operations from 1921 onwards.

The site's beginnings were modest enough. In 1917 the British Admiralty bought the land and contracted Shorts of Belfast to build an airship factory and workers' accommodation, known as Shortstown. 'Number 1 shed' ('Building 80'), the first airship hangar, was built by A.J. Main & Co. of Glasgow the same year and in 1918 the launch of the airship R31 marked the beginning of Cardington's active service. A year later the Air Ministry took over the site, renaming it the Royal Airship Works in 1921. Number 1 shed was enlarged during 1926–27 to house the R101, and a year later was joined by 'Number 2 shed', built by the Cleveland Bridge & Engineering Company for the sister airship R100, which had been fabricated at Howden in Yorkshire. Number 2 shed had been relocated from the Pulham airship base in Norfolk. The two sheds were of hitherto unthinkable size, each 245 m x 85 m x 55 m (805 ft. x 280 ft. x 180 ft.), and are still the largest pair in Western Europe. Their main doors, powered by electric motors, weigh 940 tonnes.

But Cardington's heyday proved to be short. In 1930 the Vickers-built R100 successfully flew across the Atlantic and back. However, on its maiden voyage on 5 October 1930, the Cardington-built R101 crashed in fog into wooded hills in northern France, killing forty-eight, including Lord Thomson, the Minister for Air, and other figures in the airship programme. Some commentators attributed the cause of the disaster to the overemphasis given by the Air Ministry design team to the development of suitable diesel engines to power the airship at the expense of engineering the craft itself, while the Vickers engineers had early abandoned the quest for diesel power and opted for petrol engines, enabling more time and resources to

be devoted to airframe design. Whatever the explanation, the disaster effectively curtailed the airship programme in Britain. A year later the government decided against further airship development, and the R100, despite its success in flying to Canada and back, was ignominiously sold off as £450-worth of scrap.

Cardington became a Royal Air Force station in 1936, and during World War II it played a valuable role in the development and manufacture of barrage balloons used as part of the air defence of British cities; it was used subsequently for work on balloons for meteorological research. In 1974, the Building Research Establishment took over the site, and the hangars were used by the Fire Research Station, their enormous size making them ideal for the testing of alarm systems and fire spread in mocked-up buildings. Size also brings heavy costs in terms of building maintenance, and Number 1 shed remains at risk. Yet the Cardington site still manages to retain its tradition of aeronautical innovation, with the July 2000 launch of a pioneering airborne vehicle known as SkyCat, the brainchild of the Bedford-based Advanced Technologies Group, which combines the latest super-lightweight technology with state-of-the-art power and landing systems. Reverting to its roots and *raison d'être*, Cardington continues to offer the space in which such airship ventures can prosper.

LEFT The vast hangars were sized to accommodate the largest craft envisaged during the great inter-war heyday of the airship.

Key Facts

Architects: SIAT Architektur & Technik

Structural engineers: Arup

Internal floor area: 66,000 m² (710,400 sq. ft.)

Extent of building: 363 m (l) x 225 m (w) x 107 m (h) (1200 ft. x 740 ft. x 350 ft.)

CargoLifter Airship Hangar
Brand, Germany, 1999–2001

ABOVE The hangar ends are closed by doors comprising eight innovative Z-sectioned spherical segments, powered by motors and running on tracks in the concrete base slab. The doors take fifteen minutes to open or close completely.

ABOVE RIGHT The PVC membrane spans 31 m (102 ft.) between each trussed arch. To prevent it from rubbing against the external structural bracing it is restrained by prestressed cable.

Associated in the popular imagination with an inter-war world of flag-waving and ill-fated maiden voyages, airships are currently enjoying a revival. Historically, Germany is the undoubted leader in the development of these craft, from the first experiments by Count von Zeppelin in the 1890s through to the recently proposed load-carrying CargoLifter (CL) fleet. Hangars to shelter these huge craft are an important part of the airship legacy, and many were built in Germany, France, Italy and Britain between 1898 and 1938; the largest-ever airship hangar is believed to be the Goodyear Airdock (1929) in Akron, Ohio – 358 m (1175 ft.) long, 99 m (325 ft.) wide and 34 m (112 ft.) high.

In parallel with its pre-eminence in the evolution of airships, Germany developed an expertise in hangar design, a tradition that continues with the CargoLifter Hangar at Brand, near Berlin. The design team drew on earlier research on hangars and structural membranes carried out at Stuttgart University's Institute for Lightweight Structures during the 1970s and 1980s by Frei Otto and others. The team concluded that the most promising and material-efficient structural form was a rigid semicircular arch without hinges, which, coincidentally, echoed the shape, size and structural system of early reinforced-concrete hangars and exhibition halls. Hinged structures had found favour because they proved easier to design and build, but

the rigid, hingeless structure selected for the Cargo-Lifter Hangar used less steel. This was an important advantage in constructing an enclosure 107 m (350 ft.) in height – twice that of (and at 363 m (1200 ft.) considerably longer than) the largest Zeppelin hangar (1936); its fatter and loftier shape reflects that of the more bulbous CL 160s of the future.

Hangar doors are always problematic to design. The largest possible opening is required, as well as weather protection, for the contents; in the past, various combinations of sliding, swivelling or rotating doors have been attached to the basic shed. For CargoLifter, an entirely new design was developed: a door made up of spherical segments that folds like a concertina, pivoting on a point at the crown of the last arch at each end of the central barrel-vaulted body of the hangar, on a semicircular track in the concrete base. The enormous size of each of these door segments, which have an arch length of 168 m (550 ft.) and a base width of 42 m (138 ft.), called for the lightest possible form of construction. This was achieved by designing each segment as a shell, with its inside face formed as a curved grid of identical vertical, horizontal and diagonal members. With an outer face formed of corrugated metal cladding panels spanning between the side beams that meet at the peak of the door, it produces an appearance not unlike the fan vaults of Gothic cathedrals. Each segment slides to nest behind the next, powered by a motor drive at the end of each door track.

Forming the main body of the hangar, the arch trusses are not semicircular but polygonal. Each truss consists of seventeen straight segments, 18 m (59 ft.) long, assembled as a triangular Vierendeel structure. This is connected to the next by a deep truss along the ridge that also helps the structure to resist the heavy compressive forces on the last two arches caused by the opening doors. At the bases of the trusses are concrete plinths that also act as entrances to the building. A PVC-coated membrane acts as the roof covering.

Aside from its awesome proportions, the Cargo-Lifter Hangar represents evolution in the use of materials. While the great Cardington Hangars of 1924–26 (pages 50–51) needed 4.87 kg/m of steel, the CargoLifter spans more than three-and-a-half times the distance yet uses only 1.04 kg/m to do it.

ABOVE A small version of the proposed CargoLifter airship, nicknamed 'Charlie', in front of the glazed central section of the hangar.

BELOW The main body of the hangar is formed by polygonal steel arches, each consisting of seventeen straight sections. Of the eight door segments, three on each side move and one remains fixed.

Key Facts

Port authority:	Port of Rotterdam
Port area:	10,500 ha (26,000 acres)
Area of industrial sites:	5000 ha (12,000 acres)
Total water area:	3500 ha (8400 acres)
Annual throughput:	322,000,000 tonnes (in 2002)

As an example of the scale a modern port complex can attain, the Rotterdam Europort represents a remarkable achievement in that brand of large-scale planning and engineering that is associated especially with the Dutch. Its world-beating gross throughput in 2002 of 322,000,000 tonnes, compared to that of runner-up Singapore's 258,000,000 or Shanghai's 230,000,000, also outstrips those of its principal European rivals, Hamburg, Antwerp and Marseilles, combined.

The port forms almost a region in itself, extending some 40 km (25 miles) from the city centre to the North Sea and including a total port area of 10,500 hectares (26,000 acres) and a quay length of 80 km (50 miles), served by nearly 300 cranes. Such statistics reflect Rotterdam's pre-eminence as a European hub for imports from and exports to the United States and the Far East, as well as its status as Europe's premier container port, supported by a

Rotterdam Europort
Rotterdam, The Netherlands, 1960–

high-quality infrastructure providing processing and distribution facilities. It is also an important transshipment centre, with an emphasis on the handling of raw bulk materials such as oil, chemicals, coal and ores. Its combined economic activities amount to nearly 2% of gross national product as well as providing employment for more than 60,000 people locally and 250,000 elsewhere in The Netherlands.

The city of Rotterdam owes its origins to the dam built over the River Rotte in the thirteenth century, a barrier that made it necessary to transship cargo and that gave rise to the original urban fabric of quays and warehouses. The first real pressure for massive growth in port capacity was applied by the burgeoning industries of the Ruhr cities in the nineteenth century, which used the Rhine waterway for the transport of raw materials and for the export of finished products by barge. Further impetus was provided by the cutting of the Neuwe Waterweg (New Waterway), opened in 1872. The growth of the city as an outlet for seaborne exports was supported by a set of new port basins built on the south bank of the River Meuse (Maas), allowing Rotterdam to consolidate its hold on the Rhine and on international traffic.

Following World War II more than 40% of the dock area was left in ruins, but the post-war economic resurgence and the need for more berthing capacity led to pressure for the development of new dock basins to the west, and support areas south of the Neuwe Waterweg. Rotterdam port had established its pre-eminence as a petroleum import centre with the construction before the war of its first two oil terminals at Waalhaven and Merwehaven. However, the 1960s saw the dramatic growth of tanker and supertanker fleets, which, with their requirement for a draught of at least 20 m (65 ft.), could not be accommodated in the existing port basins. The need to provide full access for these vessels drove the construction during that decade of Rotterdam's Europort. Currently the port can offer more than 25,000,000 cubic metres (883,000,000 cubic ft.) of tank refinery storage.

At a stroke Europort doubled Rotterdam's available harbour capacity and soon proved to be a very attractive location for companies, which benefited from investments made in the infrastructure. There have proved to be few competitors in Europe for port expansion on this scale and with this speed of response to the emerging markets.

Such was the commercial success of Europort that the continuing pressure for further expansion could be accommodated only by reclaiming further land from the North Sea. This was achieved by a classic Dutch polder operation in which the future site was first enclosed by a barrier, the water progressively drained off and replaced by sea-dredged sand, and then the layers of fill allowed to consolidate. First shipping operations from the expanded Europort began in 1973.

In common with other port cities, restructuring of the downtown dock basins, largely devastated in World War II, has provided a stage for urban regener- ation, with a set of high-profile projects including the Erasmus Bridge (pages 88–89), new business centres and housing. In this sense, Rotterdam's genesis as a natural trading point on the dam has now been reinforced by bringing back commerce right to its heart – with the addition of visiting cruise ships berthing near by. The foundations of Rotterdam's continuing success as a world-class port, however, were laid with the bold decision to build Europort and its subsequent extensions ready to receive the new breed of megaship.

ABOVE The dedicated East Termina on the Maasvlakte, an area of reclaimed land at the mouth of the River Meuse (Maas). The boosting of container-handling facilities reinforced Europort's position as the largest container port in Europe.

OPPOSITE TOP Aerial view of the Europort site. The photograph was taken in 2000; the high pace of change at the port is indicated by the fact that a new chemicals factory has been built between the container termina and the oil tanks (far right).

OPPOSITE The Shell Pernis refinery. The increase in petroleum imports and the subsequent need for greater refinery capacity provided the major impetus to the expansion of Europort.

Key Facts

Architects: Foreign Office Architects (FOA)

Structural engineers: Structural Design Group (SDG)

External floor area: 438,000 m² (4,715,000 sq. ft.)

Length of terminal: 400 m (1320 ft.)

Cost: US$195,000,000

Foreign Office Architects

Founded by Alejandro Zaera Polo and Farshid Moussavi in 1992, London-based Foreign Office Architects (FOA) has emerged as a leading international practice in architecture and urban design. The Yokohama Port Terminal was the major project that brought it to prominence; the design was selected to represent Britain at the Eighth Venice Architecture Biennale in 2002. FOA is remarkable for realizing a building on this scale while being a recently established practice.

Most recently, FOA has been announced as the winner of the competition to design the BBC's new Music Centre – the 'Music Box' in White City, London. This building promises to deliver FOA's particular brand of striking forms and spatial fluidity, as well as a welcoming public face. European projects on site include a coastal park in Barcelona, and a theatre and auditorium for Torrevieja, Spain. Both founders continue to combine practice with teaching as visiting critics in Europe and North America.

RIGHT A view of the exposed folded-steel framework before installation of cladding panels and timber decking.

Yokohama Port Terminal
Yokohama, Japan, 2000–02

As points of interface between land and sea, marine terminals are a distinct and unjustly neglected category of architecture. From modest riparian landing points for river-boat services to huge, complex facilities equipped to receive and service the world's greatest liners, this building type has recently enjoyed something of a renaissance, in which it has taken on an urban, place-making role. This development is exemplified by Yokohama's new port terminal, the result of an international competition in 1995 won by London-based Foreign Office Architects.

Once a small fishing village, Yokohama is now Japan's second city, a rival to Tokyo as a port, and a centre with strong civic ambitions of its own. Although it hosts a modest fifty to sixty cruise ships each year, the city's authorities decided to replace their outdated 1960s marine terminal with a facility that can welcome up to four vessels at a time. In responding to this brief for the Yokohama International Port Terminal, the architects were able to move beyond the creation of a strictly functional structure to produce a new urban destination. It includes a cavernous assembly space,

Osanbashi Hall, for public events; a substantial, boldly scaled promenade from which visitors can view ships and the city; and, most notably, a sequence of spaces and routes that become completely open to the public once the baggage consoles and immigration control points have been retracted into the floor. When there are no ships berthed at the terminal, it can become anything that the city authorities require, chameleon-like: by turns a marketplace, a floating foyer for exhibitions or the setting for outdoor performances.

Sheathed in boards of dense Brazilian hardwood and sections of grass, the terminal complex resembles an ancient earthwork more than an example of conventional maritime architecture. Yet its structure and method of fabrication are very close to those employed by shipyards, reflecting the architects' conviction that, in employing a steel superstructure, their building should pay appropriate homage to great shipbuilding and harbour-engineering artefacts. Through the use of fireproof structural steel, which does not need to be cloaked by thermal and fire insulation, it is possible to maintain the taut visual dynamism of exposed steel members resonant

BELOW The sea approach to the terminal, with the port of Yokohama beyond. The folded-plate structure of the terminal is clearly visible.

of heroic engineering structures. The parallel is further reinforced by the chosen construction method: sections of the building were designed to be fabricated in Japanese and Korean shipyards and then carried by barge to the site.

The port terminal's basic structural concept flows directly from the way in which it is organized as a set of ramps running seawards to carry passengers, goods and the general public, the overall length of the building (400 m; 1300 ft.) being determined by the length of ramp needed to span the distance from the *in situ* concrete apron to the public entrance level. In turn, these ramps provide support for the folded-steel plates that roof the two civic plazas, one external and one internal, and that span up to 30 m (100 ft.). Hence the structure consists of two elements: the girders housing the access ramps, and the folded plates spanning between them. Each more than 1 m (3.3 ft.) in height, the box girders are fabricated from steel plates, welded together and varying in thickness from 6 mm to 40 mm (0.25 in. to 1.5 in.) to reflect the different stresses to which they are subject, and are strengthened in key locations, such as the ramp landings, by concrete infilling. Special hatch openings were needed to allow access for welders to work inside the girders, once the girders had been assembled. Individual girder sections had to conform to the 50-tonne upper weight limit of the crawler-cranes used to fabricate the structure on site.

Superficially, the folded-plate sections of the terminal have the appearance of origami models, but in reality they are fabricated as metal sheets attached to a supporting framework to form a composite structure. Instead of being welded to the framing members — and thus subject to potential distortion — the thin steel plates are attached by Hilti rivets to the frames, the 1.5 m (5 ft.) module of which is matched to the roll width of the steel plate as delivered from the mill. Manufacturing tolerances were demanding: no more than plus/minus 3 mm (0.1 in.) for the girders and no more than 10 mm (0.4 in.) for the assembly of the girders and folded plates. Junctions are formed with high-tension bolts in oversized holes. The structure was put together sequentially, with the actual co-ordinates of the girders — once these members were in place — being fed back to the plant fabricating the folded plates to ensure that they synchronized exactly with their bearings.

Yokohama demonstrates convincingly how an imaginative architectural concept that flows from a demanding — and often internally conflicting — client brief can stimulate a structural-engineering solution of equal quality and suitability. It is difficult, here, to say exactly where architecture stops and engineering begins.

ABOVE The upper level of the terminal becomes an addition to the city's public realm, providing space for pedestrians to promenade and to view the arrival of passenger ships.

FAR LEFT Timber-clad routes offer constantly changing outlooks.

LEFT Interior ramp with folded-plate beams above, typical of the complex, fluid spaces inside the building.

Key Facts

Architects:	RMJM
Structural engineers:	Arup/Tony Gee & Partners
Length of aqueduct:	100 m (330 ft.)
Height between canals:	25 m (82 ft.)
Cost:	UK£78,000,000

S naking through the countryside and into the heart of industrial cities, canals have frequently been dubbed the 'motorways' of their day – linking major centres, transporting goods, and, where one meets another, creating ingenious intersections of great complexity and often beauty. They can also boast their own brand of architecture – the label 'engineering' alone hardly does such structures justice – emerging from the need to change levels, to intersect, and to tunnel beneath or bridge over natural obstacles.

The most dramatic example of such canal architecture must be the boat lift, rare on British waterways but always eye-catching. The most significant of this type hitherto was the Anderton Boat Lift in Cheshire in north-west England. It was designed and built by Edwin Clark in 1875 to transfer cargo-carrying barges from the River Weaver to the Trent & Mersey Canal some 15 m (50 ft.) above,

Falkirk Wheel
Falkirk, Scotland, 1998–2002

The new concrete aqueduct threads through five piers, before meeting the wheel that will lower boats to the Forth & Clyde Canal 25 m (80 ft.) below.

As boats travel along the aqueduct, passengers are afforded a dramatic, high-level vantage point from which to enjoy the Scottish landscape.

ABOVE Part of the wheel – with a canal boat in one of the caissons – is shown at the level of the basin leading to the Forth & Clyde Canal; the sloping windows of the visitors' centre are seen to the right.

and was reopened in 2002 following refurbishment. In its day the Anderton Lift spawned many imitators in Europe and North America.

Yet canals can still deliver innovation. The Falkirk Wheel is indisputably the most dramatic component of the Millennium Link – an £84,500,000 project to forge a continuous waterway link between Scotland's east and west coasts. This unique boat lift transfers boats vertically between two historic canals in the Scottish Lowlands, the Union Canal and the Forth & Clyde Canal. The 25 m (82 ft.) vertical transit had previously been achieved via a flight of eleven locks, which were decommissioned in 1933. The new solution is a wheel that takes two boats up and two boats down (or a load of 400 tonnes, including the weight of water) the equivalent of a nine-storey building. As well as representing a world first, the Falkirk Wheel forms a notable landmark and a tourist attraction of national importance, as was intended by project promoters British Waterways from the outset.

The drama begins when boats on the high-level Union Canal emerge from a new tunnel under the Roman Antonine Wall that narrows on to a semicircular concrete aqueduct 100 m (330 ft.) long, threaded through five piers, at 25 m (82 ft.) centres, founded in the hillside. From the aqueduct, the vessels enter a steel container, or caisson, capable

of holding two 20 m (65 ft.) boats side by side, which is then rotated half a turn on the wheel to bring them level with a new basin leading into the Forth & Clyde Canal, a process that takes fifteen minutes to complete. From below, vessels are propelled upwards at the same time, and the boats then move off along their respective waterways.

Each caisson is equipped with lock gates at both ends, allowing boats to enter or to leave, and echoing the workings of a traditional lock. Boats enter when the wheel is stationary; the caisson gates are closed, the wheel rotates, lifting or lowering the caisson, and the gates are opened to release the boats at their new level. During the wheel's rotation around its 3.5 m (11.5 ft.) central axle, the caissons remain horizontal owing to a set of five gears, the central gear being fixed in a static position around the central hub. Two smaller stability gears revolve around this as the wheel turns, meshing with the remaining two gear sets, which are fixed to the bottom ends of the caissons, making it impossible for them to rock back or forwards. This deft solution was directly inspired by the form of the wheel and the way in which the caissons are encircled by its hooked arms. The design team mocked up a Lego model to confirm that this concept could work. The turning and controlling of the wheel are achieved through a drive system based on a single hydraulic power-pack.

This pumps oil through ten hydraulic motors, each no larger than a telephone, ranged around one end of the central axle.

Given the simplicity of the wheel's basic concept, the other significant engineering challenge proved to be that of accommodating the inevitable movement of the concrete aqueduct structure while keeping a waterproof seal at the interface with the wheel structure. The solution developed by the design team involved introducing a short section fabricated in steel between the end of the main run of the concrete aqueduct and the wheel.

As an object in the landscape, the Falkirk Wheel transcends a direct expression of the engineering problems that it is required to resolve. Its form is unashamedly dramatic, enhanced by deliberate attention being paid to each functional element as part of an overall composition. Certain elements are visually suppressed, others enhanced, in the spirit of the best of the TVA dams (pages 104–107). It has the qualities of the best Millennium architecture, with visitor numbers to match.

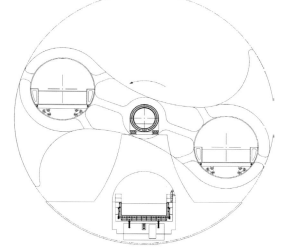

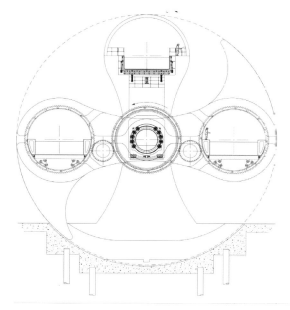

LEFT Sectional elevations showing the wheel lift in mid-rotation; (top) showing the link to Forth & Clyde Canal and (bottom) showing the aqueduct to the high-level Union Canal.

BELOW The wheel in mid-rotation, between the entry aqueduct and the lower basin.

Key Facts

Consortium: Transmanche Link (Balfour Beatty Construction, Costain, Wimpey Worldwide, Taylor Woodrow, Tarmac, Bouygues, Dumez, SAE, SGE, Spie Batignolles)

Length: 51.5 km (32 miles) (37.5 km/23 miles under water)

Diameter of two train tunnels: 7.6 m (25 ft.) (inner diameter)

Diameter of central service tunnel: 5 m (16 ft.) (inner diameter)

Boring rate: 400 m (1320 ft.) maximum per week

Cost: UK£9 billion

Channel Tunnel
Folkestone, UK–Calais, France, 1987–94

ABOVE One of the two giant tunnel-boring machines (TBMs) is trained into position. These massive machines combined the processes of drilling, removing spoil and shoring up the tunnel roof and sides with concrete linings.

OPPOSITE TOP An aerial view of the tunnel mouth on the French side, from which trains emerge into the countryside at Fréthun.

OPPOSITE Engineering of the power supply for the Eurostar train engines catered for both British and French voltages. High-speed passenger trains now make the journey between London and Paris in just over two-and-a-half hours.

Despite a long-standing historical rivalry, both Britain and France have always stood to benefit from an all-weather link between their shores for the transit of passengers and goods. Over the centuries various proposals for an underwater tunnel were mooted, including, most notably, Albert Mathieu's unworkable gas-lit scheme of 1802, to be ventilated at intervals by chimneys. Tunnel digging did actually start in earnest in the early 1880s on both sides of the English Channel, and again in 1974, the first attempt foundering in the face of invasion fears and the second as a consequence of financing difficulties, both on the British side. Today, trains make the twenty-minute underwater transit at speeds of up to 160 km/h (100 mph), for up to 500 times a day. It seems effortless, and its existence inevitable.

Commitment to build the fixed link came only in 1986, when a contract to design, build and operate a tunnel and associated works was awarded to the Anglo-French consortium Transmanche Link (now Eurotunnel), which managed ten smaller contractors and was financed by 220 syndicate banks. Work on what became the world's longest underwater tunnel (51.5 km; 32 miles), and reputedly the world's most expensive privately financed engineering project, started on site in December of the following year, with a brief to provide a rail crossing for vehicles as a shuttle service and for through-running passenger

trains. A rail tunnel was the only practical scheme, because a road tunnel of this length could not be ventilated, would require a larger cross-section and landtake, and would be clearly vulnerable to such accidents as the terrible fire that in 2001 struck the St Gotthard Tunnel (a mere 16 km/10 miles long) under the Alps.

The consortium's task was greatly eased by the presence of chalk beds along the proposed route, as chalk marl is a medium favourable for tunnelling, with low permeability, high consistency and requiring little support until sections of tunnel lining can be installed. Through this stratum, three separate tunnels were bored: two single-direction tunnels for trains – each 7.6 m (25 ft.) in diameter to accommodate the loading gauge set by the vehicle-carrying shuttle cars and the overhead electricity-supply cables – on either side of a smaller service tunnel linked to them by cross-passages. This central tunnel was bored first, and acted as a pilot for monitoring ground conditions en route before the two train running tunnels were cut. It now serves several functions: it acts as a supply duct for fresh air, maintained at a higher pressure than that of the running tunnels to prevent it from filling with smoke; it offers an emergency escape route for passengers; and it provides access for routine maintenance. The

safety function of the service tunnel proved its worth in November 1996, when a fire that took hold on a shuttle-borne lorry caused the train to halt in mid-crossing, trapping thirty passengers. They were all safely evacuated via the service tunnel, but the fire took more than six hours to extinguish.

Driving a total length of more than 150 km (95 miles) of tunnel in little more than three-and-a-half years called for prodigious technical and management expertise, as well as a workforce numbering 13,000 at its peak; the quantity of spoil removed was equivalent to more than three times the volume of the Great Pyramid at Giza, Egypt. The tunnelling was done by two enormous purpose-built tunnel-boring machines (TBMs) – each with a price tag of £10,000,000, yet in spirit and inspiration a direct descendant of the first Great Shield that the pioneering nineteenth-century engineer Marc Isambard Brunel (father of Isambard Kingdom Brunel) invented to bore his Thames Tunnel of 1825–43 in east London. Each TBM presented to the workface a rotating head holding tungsten-carbide-faced cutter discs, mounted on the front of the tunnelling shield, which could be steered. The cutting-head was pushed forwards with the pressure necessary to engage the chalk marl by thruster rams acting against the rear sections of the tunnelling shield. The shield was kept in place by radial rams forcing into place the concrete segments lining much of the tunnel, which were precast near Calais and brought to site via trains and,

finally, transferred by conveyor belt to the TBMs. By repeating this tunnelling cycle, with each TBM in effect forming its own continuous 'assembly line' for cutting, removing spoil and installing tunnel linings, progress could be rapid – one TBM moved forwards more than 400 m (1300 ft.) in the space of a week. The breakthrough of the last short section between the TBM driven from Britain and the other from France was made on 30 October 1990, with the two tunnelling teams enjoying their first handshake on the first day of December. By this time the British TBM had been driven down into its permanent resting-place in the Channel bed.

How was such a perfect match-up achieved? With an overall length of nearly 40 km (25 miles) between access shafts to be tunnelled blind, high-precision guidance was essential. Base lines were established on both sides of the Channel, co-ordinated by satellite signals, then projected optically down the access shafts and along the tunnel to be calibrated against a target point set on the rear of each TBM. Their vertical and horizontal alignments were subject to continuous monitoring and adjustment based on feedback from the positioning devices. This system produced breathtaking results: the centre-lines of the tunnel were off target by a mere 35 cm (13.8 in.) horizontally and 5.8 cm (2.3 in.) vertically. In so extreme an environment of mud, spoil, pressure, noise and heat, 60 m (200 ft.) below the seabed, this must rank as the project's greatest triumph.

OPPOSITE Each tunnel-boring machine (TBM) was capped by a rotating head holding tungsten-carbide-faced cutter discs. With the engineers appearing tiny as they work, the gigantic scale of these machines becomes clear.

BELOW A section of a TBM is lowered down the access shaft.

Key Facts

Design engineer:	Gunnar Lotsberg
Tunnel length:	24.5 km (15 miles)
Average transit time:	20 minutes
Max depth of rock above tunnel:	1400 m (4600 ft.)
Cost:	US$125,000,000

RIGHT Construction operations in preparation for drilling and blasting. More than 5000 blasts were required for the tunnel to break through, each blast releasing 500 m³ (655 cubic yards) of rock.

BELOW The drilling jumbo, guided by laser beams, runs three hydraulic drills. Each blast needed 100 holes drilled to contain explosives.

Driving through a major road tunnel offers motorists a particular experience not shared by the rail passenger, whose transit generally lacks interest, being merely a matter of looking at one's watch from time to time until there is (literally) light at the end of the tunnel. For drivers, the levels of concentration needed are far higher, as the passage is made in the company of a stream of other vehicles to a diabolic soundtrack amplified by the tunnel walls. Millions of tonnes of rock bear down on the tunnel from above, and the atmosphere of titanic grandeur is reinforced by mysterious side chambers and the glimpse of escape routes. By comparison, despite their equal engineering achievement and their great length – up to 54 km (33.5 miles) in the case of the world-record-holding Seikan Tunnel in Japan – rail-only tunnels seem prosaic.

Thanks to its dramatic topography and to the need to keep routes open during winter, Norway

Laerdal–Aurland Road Tunnel
Norway, 1995–2000

has constructed more than its fair share of road and rail tunnels: the Gudvanga Tunnel (Bergen–Oslo, 11.4 km; 7.1 miles) and the Folgefonn Tunnel (Odda–Gjerde, 11.2 km; 6.9 miles) are both for road traffic, while its most notable rail tunnel (Romeriksporten, 14.6 km; 9.1 miles) carries the link from Gardermoen Airport to Oslo. More recently, however, the scale of operations has been increased dramatically, with the boring of a new link costing $125,000,000, between Laerdal and Aurland. The world's longest road tunnel, this connection provides an alternative to the ferry crossing between the Bergen region and the east of Norway, where Oslo is situated. This route had previously been traversed by a mountain pass dubbed the Snow Road, which was subject to periodic closures and only reliably passable for a few months during the summer. Remarkably, in view of its length – 24.5 km (15 miles) – and the need to remove more than 2,500,000 cubic metres (3,300,000 cubic yards) of spoil, the Laerdal–Aurland Tunnel required a mere five years from its inception to its opening by King Harald of Norway on 27 November 2000. Such progress was facilitated by the decision to drill a 2 km (1.3 mile) long access tunnel from a side valley to meet the main bore, thus allowing drilling to take place from both ends and the centre simultaneously.

Lacking the usual reference points of passing landscape as a visual stimulus to motorists, road

tunnels of this great length need to be stage-managed to break the monotony – and hence danger – of the passage. In the case of Laerdal–Aurland, the transit, taking twenty minutes to complete, is broken down into four sections by three caverns, or aptly named 'mountain halls', grand enough to gladden the heart of the most demanding troll. Two are located 6 km (3.7 miles) from each end of the tunnel and the third at the mid-point. Their drama is further enhanced by change in the colour of the lighting, from the white used for the tunnel to blue and yellow for the caverns, creating at intervals the illusion of driving into daylight. The caverns have even found favour as a tourist draw in their own right and as an unconventional wedding venue.

As in the case of any road tunnel of comparable length, maintaining air quality is a primary concern, and involves a combination of efficient extraction and cleansing of polluted air. The extraction method involves drawing fresh air into the tunnel by huge fans at both entrances and then expelling it in a polluted state through the Tynjadalen access and ventilation side tunnel. Cleansing occurs in the world's first in-tunnel treatment plant, located in its own cavern some 9.5 km (6 miles) from Aurland. Polluted air is cleansed of dust and soot by passing it through an electrostatic filter, and the nitrogen dioxide is removed by a giant-sized carbon filter.

Safety and security measures in the tunnel are predictably extensive following such disasters as the St Gotthard Tunnel fire of October 2001, in which a blaze started by a vehicle collision caused eight deaths. Photo-monitoring of all vehicles as they enter and leave the tunnel, and failsafe communication networks to security centres in Bergen and Laerdal – linked to fire, police and hospital emergency departments – comprise the electronic infrastructure protecting motorists in transit. Apart from the refuge provided by the three 'mountain halls', the tunnel cross-section has been fashioned to include niches every 500 m (1640 ft.) for emergency use; fifteen turning areas for buses and articulated vehicles complete the physical measures in place. Emergency telephones and fire extinguishers are provided at more frequent intervals than previous best practice. In the event of an incident signalled by an emergency phone, stop-lights and signs instructing motorists to "turn and drive out" come into operation.

ABOVE Three caverns, or 'mountain halls', along the length of the tunnel provide spatial relief for drivers and additional opportunities to turn vehicles around.

BELOW LEFT The gondola in its original form. The timber decking of the platform has since been replaced to allow vehicles to be carried.

BELOW RIGHT A view during construction, showing how the bridge resembles two independent structures joined together.

Key Facts

Design engineers:	George Camille Imbault/Cleveland Bridge & Engineering Co. Ltd
Contractors:	Sir William Arrol & Co.
Overall lengtn:	260 m (855 ft.)
Total span:	90 m (295 ft.)
Height of gondola above river level:	50 m (165 ft.)
Gondola transport capacity:	approx. 9 cars and 250–300 passengers
Crossing time:	2–3 minutes
Cost:	UK£84,000

Ferdinand Arnodin

The French construction engineer Ferdinand Arnodin (1845–1924) was a decisive figure in the development of the transporter bridge. With a rare speciality in cable design and a patent application in place, he joined forces with the Spanish architect Alberto Palaçio, who had independently developed the concept, to build such a bridge in Spain, crossing the River Nervion, near its mouth and at the entrance to the port of Portugalete. With a span of 164 m (540 ft.) and horizontal deck, from which the transit car was suspended at a height of 45 m (150 ft.), the bridge opened in July 1893.

From 1898 onwards, Arnodin proceeded to build further transporter-bridge crossings at Bizerte, Rochefort, Rouen, Nantes and Marseilles in France and at Newport in Wales, usually acting as operator as well as constructor. He continued to experiment with new systems and to refine his bridge constructions until his death.

Transporter Bridge
Middlesbrough, England, 1909–11

More, perhaps, than any other industrialized region in the world, north-east England can lay claim to a sustained tradition of innovation in the building of bridges. These range from the first Roman structures, through Newcastle's many bridges high and low, to Gateshead's newly opened 'winking eye' bridge spanning the River Tyne. Some commentators explain this pre-eminence in terms of the region's topography – steep ravines, slopes and valleys – but such analysis fails to take into account those notable structures bridging flat expanses of river or estuary. The building of such bridges tends to require long and expensive approach spans.

One solution to this problem, especially where the traffic is light and consists largely of foot passengers, is the transporter bridge, or 'aerial ferry'. This family of structures enjoyed its heyday at the beginning of the twentieth century, when fifteen examples were built in Europe and the United States, of which about half survive. In essence, this form of bridge consists of an enormous girder supported or suspended high enough above a river to allow clearance for shipping below. A car, or 'gondola', carrying passengers and vehicles is suspended from the girder and makes the transit across the river under steam or electric power, being raised from ground level on one bank and lowered to ground on the other. Typical applications include sites where industry has developed faster on

one bank of a river than another and existing ferry connections prove inadequate to carry the workforce across twice a day.

Such was the reason behind the building of the Middlesbrough Transporter Bridge. As heavy industry consolidated at Port Clarence on the north bank of the River Tees, while workers – upwards of 4000 men in 1906 – lived on the other side, the difficulties in crossing the river became acute. With a crossing time of fifteen minutes, the existing ferry operations had become bottlenecked, and were further hampered by strong tides. As a short-term expedient, river steamers were brought in to service the crossing, but the ultimate solution proved to be a permanent high-level bridge that would not impede river traffic. Advice was sought by the local council from the French engineer Ferdinand Arnodin, by then established as leader in the field of transporter-bridge design, and from the Cleveland Bridge & Engineering Co. Ltd, another experienced authority.

Built by the Glasgow firm of Sir William Arrol & Co. within a period of twenty-seven months and opened by Prince Arthur, Duke of Connaught, on 17 October 1911, the Middlesbrough Transporter Bridge was effectively conceived as two independent structures joined mid-way across the river; each of the twin pylon towers supports a back span of 45 m (150 ft.) acting as a counterbalancing cantilever to the main span of about 90 m (295 ft.). Below the main girder, a gondola is suspended some 50 m (165 ft.) above the river on a wheel-and-rail system; it makes the crossing in two to three minutes every quarter-hour, eighteen hours a day. Besides its continuing importance as a convenient all-weather river crossing – it can withstand winds of up to 70 km/h (45 mph) – the Transporter Bridge has attained iconic status as a symbol of Teesside, a distinction underlined by its award in 1993 of the Institution of Mechanical Engineers' highest honour, the Heritage Plaque.

Notable survivors of Europe's once-numerous group of transporter bridges include that spanning the River Charente at Matrou, near Rochefort in France (span: 140 m or 460 ft.; girder height: 50 m or 165 ft.); a crossing of the Kiel Canal at Rendsburg in Germany (span: 150 m or 490 ft.; girder height: 40 m or 130 ft.); one over the River Nervion, in Spain (span: 164 m or 540 ft.; girder height: 45 m or 150 ft.); and the Newport Transporter Bridge over the River Usk in Wales (span: 200 m or 655 ft.; girder height: 55 m or 180 ft.). The bridge at Newport ranks as the most spectacular remaining monument to the talents of Ferdinand Arnodin, the engineer who will always be regarded as the inventor of a type of structure that still impresses by its lightness and apparent fragility; Middlesbrough, however, retains its status as the largest operational transporter bridge in the world.

ABOVE The distinctive profile of the bridge has become synonymous with Teesside.

OPPOSITE The gondola is suspended from a travelling gantry running beneath the main bridge girder.

Key Facts

Structural engineer: Eugène Freyssinet

Contractors: Enterprises Limousin

Total span: 888 m (2915 ft.)

Main spans (3x): 188 m (615 ft.)

Rise: 27.5 m (90 ft.)

RIGHT Eugène Freyssinet (on the left) was one of France's most innovative engineering talents. Here he is pictured with the builder, Limousin, visiting the site of the Orly airship hangars, the most famous of his pioneering shell-roof structures.

There is often a moment in the career of a great engineering pioneer that can be identified subsequently as a turning-point in the development of personal themes, obsessions or insights. Sometimes this watershed takes the form of a published paper or of a lecture to one's peers, but more often than not a single structure provides the visible proof. For one of France's most eminent *grands constructeurs*, Eugène Freyssinet (1879–1962), that moment was the completion of the Albert-Louppe Bridge at Plougastel, spanning the estuary of the River Elorn close to the port of Brest, France. Declared open by the then president of France, Paul Doumer, on 9 October 1930, the bridge crossed the 560 m (1840 ft.) wide river using three reinforced-concrete vaults, each spanning a new world-record distance of 188 m (615 ft.) between pier centre-lines. The Albert-Louppe bridge, carrying a roadway and a railway track below, was also remarkable for

Albert-Louppe Bridge
Plougastel, France, 1923–30

costing only half the sums estimated by competing design proposals.

Freyssinet's career was no less impressive than his bridge. His quest for utility and economy of means began in earnest with his appointment to the local office of Ponts et Chaussées (Bridges and Roads) at Moulins in the Allier département, where in 1909, at the age of thirty, he designed and had built three bridges over the River Moulins. Each bridge had a reinforced-concrete span of 73 m (240 ft.) with a remarkably flat arch and cost little more to build than the budget for a single bridge of conventional design. After World War I, Freyssinet embarked on a second period of innovation, this time in the design and construction of shell-roof structures in concrete, the most famous of which were his twin airship hangars (1921) at Orly. Although renowned as the pioneer of prestressing techniques, Freyssinet also proved to be a master in the use of *unreinforced* mass concrete, as is triumphantly visible in the 100 m (330 ft.) arch of the Pont Neuf at Villeneuve-sur-Lot (1914–19), in Aquitaine.

The designer's boldness and ingenuity are everywhere evident in the building methods adopted for the Albert-Louppe Bridge. Each of the three great arches was cast using a single timber shutter, the largest such wooden assembly in the history of construction. The arches were floated into place on two specially designed barges, themselves inevitably of reinforced-concrete construction, and each 35 m x 8 m (115 ft. x 26 ft.). Despite its enormous size, the shutter was built entirely from

standard planks of pinewood 4 cm (1.6 in.) thick, fixed together simply by staggered nails, and with its shape and alignment controlled by a network of tensioned steel wires. A further innovation was a world first in the use of the now commonplace technique of corbelling an arch outwards and upwards on each side of a bridge pier, so that the structure is always balanced during construction. A temporary funicular gantry, with a range of 800 m (2625 ft.), advanced across the estuary along the centre-line of the bridge. An operator in the cabin at the top of the gantry could control the manoeuvring into place of such prefabricated components as the metal sections that formed the lower deck of the bridge and carried the railway.

Freyssinet himself rated Albert-Louppe as one of his most significant achievements, remarking that "Plouçastel is the most successful of all my bridges. The bridge has a certain scale, not the scale of man-made artefacts but that of Nature itself." The clear, leaping spans of the three great arches, the muscularity of the vertical diaphragms and the filigree of the trelliswork supporting the railway deck combine to create an impressively robust design.

In retrospect, however, this monumental structure could be said to represent the zenith of reinforced concrete as the preferred material for realizing major civil-engineering projects. The era of prestressed concrete, with the potential for creating spans of unprecedented lengths, lay ahead. In this field, Eugène Freyssinet would again prove himself to be a pioneer.

ABOVE The three great arches were each cast in turn, using a huge timber shutter, and were then floated into place using two barges.

OPPOSITE The scale of Freyssinet's achievement is evident from this view of the river estuary. Since 1994 the Albert-Louppe Bridge has not been used for cars. The new road bridge can be seen under construction parallel to Freyssinet's bridge.

Key Facts

Structural engineers: Sir Ralph Freeman/Dr J.J.C. Bradfield, New South Wales Public Works Department

Contractors: Dorman Long & Co.

Overall length: 1149 m (3770 ft.)

Span: 503 m (1650 ft.)

Width of deck: 49 m (160 ft.)

Cost: AUS$4,100,000

Freeman Fox & Partners

Sir Ralph Freeman's involvement as structural consultant on the Sydney Harbour Bridge is characteristic of the career of one of the most notable bridge designers of his time and of a key figure in the growth of the firm of consultant engineers Freeman Fox & Partners (now known as Hyder Consulting Ltd).

Founded by Sir Charles Fox, builder of the Crystal Palace for the Great Exhibition in London of 1851, the firm designed railways, tunnels and such bridges as those crossing Sydney Harbour and Victoria Falls under Freeman senior. It acted as consulting engineer, under Freeman's son, to the 1951 Festival of Britain and subsequently became a world leader in the design of long-span suspension bridges. These include the two over the Bosphorus Strait (see page 9), and in Britain, the Forth, the Severn and the Humber estuary crossings.

Later growth and diversification of the firm led to its involvement in the building of the Hong Kong Metro and of power stations and motorways, with important innovations being made in all areas of structural design.

Sydney Harbour Bridge

Sydney, New South Wales, Australia, 1922–32

ABOVE The bridge arch rises in strong, almost surreal, contrast to the tightly packed terraces of housing, and its massive scale is clear.

As a world-renowned city, Sydney is thrice blessed: it has a magnificent natural harbour with picturesque views at every turn; an opera house with a memorable profile that serves as a symbol for the city; and the Sydney Harbour Bridge, a structure, though utilitarian, that far transcends the job it was built to do. Few visitors – and especially those coming by ferry to the terminal on Circular Quay – can fail to relish the visual counterpoint between the white 'sails' of Jørn Utzon's Opera House and the robust elegance of the steelwork of the bridge – the 'old coathanger', as it is sometimes called – opened half a century earlier.

While the idea of a bridge crossing Sydney Harbour to link Dawes Point and Milson's Point had been mooted several times from the end of the nineteenth century and into the twentieth, the driving force behind its construction came in the determined person of Dr J.J.C. Bradfield. A staff member of the New South Wales Public Works Department, Bradfield became chief engineer of the project, and was responsible for the outline structural concept and documentation on which worldwide design-and-construction tenders were called in 1922. From the six finalists, the long-established Middlesbrough-based British firm of Dorman Long & Co. was awarded the contract and brought in the noted structural engineer Sir Ralph Freeman as consultant to oversee the

detailed design. His specialist expertise was highly necessary, as every change in the bridge design required the recalculation of the entire single-arch structure that emerged from the bidding process.

The structure as built exemplifies an evolutionary period in bridge design, when conscious efforts were being made to heighten the dramatic contrast between the familiar assembly of standard steelwork sections and a more deliberately 'architectural' treatment of other elements. Here, the unadorned steel framework that forms the great arch of the bridge – the profile of which has many antecedents worldwide – contrasts most effectively with the four 90 m (300 ft.) high pylons. Built of concrete, the pylons are faced with 18,000 cubic metres (23,500 cubic yards) of granite quarried near Moruya and shipped in purpose-built barges over the 300 km (185 miles) north to Sydney. The foundations for the four bearings that carry the full load of the arch and deck are concealed. These rest on sandstone rock and were infilled with specially mixed high-strength concrete laid in a hexagonal matrix.

Once the approach spans were complete and the pylon towers in place, the central arch, spanning just over 500 m (1640 ft.), was formed by two half-arches built out progressively from each shore. The structures were stabilised using 128 temporary steel cables passing over concrete saddles and running

ABOVE A view under the bridge towards the city centre, the Circular Quay ferries and Sydney's other major landmark, the Opera House.

back to anchor points underground; these cables were released once the arch had been completed. The arch sections were prefabricated on land, transferred by barge into position and then raised by an electrically powered creeper-crane located at each end of the arch and advancing with the lengthening span. The sections of the arch were successfully joined on 19 August 1930. It took a further nine months to install the bridge deck, which was built outwards from the centre to make best use of the creeper-cranes that were now situated in that central position. In February 1932, the bridge was ready to be load-tested using ninety-six steam locomotives, and 19 March saw the official opening ceremony, performed by the premier of New South Wales, the Hon. John Lang.

Perhaps less widely known are the wider social implications of building the bridge. Finding space at a constricted point in the harbour for the construction sites and lay-down areas, not to mention the extensive access roadworks and approaches required, led to the demolition of more than 800 houses without any compensation being paid to their owners. A more favourable result arose directly from the method of construction chosen. The complex design of the bridge was highly labour-intensive, and it still requires heavy maintenance. Cold-chisel riveting techniques, more typical of the nineteenth century, were extensively used to assemble the steelwork – six million rivets in the bridge deck alone, some up to 10 cm (4 in.) long and weighing 3.5 kg (7.7 lb). As a consequence, the building of Sydney Harbour Bridge proved to be an important generator of employment at the height of the Depression – for those working in Sydney on the structure itself, or in the fabrication workshops at Milson's Point, and for the steelworkers of Dorman Long & Co. in Middlesbrough, who provided almost 80% of the 52,800 tonnes of steel needed, including 39,000 tonnes for the arch alone.

For most visitors to Sydney, it is difficult now to imagine the harbour skyline without a bridge of such distinctive character that still qualifies as the widest long-span arch bridge in the world.

Key Facts

BELOW Construction drawing of the Schwandbach Bridge. The bridge deck is curved on plan, with the vertical cross-walls leaning outwards from the base of the arch to support it.

Structural engineer: Robert Maillart

Salginatobel span: 90 m (295 ft.)

Schwandbach span: 37.5 m (123 ft.)

Salginatobel rise: 13 m (43 ft.)

Schwandbach rise: 6 m (20 ft.)

Robert Maillart

Celebrated for a series of remarkable bridges and other structures in reinforced concrete, the Swiss engineer Robert Maillart (1872–1940) combined bold experiments in the use of this material with a refined aesthetic judgement. Structural engineer, teacher at his alma mater, Zurich Polytechnic, and sometime contractor for his own projects, Maillart achieved pre-eminence in bridge design in Switzerland from the first decade of the twentieth century, and was a frequent winner of design competitions.

His most celebrated structure, the Salginatobel Bridge, exemplifies his preferred working method, which involved building on lessons learned from earlier designs. From one project to the next, each element was progressively refined and then combined with others to produce structures of great strength and elegance.

Such is their enduring quality that Maillart's designs have continued to be exhibited, published and discussed, a tribute to his ability to create structures that, while serving their purpose, are also works of art. Of his forty-seven bridges, almost all are still in use.

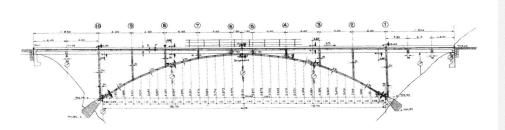

Salginatobel and Schwandbach Bridges
Switzerland, 1930 & 1933

Despite their relative isolation in remote Alpine sites, two bridges designed by the great Swiss engineer Robert Maillart are among the most celebrated structures of the twentieth century. Maillart's reputation as a pioneer of bridge design, whose structures consistently advanced the applications of reinforced concrete, has never been higher.

The Salginatobel Bridge (1930) is the most famous example of a structural type invented by Maillart – the three-hinged hollow-box arch built in reinforced concrete. His earliest (and the world's first) use of this form was in the bridge over the River Inn at Zuoz (1901). He followed this in 1905 with the three-hinged arch design of the Tavanasa Bridge over the Rhine at Grisons, at the time of construction the longest-spanning reinforced-concrete arch bridge in Switzerland (51 m; 170 ft.). Its form is a direct expression of the physical forces acting upon it. It also embodied all the key attributes of a Maillart design – tautness, powerful elegance, efficient use of materials, and best value to build and maintain.

Maillart's proposal for the Salginatobel Bridge won a design-and-construct competition as it had the lowest costs; the bridge as built has the longest span (90 m; 295 ft.) of all Maillart's structures. The central section is a hollow-box, light structure with internal fins, on the model of the Zuoz Bridge; for the outer sections these fins are exposed as vertical supports linking the arch to the bridge deck. Subtle visual adjustments, such as the projection of the parapet to create a powerful shadow, add drama to the bridge's profile.

With the Schwandbach Bridge, with a span of 37.5 m (123 ft.), Maillart produced what many consider to be the most perfect synthesis of bridge form, in what proved to be his last deck-stiffened arch structure. As the designer and critic Max Bill noted in his 1949 monograph on Maillart: "It can be claimed without exaggeration that it combines a maximum of economy and beauty while perfectly fulfilling its purpose." What is most notable about the structure is that, rather than being placed straight across the deep ravine, it curves elliptically on plan so that the smooth flow of the roadway is uninterrupted, and clumsy transitions at each end where the approach road flows on to the bridge deck are avoided. The structure's elegance is further enhanced by the absence of closed masonry or concrete abutments on the approaches and by maintaining a constant depth of edge for the deck, so that the line of the bridge elevation is unbroken despite the greater width of the approach span.

The structural problem posed was that of how to connect this curving plan of the deck with the vertically curved arch below and yet create a form whose performance could still be calculated. Maillart solved this by sloping outwards the vertical trapezoid cross-walls from the base of the arch to the deck, their widths varying according to their relative positions along the span. Hence the inside face of the arch follows the curve of the bridge deck, while the outer face remains straight, projecting beyond the arch above. This extra width towards the springing points had the further benefit of providing additional resistance to the twisting loads produced by the curving bridge deck.

Instead of the solid parapets that are found on earlier bridges, here the bridge is edged with nothing more substantial than a metal railing; the necessary rigidity is provided by an edge beam on each side of the roadway, achieving a smooth, sweeping elevation. Yet visually the most notable innovation achieved by Maillart at Schwandbach is the way in which the line of the arch remains unbroken without appearing to merge with that of the bridge deck above.

These two bridges, daring and innovative in form, retain an immense power to impress. In 1991 the Salginatobel Bridge, along with twelve other notable structures worldwide, gained the accolade of International Civil Engineering Landmark, awarded by the American Society of Civil Engineers. As the English critic Philip Morton Shand wrote: "What Maillart accomplished is far better and more directly apprehended by the eye than by the brain."

OPPOSITE Erection of timber shuttering to support casting of the *in situ* concrete arch of the Schwandbach Bridge.

BELOW LEFT The Salginatobel Bridge's dramatic leap across the valley is one of the iconic images of structural engineering. It was the longest bridge span Maillart ever built.

BELOW Timber shuttering for the Salginatobel Bridge was built up from the valley floor.

Key Facts

Designer:	Sir Donald Bailey
Span range:	10–60 m (33–195 ft.)
Loading capacity:	40 tonnes
Average construction time:	3–5 hours
Total length of bridges constructed during World War II:	320 km (200 miles)

RIGHT Bailey bridges were crucial in keeping open essential lines of supply and for deploying troops during the Allies' advance across Europe.

Many an ingenious invention has been the result of a hobby. When British civil servant Donald (later Sir Donald) Bailey showed colleagues at the War Office the home-made models of temporary bridges for military use that he had devised in his leisure time, his ideas were supported, and full-size prototypes were built, despite initial scepticism. Production of Bailey bridges, as they were named, began slowly, yet by D-Day (6 June 1944) they were available in sufficient quantity to prove an invaluable tool in the campaign to liberate Europe.

Bailey's approach was entirely novel. Any system to build temporary bridges under battlefield conditions needed to be robust, portable, foolproof and flexible in use. Bailey made sure that the erection of his bridges would require the use of only simple hand tools such as jacks, hammers and rope. His 'kit of parts' could be transported on army trucks and its

Bailey Bridges
Worldwide, 1936–

largest component was of a size that could be handled by only four or five men. The other major innovation was the method used for constructing the bridge: the assembled bridge sections were slid forwards on rollers – rather like a nearly horizontal ladder – then 'launched' out across the opening, with the landward side counterbalanced, and, finally, jacked down on to spreader footings on the far bank. In this way, the structure was self-supporting.

Essentially unchanged, Bailey bridges are still in use today. The 'kit of parts' contains three principal components: a set of 6.25 m (20 ft.) transoms, which run across the width of the bridge; a set of 3 m (10 ft.) stringers, which are linked to the topsides of the transoms to form rectangular units; and the 3 m (10 ft.) side panels, which as open trusses provide the structural 'muscle' of the bridge. The side panels are clamped to the stringers to form the 3 m (10 ft.) long sections of the bridge, which has a 3.6 m (12 ft.) wide roadbed. As these sections are pushed forwards progressively on rollers, the next bridge section is built behind. Structural continuity between sections is achieved by driving steel pins into overlapping holes in the corners of the panels. Although lacking its bridge deck, which is formed by timber boards laid over the steelwork, the Bailey is now ready for 'launching'.

During World War II, the key attribute of the design was its inherent flexibility. Instead of needing to develop a bespoke structure for every crossing, military engineers could readily adjust the Bailey according to the span length required, the condition of any remaining bridge abutments and, crucially, the weight of vehicles needing to make the crossing. This last factor could often prove decisive as the weight of the newer tanks, such as the Grant and the Sherman M4, had increased to 35 tonnes. To cope with span requirements ranging from 10 m (33 ft.) to more than 60 m (195 ft.), it was a simple matter with the modular design to bolt on extra standard panels, either vertically to form a deeper side girder or side-by-side to increase cross-sectional area. Most ingenious of all, this flexibility meant that any panels damaged by shellfire could simply be bypassed by bolting on new panels above or beside them, to form an instant 'splint' for the defective section. Designs were limited only by expediency and imagination.

As preparations for Operation Overlord – the Normandy invasion – were ramped up, Sir Donald's design was licensed for manufacture in the United States. There and in Britain a total of nearly 500,000 tonnes of bridges were fabricated – 320 km (200 miles) of fixed bridges and 65 km (40 miles) of floating crossings. Notable achievements in Bailey bridge construction include the forty-one bridges totalling more than 1.5 km (1 mile) built by a single 600-man engineering battalion of US General George Patton's Third Army, on the advance towards Germany. Many bridges remained in use to serve the civilian population, pending permanent crossings. Both Generals Eisenhower and Montgomery placed the Bailey bridge high among the hardware that made victory possible.

Today updated versions of the basic design continue to serve in military conflicts worldwide; transport authorities use them for temporary crossings; and refurbished Baileys provide low-cost, rural links.

ABOVE Longer spans were sometimes achieved by using river barges as support piers.

OPPOSITE The Bailey bridge proved invaluable in reopening river crossings where conventional bridges had been destroyed.

Key Facts

Structural engineer: Christian Menn	
Total length: 678 m (2225 ft.)	
Main span: 174 m (570 ft.)	
Side spans: 127 m (415 ft.)	
Pier height: 150 m (490 ft.)	

RIGHT The bold form of the bridge remains imposing against the backdrop of the steep Alpine valley.

FAR RIGHT The piers extended above the deck level create an effective contrast with the horizontal profile of the bridge deck.

Ganter Bridge
Eisten, Valais, Switzerland, 1976–80

Certain bridge designs are so distinctive that they appear to have come into the world fully formed, lacking apparent precedent and having a form in which nothing can be altered, added or removed without detriment. Yet the emergence of such structures is never an isolated event; they inevitably represent a key point in the development of their designer's career and derive from a background of experience in teasing out the most efficient and telling forms for the purpose.

The pedigree of the Ganter Bridge, designed by the veteran Swiss engineer and educator Christian Menn, is a long one, and includes a direct link to the work of the great Swiss engineer Robert Maillart (see pages 76–77) through his father Simon Menn, a renowned civil engineer who had been associated with Maillart on his later projects. Christian Menn began his own civil-engineering career imbued with a knowledge of Maillart's work, and the earliest bridges that he designed show a strong direct influenc. However, by the time he had the opportunity to design a crossing for the Ganter Valley in the canton of Valais in southern Switzerland, he had already mastered not only the engineering parameters of high, long-span bridge design but also the aesthetics of such structures in terms of a visually resolved solution.

The beginning of what many regard as Menn's most notable design occurred in 1974, when by invitation he developed, as an alternative to a costly tunnel, a proposal for a two-lane autoroute bridge, to cross the Ganter Valley and join the road leading to the Simplon Pass, which links Switzerland and Italy across the Alps. The engineer's solution as built evolved from an initial study of possible locations in which to found the support piers in the challenging ground conditions of the valley. These positions were changed over the course of the design development to balance the length of the side and central spans and to regularize the overall configuration of the bridge.

Menn's choice of hollow-box pillars slightly wider than the roadway as his two bridge-supports brings great visual strength to the bridge in profile without obstructing the great open sweep of the valley; this impression is reinforced by the wide spacing between them. The hollow-box form is particularly efficient in resisting side loads, especially from wind forces, and the pillar positions chosen enabled economies to be made in the reuse of formwork needed to cast the hollow box that forms the bridge deck.

With spans of this length – a central span of 174 m (570 ft.), the longest in Switzerland, and 127 m (415 ft.) for each of the curved side spans – a girder of great depth would normally have been needed where it met the support pillars. Instead, Menn used cable stays to create additional structural support, thus reducing what would otherwise have been cantilevers 87 m (285 ft.) long to spans of only 40% of that length and keeping the cantilever depth at a maximum of 5 m (16 ft.). These stays he encased in concrete so that they follow the curve of the side spans, and also to protect them from corrosion. As the cables are bonded to the concrete, they benefit additionally from stresses lower than those that would occur if they were exposed.

Although the decision to enclose the stays was made for functional reasons, it has resulted in the most memorable and distinctive part of the bridge's profile; exposed stays would have proved visually weak, especially in the central span.

One of the most obvious aesthetic issues needing to be resolved by Menn was how to reconcile the relatively thin horizontal profile of the narrow bridge deck with the powerful verticality of the support pillars. One part of his solution was to extend a section of each pillar 10 m (33 ft.) above the deck and to use it as a support for the encased cable stays so that the junction profile is smoother. The pylons are also flared outwards towards the top, a further aesthetic refinement that appears absolutely inevitable in retrospect.

Menn's unique and unprecedented design proved in the event to be a very economical solution, costing only about half the amount estimated for the tunnel alternative. Its great interest lies not only its visual distinctiveness but also in the way in which Menn has weighed the various technical possibilities for each element of the structure against the aesthetic consequences of their use and has combined them in a powerful and fitting solution. Here the architecture is not applied – it flows from the mind and the lifelong experience of a single great engineer

BELOW The cable stays of the Ganter Bridge are encased in concrete to allow them to retain the curved alignment of the bridge, and at the same time heightening the visual strength of its profile.

Key Facts

Architect/Engineer:	Santiago Calatrava
Total length:	250 m (820 ft.)
Main span:	200 m (655 ft.)
Pylon height:	142 m (465 ft.)

LEFT The pylon requires no back-stays; cables are tensioned by the weight of the steel and concrete structure alone.

BELOW Pedestrians enjoy a central route elevated above the level of the roadway on either side.

Cable-stayed Bridges

The Alamillo Bridge in Seville takes its place in a line of dramatic cable-stayed bridges that form part of an urban waterside landscape, often at the heart of a city centre; other examples include the Charles River Mainline Bridge (2001) in the centre of Boston, Massachusetts. A cable-stayed bridge structure differs from that of a suspension bridge in that the deck is supported directly by a set of cables anchored to single or paired pylons. The first extensive use of this structural principle was in the late 1950s, in a group of bridges crossing the River Rhine; these were followed by innovative French designs such as the Pont de Brotonne in Normandy and the bridge at St-Nazaire (1975).

In other cases such as the Erasmus Bridge in Rotterdam (pages 88–89) these urban water crossings can signal a 'gateway' to a quarter earmarked for regeneration. The high mast – often single – and fan of cables signify an optimism and dynamism that can make such bridges effective symbols of a progressive city administration.

Alamillo Bridge
Seville, Spain, 1987–92

World's fairs, exhibitions, congresses and other causes for celebration have always proved fruitful in terms of new public works, in particular great bridges and major elements of road infrastructure. Many such works are, from the outset, intended to continue to serve the host city once the visitors have departed. In the case of Seville's Expo '92, bridge-building was an essential stage in the opening up of road and pedestrian connections from the city proper westward to the (then) deserted Expo site, the island of La Cartuja. Besides creating the necessary physical links, the new bridges presented an unmissable opportunity to advertise the presence of Expo '92 and, as a bonus, to form a symbolic gateway to the rest of Spain. Four bridges were built, two following the designs of Santiago Calatrava, the noted Spanish architect–engineer.

Calatrava's original concept envisaged a pair of identical bridges to cross the Meandro San Jeronimo branch of the River Guadalquivir, providing access to La Cartuja island, with a new 1.5 km (0.9 mile) road along the bank between them. The road would also have incorporated the Puente de Cartuja viaduct, a remarkable design featuring a vaulted soffit and cantilevered dual carriageways shading the pedestrians below. The design of one bridge was intended to mirror that of the other along the centre-line of the river to create a mutually reinforcing

symmetry that would represent the hoped-for 'gateway'. In the event, only the Alamillo Bridge was realized, along with the viaduct, yet it is a design of such singularity and sculptural power as to make any cloning of it ill-advised.

To certain commentators, Seville's Alamillo Bridge clearly belongs to, and has evolved from, that family of cable-stayed bridge structures including those that graced the German Rhine from the late 1950s, many of which were designed by Professor Fritz Leonhardt and his colleagues, as well as subsequent bridges in France. The Alamillo Bridge, however, represents an imaginative leap forwards in this bridge typology. The single 142 m (465 ft.) high pylon from which the deck is supported, rakes back away from the city and the river towards the exhibition site, at an angle of 58 degrees, reputedly echoing the profile of the Great Pyramid at Giza.

The inspiration for this raking profile can be traced back to the sculptures that Calatrava has used to explore promising structural concepts, most notably his *Running Torso* (1986) in Zurich's Bauschanzil Restaurant. In this work five marble cubes stacked in a rising diagonal are counterbalanced by a wire stay, creating visual tension and a sense of forward movement. The bridge remains a notable example of the successful translation of a structural concept from model scale to full size.

Apart from its self-evident dynamic profile, the raking pylon of composite concrete and steel construction that supports the 200 m (655 ft.) bridge span is sufficiently heavy to tension the thirteen pairs of cables that hold the deck; its weight obviates the need for any back-stays on the other side. No further

bracing to stabilize the structure is required. This concept of the raking pylon, requiring only one set of stay cables, and visually analogous to a harp and its strings, can claim to be an important innovation in bridge design. It has led to further refinements by Calatrava himself and by others. A comparison could also be drawn with a Gothic cathedral, in which the weight of the pinnacles counterbalances the thrust of the buttresses.

Construction of the pylon proceeded upwards from massive mass-concrete foundations in the river bank, using a giant crane to lift the hollow steel sections into place prior to their being welded together and filled with reinforced concrete. Initial assembly of the bridge deck took place on continuous falsework erected on the riverbed, aided by the fact that the river dries up seasonally. The deck is made up of a central spine beam, a hexagonal box girder in section, to which the cable stays are fixed and from which the two carriageways are cantilevered on each side. This central beam doubles as a pedestrian and cycle route raised well above the level of the traffic.

A less dramatic but nonetheless notable feature of this Calatrava design, and indeed of many others from his studio, is the respect accorded to pedestrians, a group all too often given short shrift in the planning of major civil-engineering infrastructure. At Seville, the Expo '92 visitor and those who have followed enjoy panoramic views of the city, the river and the exhibition site as they cross. Moreover, in places their route is deftly shaded by other parts of the bridge structure — a great benefit during the heat of a southern Spanish summer.

Key Facts

Designer: Michel Virlogeux/Service d'Etudes Techniques des Routes et Autoroutes (SETRA)

Architects: François Doyelle, Charles Lavigne

Main span: 856 m (2800 ft.)

Total length: 2141 m (7025 ft.)

Height of pylons: 215 m (705 ft.)

Michel Virlogeux

After studying at the Ecole Polytechnique and then at the prestigious Ecole Nationale des Ponts et Chaussées, and graduating in 1970, Michel Virlogeux (born 1946) spent two decades with Service d'Etudes Techniques des Routes et Autoroutes (SETRA), the French government design office for public works, where he became technical director. During that period he was responsible for the design of a large number of cable-stayed structures in France, including the bridge over the Gulf of Morbihan and the viaduct at Millau (pages 94–95).

Since 1994 Virlogeux has been a consultant engineer. Among other honours, he was the first recipient of the Fritz Leonhardt Prize, in 1999. His work is notable for its concern for the aesthetics of bridge structures, and he has successfully collaborated with such architects as Charles Lavigne to produce designs of great power and refinement.

Pont de Normandie
Honfleur–Le Havre, France, 1989–95

ABOVE The first bridge elements of the central span are attached to the pylons.

OPPOSITE TOP LEFT Crane-lifting of a typical deck section.

OPPOSITE TOP RIGHT The final bridge deck section is lifted into place to close the span.

OPPOSITE The two decks extend outwards from land, to meet only when all of the final pieces have been winched into place.

Although not in general a part of the seemingly inexorable rise of urban 'signature' buildings, which are designed to put their host cities on the map, certain great bridges have managed to achieve much the same iconic quality, coming to serve as proxies or silent ambassadors for a city or a region. While performing their primary, functional purpose of providing a safe transit over a river or a valley, such bridges may also carry an emotional charge as points of arrival or departure, gateways or thresholds, the crossing of which signals an important stage of a journey. On occasion, a great bridge can encapsulate the technical innovation and constructive daring of a nation or, at a more mundane level, the relative clout of local politicians when funds for development are on offer.

It would be hard to find a better example of these qualities than the bridge that links the northern French seaport of Le Havre with the historic town of Honfleur – the Pont de Normandie. Conceived as much as a symbol of Normandy's status and importance in French national life as to provide a further crossing near the mouth of the River Seine, the 2141 m (7025 ft.) long structure boasts a memorable profile, which is particularly effective in its low-lying, estuarial setting, uncluttered by urban development. When completed in 1995, its cable-stayed central span of 856 m (2800 ft.) held the

world record as the longest of its type; overtaken three years later by Japan's Akashi Kaikyo Bridge, with its still unsurpassed central span of 1991 m (6530 ft.), the Pont de Normandie retains its record as the longest in Europe. It is also unusually high: at 215 m (705 ft.), its pylons are taller than the Tour Montparnasse in Paris.

The choice of a cable-stayed design directly reflected the nature of the site. A conventional suspension bridge was ruled out because of the difficulty of securing adequate anchorages for the suspension cables in the soft river mud. As the new bridge would be required to carry only light traffic, as opposed to the many traffic lanes that typically are carried by suspension bridges, the lighter, more elegant and more materials-efficient cable-stayed design was especially well suited to the task. In addition it would demonstrate a visibly daring technical innovation that would enhance the reputation of French civil-engineering expertise as the twentieth century drew to a close.

In essence, the structural principle of a cable-stayed design such as that of the Pont de Normandie can be understood as a pair of scales. Each pylon is balanced against the other, with the weight of the bridge deck carried on cable hangers, either parallel to one another or splayed, fixed at regular intervals to the sides of the deck.

The construction sequence differs from that of a suspension bridge, in which the wires forming cables that comprise the catenary arch are spun together and then pulled across the span: with these suspension cables in place, the individual sections of the bridge deck are floated out (in the case of a river crossing), or lifted from the ground (in the case of a land crossing), to below their ultimate position, before being lifted into place with the support of the cables above.

By contrast, cable-stayed bridges – and box-girder bridges, for that matter – are constructed outwards from each pylon, with each new section of deck being pushed forward beyond the previous one by purpose-designed support gantries and then secured by the next pair or pairs of cable stays until the final section of the central span is locked into place. Deck sections are added on each side of the pylon in sequence, so that each pylon remains balanced as the deck installation progresses and avoids excessive bending moments acting on the pylon.

Because the River Seine is wide and open at this point, wind pressure and squalling were particular concerns for the design team; the new structure had to be capable of resisting winds of up to 300 km/h (185 mph). In addition to computer modelling of the structure in such conditions, extensive wind-tunnel testing at the renowned ONERA facility (pages 152–53) was needed to refine the profile of the bridge deck, in order to increase its torsional resistance and to finalize the layout of the cable stays. There are a total of 184 of these, which are arranged in two groups of twenty-three paired cables on each pylon. These stays represent more than 60% of the surface area exposed to wind forces and have been designed in such a way as to allow the removal of any single stay for maintenance, independently of the others.

The two concrete pylons of the Pont de Normandie are a telling instance of a design concept that moves beyond mere functional purpose. Their form as an inverted Y offers exceptional rigidity and stability to carry the weight of the bridge deck and to resist wind loads, but it also can be read as a symbolic 'gateway' through which travellers pass. So exceptional is the span of this bridge that, owing to the curvature of the earth, these pylons are 2 cm (0.8 in.) further apart at their summit than at their base.

RIGHT The dramatic thrust of the inverted Y-shaped pylons is reinforced at night by powerful floodlighting.

Ben van Berkel

Ben van Berkel (born 1957) studied architecture in Amsterdam and in London. He has established himself as a leading contemporary designer with such innovative projects as the Aedes East Gallery in Berlin, an electricity substation for REMU (the Dutch electricity supplier) at Amersfoort, and the Möbius House near Amsterdam. Current projects include housing and offices in Almere, The Netherlands; the new Mercedes-Benz Museum in Stuttgart, Germany; and a music faculty in Graz, Austria.

Together with Caroline Bos, Van Berkel set up the architectural practice Van Berkel & Bos Architectuurbureau in 1988 in Amsterdam, which concentrated on urban development projects, architectural designs and infrastructure plans. In 1998 they established a new firm, UN Studio, as an interdisciplinary network of specialists in these three fields. Ben van Berkel is also active as a theorist and has taught at New York's Columbia University, at the Architectural Association in London, and at Harvard and Princeton universities.

Erasmus Bridge
Rotterdam, The Netherlands, 1996

ABOVE Using floating cranes, the pylon is manoeuvred into position.

OPPOSITE TOP The bridge is a distinctive landmark on the skyline of Rotterdam, strikingly modern and yet with echoes of the functionality of dockside structures.

OPPOSITE The cables are aligned to avoid bending stresses in the pylon.

When a city searches for a structure that can stand as its unique symbol or 'trademark', new bridges can sometimes make excellent candidates, especially if they can offer a distinctive skyline profile uncluttered by high-rise buildings or structures. From its inception, the Erasmus Bridge was a clear favourite to fulfil this role for Rotterdam. It was designed to link the city centre southwards across the River Meuse (Maas) with the former docklands and the quarter of Kop van Zuid undergoing regeneration, and hence enjoys a high visual and political profile. Completed in 1996, the form of the 'Swan Bridge', as it is known to Rotterdamers, duly became part of the city's official logo. Cyclists, pedestrians, trams and motor traffic cross the main bridge span and then a side span, which can be lifted to allow vessels to pass through a side channel. In its wide, estuarial setting, the bold, angular forms of the Erasmus Bridge are seen to best advantage.

Structurally, the Erasmus Bridge is a cable-stayed design, comparable to a number of other European examples, but subject during its development by a combined architectural/engineering team within Rotterdam's Public Works Department to an exhaustive process of refinement in both its overall form and its details. With its total span of 800 m (2625 ft.) and main span of 280 m (920 ft.), the bridge has no claim to inclusion in the record books on dimensions alone. Yet as a visual anchor to a Rotterdam waterfront lacking a cohesive character, the Erasmus Bridge makes its presence triumphantly felt, much as Santiago Calatrava's Alamillo Bridge (pages 82–83) does in its Seville setting. Both bridges employ a backward-leaning pylon to tension the cables supporting the steel bridge deck; in the case of the Alamillo Bridge the rake and weight of the pylon obviate the need for back-stay cables, while eight such cables restrain the pylon of the Erasmus Bridge. From each leg of the 140 m (460 ft.) A-frame pylon, which tilts towards the vertical in its uppermost section to provide a more efficient configuration for the cable anchorages, a fan of cables descends to raise the bridge deck. After the bridge came into service, it was found that, under certain conditions, the prevailing winds tended to cause these fan cables to vibrate, and, to correct this, rubber dampers were installed at the bottom of the cables and elsewhere at deck level.

The whole bridge structure sits upon foundations formed of long steel piles that were hammered down from barges into the bearing strata, providing a sound base for construction as well as a protection against potential damage from vessels straying off course. The pylon and bridge deck sections were fabricated off-site as steel boxes, which were then manoeuvred into position against one another using that breed of floating crane that the Dutch have made very much their own.

In deciding to replace the concrete pylon in the original proposal with one of steel, chiefly in order to reduce its weight and improve handling, the design team has created a form that follows the constructional logic of the latter material. Steel structures are best configured as angular forms with sharp arrises, as opposed to the smoother, more fluid lines achievable with a comparable structure in concrete. The resulting welded-box profile of the steel pylon may lack the sinuous elegance of a concrete mast, but it sits well enough in the company of other harbourside structures made of the same material.

A structure of this scale and prominence called for an innovative lighting solution. While the light-blue colour chosen for the steelwork tends to make the bridge pylon merge into the sea- and skyscape by day, at night dramatic and precisely directed white

light illuminates the pylon and cables, imbuing the structure with a graceful aura that belies its weight of nearly 7000 tonnes. By further abstracting and heightening the form of the bridge, the lighting scheme dematerializes the structure to the point at which it begins to assume something of the iconic status of the Eiffel Tower or the Sydney Opera House, the profiles of which are instantly recognizable symbols of their host cities.

At the same time, the aesthetic of the bridge manages to echo that of the structures that still populate the Rotterdam dockside – the huge handling cranes and other machinery – as well as evoking the tradition of shipbuilding, with its working of large steel plates and sections into clean, robust and very obviously functional structures. Notable, too, is the consistency of detailing throughout and the use of the same 'family' of forms at different scales, which give a powerful unity to the whole design.

Key Facts

Architect: Georg Rotne	
Engineers: ASO Group (Arup, SETEC, Gimsing & Madsen, ISC and Tyréns)	
Total length of crossing: 16 km (10 miles)	
Daily traffic: 10,250 vehicles, 16,000 railway passengers	
Cost: DK Kr14.8 billion	

RIGHT The concrete trough carrying the railway tracks is slung beneath the bridge girders below the road deck.

FAR RIGHT The four main pylons were cast *in situ*, using sliding formwork.

Øresund Link

Copenhagen, Denmark–Malmö, Sweden, 1995–99

OPPOSITE TOP The heavy-lift vessel *Swanen* places the final girder section into the approach span.

BELOW The High Bridge has the longest free span in the world of any cable-stayed bridge carrying both road and rail traffic, as well as the highest free-standing pylons.

F ew structures in the history of 'great engineering' have been sealed – or opened – with a kiss, but such was the royal exchange between Crown Prince Frederik of Denmark and Crown Princess Victoria of Sweden on 14 August 1999, when they met as the final span of the High Bridge over the Øresund waterway was lifted into place and their two nations were linked for the first time since the Ice Age. Sweden was now physically joined to continental Europe, with a transit time of only ten minutes to Denmark. A motorway link connects Copenhagen with the crossing leading to Sweden's third city, Malmö.

After a century of debate in both countries, the governments of Denmark and Sweden signed a

binding agreement on 23 March 1991 to construct a fixed link to carry road and rail traffic. The crossing was expected to bring important economic benefits to the Øresund region as a whole, a promise that has been amply fulfilled.

Following an international design competition held in 1992, a team comprising bridge specialists from Britain, France, Denmark and Sweden – the ASO Group – developed the scheme as it was ultimately built; the central concept was a two-level arrangement in which the motorway is placed above the railway on the bridge sections of the crossing. The construction of a public transport link, in the form of a railway, was started before that of the road

ABOVE The existing navigation channel was kept open until the completion of the bridge, then moved to its final location through the central span.

LEFT The sweeping curve of the High Bridge as it nears the artificial island of Pepperholm.

TOP The main span of the High Bridge, seen here nearing completion, was erected in four sections supported by temporary towers.

crossing. However, construction delays in tunnelling for the former meant that in the end both routes opened almost concurrently.

From west to east, the Øresund Link consists of three distinct sections: an immersed tunnel 3.5 km (2.2 miles) long, a man-made island 4 km (2.5 miles) long and a bridge 7.9 km (4.9 miles) long, the length of the bridge being about half the total distance coast-to-coast.

Leaving the Danish shore close to Kastrup Airport in Copenhagen, the parallel road and rail routes dive down into what is the world's longest combined road and rail underwater tunnel. The tunnel is constructed from precast concrete boxes 22 m (72 ft.) in length and 39 m x 8.6 m (128 ft x 28 ft.) in cross-section, joined together to form larger units 176 m (580 ft) long and weighing 55,000 tonnes. These were towed into position from their casting yard in Copenhagen North Harbour and then lowered into a prepared trench dredged in the seabed.

The routes emerge from the tunnel on to the man-made island of Pepperholm. The island was formed by filling settlement basins with 9,000,000 cubic metres (11,770,000 cubic yards) of dredged material (mostly stone and sand), behind bunds (dykes) of coarse pebbles that were shaped to the outline of the island. On the island, a viaduct is used to separate the road and rail carriageways on to two levels, with the road above the railway, before the bridged section of the crossing is entered.

To achieve this double-decking of carriageways on the High Bridge, the most efficient structural form proved to be one utilizing steel trusses on a 20 m (65 ft.) module, with diagonal members linking upper and lower decks; every other diagonal member follows the direction of the cable stays. This truss form is inherently strong enough to act as a deck for the central section of the High Bridge, which, with a

main span of 490 m (1610 ft.) and a total length of 1092 m (3580 ft.), ranks as the world's longest cable-stayed structure carrying both road and rail traffic.

Building the bridge involved a high level of on-shore prefabrication, the design being well suited to factory-type production of standardized elements. The concrete caissons and pier shafts for the forty-nine approach spans, for example, were cast in a yard in Malmö North Harbour and shipped out to site on the heavy-lift vessel *Swanen*. Each caisson, weighing between 2500 and 4700 tonnes, was then set down on to three pre-positioned concrete pads on the seabed. The pier shafts, which varied from 13 m (43 ft.) to 57 m (187 ft.) in height, were then lowered by the *Swanen* on to the caisson foundations.

Deck girders for the approach spans were prefabricated in Cadiz, Spain, and transported in pairs on an ocean-going barge to Malmö, where the prefabricated concrete troughs to carry the railway were then added. The larger cable-stayed deck girders had a shorter journey, of 200 km (125 miles), from Karlskrona to Malmö North Harbour, where the concrete roadway deck was cast over them. Only the four pylons were cast in place, using a moving shutter that was raised in 4 m (13 ft.) lifts. Construction of the main span was made easier by the fact that the main navigation channel could remain in its original position until completion of the bridge, when it moved to its final location beneath the central span. This central span was erected in four sections supported by temporary towers.

The Øresund Link is an object lesson in several respects — the clear thinking behind the design concept and the best ways of implementing it, the extensive use of prefabrication, and, above all, the spirit of openness and co-operation that typified the great venture, which was completed on time and on budget.

Key Facts

Architects: Foster & Partners/SETRA	
Structural engineers: Bureau d'Etudes Greisch/EEG Simecsol	
Total length: 2.5 km (1.5 miles)	
Central spans: 26 m x 342 m (85 ft. x 1120 ft.)	
Pylon height: 340 m (1115 ft.)	
Height above valley: 270 m (885 ft.)	

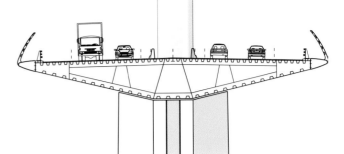

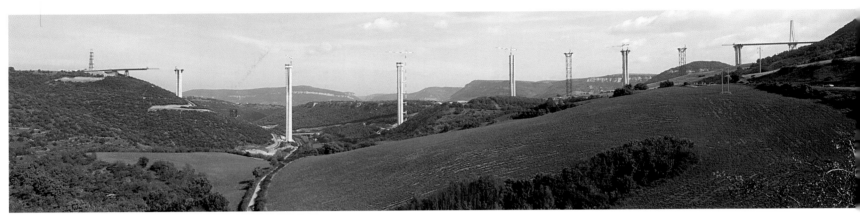

Millau Motorway Viaduct
Tarn Valley, France, 1993–2005

TOP Section through the bridge deck showing wind shields on either side.

ABOVE The giant piers begin to rise from the valley. They include the highest pier in the world, at 245 m (805 ft.).

OPPOSITE Visualization of the completed structure stretching across the Tarn Valley. The tapering pylons and cable stays minimize the impact of the structure on the landscape, though its drama and elegance are undeniable.

The building of bridges across inconvenient valleys or gorges has long provided a staple diet for progressive engineers. From the seemingly fragile cat's-cradles of timbers that carried the great American railroads westwards, through Gustave Eiffel's filigree metal viaducts spanning the river gorges of central France for the coal trains heading to Paris, to the high span of Austria's Europabrücke, the particular engineering challenge of providing high-level crossings over a valley has provoked – and continues to produce – invariably elegant and occasionally ethereal responses.

The French toll-motorway network features more than its fair share of notable viaducts, which can stand favourable comparison with their better-known Italian, German and Swiss counterparts. The competition between these countries is likely to intensify still further with the anticipated completion in 2005 of the Millau Viaduct, a 2.5 km (1.5 mile) long structure designed to take the A75 autoroute across the Tarn Valley as part of the motorway link from Paris to Barcelona ('La Méridienne'). Stretching southwards from Clermont-Ferrand to Béziers, Montpellier and the heart of the Midi, it will divert the traffic that currently grinds its way through the town of Millau and the historic villages along the valley floor. Such was its potentially detrimental impact on the environment that the A75's ultimate

alignment over the Tarn was the outcome of an exhaustive route options study in 1988, approved by ministerial decree the following year.

The best alignment for the route to link the two plateaus either side of the Tarn was further analysed through more detailed studies of a high-level and a low-level group of possible new viaduct structures undertaken by the Centre for Technical Design Studies (CERT) in Aix-en-Provence. The high-level group involved the use of a 2.5 km (1.5 mile) long viaduct and a crossing of the Tarn at a height of at least 200 m (660 ft.); the low-level group, located further down the valley, envisaged two viaducts, 600 m (2000 ft.) and 2.4 km (1.5 miles) long, extended by a tunnel. Within each group various structural options were tested, including the use of under-bracing or a central arch support, profiles of constant depth and of varying depth, and – as in the design eventually selected – a series of eight cable-stayed spans tied back to masts rising centrally above each pier. This last, preferred solution had the various merits of attracting strong support at a public inquiry, of being simpler to design and construct, of avoiding the need for a tunnel, of having a low overall cost, and of promising to make less of an impact on existing urban development than the other options considered.

The studies undertaken by CERT in turn formed

part of the competition brief to five invited teams of architects and engineers to develop a group of solutions. The international jury favoured the multi-stayed viaduct option proposed by the team of Sogelerg–Foster, which has subsequently been developed into the scheme now under construction. This configuration consists of eight separate cable-stayed spans just short of 350 m (1150 ft.) each, set on piers ranging in height from 75 m (245 ft.) to 245 m (805 ft.). The cable-stay masts rise a further 90 m (295 ft.) above the bridge deck, thereby making the Millau Viaduct, at 340 m (1115 ft.) higher than the Eiffel Tower (300 m; 985 ft.), one of the tallest bridges in the world.

The two-lane dual carriageway of the A75 will follow a slight curve as it crosses the river, and will rise at a gentle 3% gradient to improve forward visibility and safety for drivers; lateral screening attached to each side of the bridge deck will help to reduce the effect of wind on vehicles crossing. Particular attention has been paid to the design of the piers, which split below road level into two thinner columns to provide the necessary flexibility to accommodate thermal movements of the deck spans, and above road level form pyramidal A-frames tapering into a V-shaped apex. This profile provides the rigidity required for anchorage of the cable stays.

Such a project is characterized by gargantuan statistics, involving a 'menu' of 127,000 cubic metres (166,000 cubic yards) of concrete, 19,000 tonnes of prestressed reinforcing steel and a further 5000 tonnes to form the cables and stays, and a workforce of 400 employed during the four-year building programme. It is an undertaking to which Gustave Eiffel, his own memorable Garabit Viaduct of 1884 to the north near St Flour, would surely have tipped his silk top hat in salute.

Key Facts

Number of Chain Home radar towers: 50

Transmission range: 210 km (130 miles)

Height of steel transmitter masts: 105 m (385 ft.)

Height of wooden receiver masts: 73 m (240 ft.)

Distance between towers in rhomboid pattern: 55 m (180 ft.)

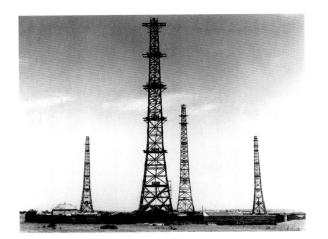

Sir Robert Watson-Watt

The Scottish physicist Sir Robert Watson-Watt (1892–1973) trained at St Andrews University in Scotland. He joined the Royal Aircraft Factory at Farnborough and during World War I investigated methods of displaying radio signals from aircraft. In 1933 he became superintendent of a new radio department at the National Physical Laboratory and subsequently undertook research into the use of radio waves to locate aircraft.

The real breakthrough came with his 1935 paper and demonstration of the effectiveness of radio detection methods, which led to his appointment as the director of the Bawdsey Research Station at Felixstowe, on England's east coast. From here, he masterminded the design and installation of the chain of radar stations along Britain's south and east coasts that would provide the all-important early warning of approaching enemy aircraft during wartime. He was knighted in 1942 for his role in the development of radar.

Chain Home Radar Towers
England, 1938–45

ABOVE A typical formation of Chain Home transmitter and receiver aerial towers.

OPPOSITE LEFT The geodesic radomes house the latter-day equivalent of the Chain Home warning system.

OPPOSITE RIGHT One of the last remaining Chain Home towers can be seen at BAE Systems Advanced Technology Centre at Great Baddow, Chelmsford, Essex.

Defences and fortifications, when not made of stone, concrete or solid steel, may seem fragile and far from visibly functional. While the reason for constructing battlements and strong-points is evident enough, a series of 105 m (385 ft.) high open-lattice towers, each with a horizontal platform halfway up, does not immediately reveal its true purpose. Combine the towers' insect-like appearance with tight security, and the sense of mystery is compounded. Few observers in the 1930s would have concluded that such towers were the direct result of certain demonstrations made by Robert Watson-Watt to the chairman of the Committee for the Scientific Survey of Air Defence at the Daventry BBC short-wave radio transmitter in 1935. These tests proved that it was possible to detect an approaching Heyford bomber at a range of 13 km (8 miles) and a height of 1800 m (5900 ft.) by the aircraft's reflection of radio waves.

Unlike the nature of other spheres of defence during the war, for which Britain seemed ill-prepared, the likelihood of air attack had prompted a climate of open-mindedness towards new inventions. Watson-Watt's theory that radio waves could be used to detect the range of approaching aircraft, as described in his 1935 paper, 'The Detection of Aircraft by Radio Methods', rapidly progressed into a programme of practical applications, with little concern for what they might cost. By the time war was declared, the east and south coasts of England were protected by a chain of radar (an acronym derived from *Radio Detection And Ranging*) stations, which were to prove vital in waging the Battle of Britain.

All radar systems work on the principle that if an aircraft or other target is intercepted by radio waves, part of the waves' energy will be reflected back and can be detected by a receiver. The section of sky under observation is 'floodlit' with radio-frequency pulses of energy, and the echoes from any aircraft within the search area are processed by the ground station and displayed via the cathode-ray tube.

Other parties involved in the conflict, including Germany and the United States, had their own versions of workable radar systems, initially land-based although later installed in aircraft. The British version based on the work of Watson-Watt and his team was fully integrated into the overall air-defence strategy, a factor decisive in its great success. Because the radar installations were linked by first-rate, dedicated communications, precise information on the height, range and speed of incoming aircraft in any weather conditions could be transmitted directly to fighter control and thence to individual squadrons.

A typical installation of the first system put in place, the so-called Chain Home (CH) network, consisted of four steel towers 105 m (345 ft.) high, carrying the transmitting aerials, and four 73 m (240 ft.) high wooden towers for the receiving aerials, which were linked to equipment that processed and displayed the reflected signals. The CH network proved effective in detecting high-flying aircraft approaching from a distance.

But a series of radar experiments with the RAF in 1938 indicated, disconcertingly, that the CH system had a serious problem in its ability to detect low-flying aircraft – that is, those flying below a 2% angle of approach to the horizontal. Intruders flying at this height could escape detection entirely.

The solution proved to be a gap-filling radar system dubbed Chain Home Low (CHL), which was developed from the existing use of narrow-band radar to guide anti-aircraft guns and coastal artillery. This radar operated at a frequency of about 200 MHz, compared to CH's much shorter one of 10 MHz. By the eve of hostilities, a CHL installation in conjunction with CH coverage could detect an aircraft at a distance of 40 km (25 miles) flying at a height of just 150 m (500 ft.), and provide accurate information on its speed and altitude.

The huge steel and wooden towers that characterized the CH system along the south and east coasts of England gave way on the west coast to simpler guyed masts fed by an improved form of transmitter. In view of the vital importance of CH and CHL radars in the air defence of the country, it is fortunate that their precise purpose was not fully understood at the time by the enemy and the chain vigorously attacked.

Key Facts

Architects: Foster & Partners

Structural engineers: Arup

Total height: 288 m (945 ft.)

Height of observation deck: 135 m (445 ft.)

Transmission range: 70 km (44 miles)

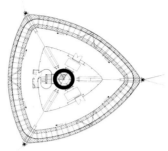

RIGHT Plan of the observation deck. The curved shape of the platforms provides structural rigidity and reduces wind resistance.

OPPOSITE The view of the tower at night clearly shows both upper and lower restraining cables.

BELOW The steel radio mast was drawn up through the centre of the platforms.

Telecommunications Towers

Since the mid-1950s, television transmission and telecommunications towers have become a familiar skyline feature. The Stuttgart TV tower (1954–55) established the model for a circular concrete structure and was followed by many others, including that in Hamburg (1962), the Munich Olympic Tower (1968) and Moscow's Ostankino Tower (1959–67). At 536 m (1760 ft.), this last was once the tallest structure in the world; its distinctive form features a tapering cone base punctuated by triangular openings.

Rising to 553 m (1815 ft.), Toronto's Canadian National Tower (1973–76) now supercedes Ostankino as the world's tallest structure. Its cross-section is also innovative – a hexagon with three tapering fins attached, more resistant to wind forces but also more striking in profile, with a greater sense of *élan*. Commercial considerations, as well as opportunities for viewing vast panoramas, ensured that a revolving restaurant and an observation deck found their place in the 'Skypod' high on the tower.

Torre de Collserola
Barcelona, Spain, 1987–92

Originally symbols of modernity and progress, television signal and telecommunications towers seemed in the 1980s and 1990s to enter a period of comfortable 'middle age', no longer appearing as fresh and striking elements on the urban skyline. Instead, the tapering towers, topped by revolving restaurants or viewing galleries and a revenue-generating array of antennas, became objects of nostalgia. Yet the familiarity of such structures, especially in Eastern Europe and North America – two fertile breeding grounds for the species, led to a demand for them to be updated. The original towers were vulnerable also to the rapid changes in telecommunications technology, which rendered them less important to emerging networks and less likely to be proudly promoted by local television stations. They were, moreover, often problematic in sensitive landscape settings, where their presence could seem strident and overbearing.

It was the prospect of a world-class event – the 1992 Olympic Games – coming to Barcelona that inspired the city authorities to promote a reinvention of the telecommunications tower. They envisaged it as a fusion between civic ambition and precise, if open-ended, technical requirements, aiming to create a new structure that would be as potent a modern monument as the towers of Stuttgart, Toronto or Berlin had been in their day. As an alternative to a series of transmitter masts on the hillside of Tibiudabo above the city, Pasqual Maragall, the then mayor of Barcelona, eventually developed a design brief for a *single* tower to carry transmissions from the local and national television networks and from Telefonica, the national telephone company. A lone tower of innovative design would have far less adverse impact on the environment and far greater visual potency and elegance than a group of unrelated structures.

Conventional solutions had no place here. Whereas a standard design in reinforced concrete would have needed a base some 25 m (82 ft.) in diameter to support the 288 m (945 ft.) tower height required, the design selected through an international competition in 1988 proposed a base of only 4.5 m (15 ft.) in diameter, minimizing the physical impact of the structure on the mountainside. Innovative in concept, the Torre de Collserola, as it is called, was designed as a hybrid concrete-and-steel braced tube, more characteristic of the world of ships' rigging and cable-stayed bridges, where the design team found their structural precedents, than in that of heavyweight civil engineering. The nub of the problem, fully embraced by the designers, was that the tower is essentially a platform for equipment that is subject to alteration: in telecommunications, as in much else, the only certainty is change.

With a period of only twenty-four months available for construction, it was essential to overlap production of the constituent parts – the shaft, the mast and the thirteen steel decks that were to carry the telecommunications equipment. Prefabrication began with the mast, which was then manoeuvred up inside the hollow concrete shaft; construction of the latter simultaneously progressed upwards using sliding formwork. At the same time, the equipment decks and public observation platform were fabricated on site and then lifted up into their final positions as sections of the tower were completed, finally to be crowned by the steel radio mast, a mere 30 cm (12 in.) in diameter. The whole city watched as the tower rose and was ringed by each platform in turn.

The supporting structure for the platforms consists of three huge trusses made of Kevlar, a material with a high strength-to-weight ratio that reflects broadcasting signals. Three pairs of cables provide further stability to the platforms, the lower guys consisting of 180 parallel-strand cables with a polyethylene covering, and the upper guys comprising three series of seven parallel cables, made of aramid (a strong artificial fibre). Broadcasting antennas – subject to periodic maintenance or replacement – are hoisted up to the platforms by a crane mounted at the top of the tower, while smaller pieces of equipment are taken up by a lift in the hollow shaft.

More, perhaps, than any other recent structure of note, the Torre de Collserola succeeds in translating a demanding technical brief into a design that achieves a fitness for purpose such as that normally associated with tools refined over long periods, for example the smoothing plane or a pair of binoculars. Although its form was subject to modelling and refinement as the development of the design progressed, there is no visible evidence of deliberate 'styling'. Like the towers of Stuttgart and Toronto, it has won its place in the affections of its host city.

100 Energy and Natural Forces

RIGHT Water to irrigate distant farmland gushes from a bank of tubes housed 55 m (180 ft.) above river level at the Hoover (Boulder) Dam in Nevada, USA, forming a cascade roughly as high as that of Niagara Falls.

OPPOSITE TOP Night-time construction on the Hoover (Boulder) Dam site in 1935. Still one of the world's largest hydroelectric dams, it retains the waters of the Colorado River between Arizona and Nevada.

OPPOSITE BOTTOM Solar reflectors in Australia; the country is a leading exponent of the potential of solar energy.

BELOW Wind farms such as these horizontal axis turbines in Altamont Pass, California, USA, are the visible expression of a significant alternative energy source.

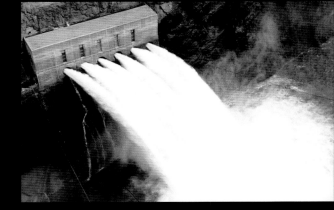

Whether as landform, water or weather, nature continues, as it always has done, to present challenges to engineers and constructors. Structures designed to control, direct and harness natural forces form an important part of the portfolio of great constructions. Some of these structures have a visible and direct purpose that has made them ready symbols for progress and modernity. Wide-ranging in impact, the greatest of these structures may have a regional or even a national dimension.

The quest for readily available, affordable electric power has underpinned the planning of countless dams and river-control systems, but few have matched the ambitious programme of the Tennessee Valley Authority (TVA) in the 1930s (pages 104–07), which must rank as one of the most notable material results of President Roosevelt's New Deal. Its dams and associated works on the Tennessee River and its tributaries, with their spacious, streamlined turbine halls and gantry cranes, are broad-shouldered, robust and striking examples of a heroic period of industrial-engineering design and are justly celebrated as such; yet the great social and economic benefits that the TVA brought to an impoverished region of the United States remain an equally important legacy. In the

cases of Egypt's Aswan Dam on the Nile (pages 110–13) and China's still unfinished Three Gorges Dam on the Yangtze River (pages 114–17), the wider environmental issues are more controversial.

The building forms emerging from the process of power generation are familiar and have progressively developed from the 1920s onwards. An evolving refinement in design has yielded structures as visually satisfying as many of the dams and power plants built under France's hydroelectric programme of the 1930s or the Hoover Dam (1931–35) and its contemporaries in the United States. More recent projects such as Vienna's Freudenau hydroelectric power station on the River Danube (pages 118–19) display their own taut elegance, which derives from direct expression of their function.

In their turn, experiments with other sources of energy and power have generated their own distinct stable of structures. Solar furnaces can take the form of major buildings in their own right; the Odeillo *four solaire* (pages 120–21) in the south of France is higher than a typical apartment block, while solar projects completed or contemplated in the United States and Australia are of equally impressive dimensions. Solar furnaces are built primarily to create high tempera-tures for experiments with materials, whereas solar cells or photovoltaic panels generate electricity and are now used as building façades or integrated with the roof structure of major buildings, as seen in Berlin's new Lehrter Station (pages 24–27).

Wind and tidal energies have yet to play as significant a role in the total energy supply as their advocates hope for, but wind farms have been built on a scale to make their presence in the landscape a matter of frequent controversy. Power generation using the action of the tides or the run of a river has a less dramatic impact because of the lower profile of the structures involved. Dramatic, without doubt, are the exploration and production platforms built by the oil and gas industry. Huge in scale, at the head of complex pipe networks and often operating under severe conditions, these are engineering structures that are no less worthy of attention than the finest bridge. And, as with a great bridge, the logistics of fabrication and assembly of the component parts are an important determinant of form.

Barriers to protect against rising river or sea waters have always formed part of coastal or riparian defence systems, and most major rivers have long had some form of regulatory system in place, but the strongest prompt to action, in Europe at least, appears to have been a series of disastrous floods during the 1950s. In some cases, such as that of Kingston-upon-Hull near the east coast of England, the city centre itself was at risk, a risk compounded by regular surge tides in the river, while on the largest of scales, the delta region of The Netherlands suffered flooding in 1953 that inundated thousand of hectares of farmland and caused great loss of life. The Thames Estuary in England proved equally vulnerable. The challenge of creating controllable protection that does not impede the passage of vessels or cause unacceptable environmental impact has led to engineering solutions of ingenuity and boldness that are major structures in themselves, offering a prominent and reassuring presence in the landscape and waterway they protect.

Superstructures such as these are doubly impressive, not only because they are great works of civil engineering often built under demanding conditions, but also for the balance that they strike with the forces of nature, not to dominate but to control.

Key Facts

Engineers: Tennessee Valley Authority	
Original number of dams to 1964: 20	
Longest dam (to 1964): 2620 m (8650 ft.) (Kentucky Dam)	
Highest dam (to 1964): 95 m (310 ft.) (Hiwassee Dam)	
Current TVA system: 34 flood dams, 29 hydroelectric plants	
Power-service area: 210,000 km² (80,000 sq. miles)	

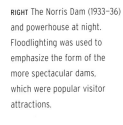

RIGHT The Norris Dam (1933–36) and powerhouse at night. Floodlighting was used to emphasize the form of the more spectacular dams, which were popular visitor attractions.

Letters from the Field

A fascinating insight into the Tennessee Valley Authority (TVA)'s early days is gained from letters written by the journalist Lorena Hickok to Harry L. Hopkins, one of President Roosevelt's inner circle of New Deal advisers, as she travelled through the Tennessee Valley in June 1934. She came into contact with the extremes of rural poverty that the formation of the TVA was intended to relieve, but saw also the first evidence of change.

Her message to Hopkins is optimistic. She writes: "A promised land, bathed in golden sunlight, is rising out of the grey shadows of want and squalor and wretchedness down here in the Tennessee Valley. ... Ten thousand men are at work, building with steel and concrete the New Deal's most magnificent project."

She did not underestimate the task facing the fledgeling TVA. The private utility companies, the land-owning interests and the local politicians were often strongly opposed to its work. Yet public support for Roosevelt seemed solid enough. She concludes: "They are strong for the President. They seem to have absolute confidence in him."

Dams of the TVA

Tennessee Valley, USA, 1933–64

OPPOSITE TOP Watt's Bar Dam (1939–42), seen here during its construction, has an unusual layout, in which the control building is located high on a cliff above the hydroelectric plant.

OPPOSITE The Hiwassee Dam (1940), with (in the foreground) the giant crane used to install and remove the generator units. The elegant design of the crane enclosure typifies the mature and robust styling achieved by the TVA engineers and architects.

Great engineering projects do not always stand alone. Some of the most notable of those described in this volume form part of a larger co-ordinated strategy applied to a whole region, or involve close technical collaboration between neighbouring countries. Yet few can rival the boldness and impact of what, to many observers, turned out to be the greatest success of President Franklin D. Roosevelt's New Deal – the Tennessee Valley Authority (TVA), the formation of which Roosevelt authorized on 18 May 1933, less than three months after he took office.

The seeds of this enormous project, encompassing the whole basin of the Tennessee River – an area almost four-fifths the size of England and Wales combined – were sown at Muscle Shoals, Alabama. The American government had bought this site in 1916 in order to build a dam destined to supply hydroelectric power for the war effort. Here the river drops more than 40 m (130 ft.) over a distance of 50 km (30 miles). The development of the site remained on the political agenda during the 1920s, when some members of Congress advocated its sale privately while others wished to retain it in the public sector. Senator George W. Norris of Nebraska campaigned vigorously for public control of this asset, but it was only in the climate of the Depression and with the incoming president's belief in the importance

of regional planning, especially in relation to its role in improving infrastructure, that the Tennessee Valley Authority became a feasible prospect. Fearful of what were thought at the time to be Socialist or even Communist tendencies within the TVA, Congress defined its role in specific and practical terms. The new authority was to make the Tennessee River easier to navigate, to provide flood-prevention measures, to plan reforestation and the improvement of marginal farmlands, to promote industrial and agricultural development, and to aid national defence through the development of nitrate and phosphorous plants at Muscle Shoals.

A central element of the TVA's programme was a dramatic upgrading of the electricity supply to the rural population. Whereas nearly 90% of urban residents in the United States had electricity by the 1930s, only a tenth of rural dwellers did; private power companies argued that to supply farmsteads and small settlements was uneconomic unless the residents paid handsomely for the connections. Via a new agency, the Rural Electric Administration, areas such as the TVA heartland could now be served through rural electricity co-operatives. By 1939 more than 400 of these were in place, serving nearly 300,000 households.

To generate cheap hydroelectricity on this scale – 2,500,000 kilowatts by the early 1940s, equivalent to

the (then) total power production of the whole of Central and South America combined – called for civil-engineering works far more extensive than those needed to build the Panama Canal. Seven new dams were built on the Tennessee River itself, eleven more were sited on its tributaries, including the rivers Holston, Clinch and Hiwassee, and two others were acquired. The total area of the lakes and reservoirs in the TVA system would exceed 285,000 hectares (1100 square miles) – by comparison, the English Lake District covers a mere 6500 hectares (25 square miles) of water – and included a navigable channel 2.7 m (9 ft.) deep that extended more than 1000 km (620 miles) to Knoxville, Tennessee.

The dams built by the TVA divide into two broad groups – those located on the tributaries of the Tennessee River and those on the river itself; the former are high and narrow, impounding bodies of water as permanent lakes, while the latter are wider in order to span the broad river, and include openings for the passage of river craft.

Notable examples of the first group are the Norris Dam (1933–36), named in honour of Senator Norris, the 'father of the TVA', and the Fontana Dam (1942–43). The Norris Dam was the first of what could be described as TVA's production line of dams, and set

the pattern for the structures that followed. Of generous proportions – 80 m (260 ft.) high and 570 m (1870 ft.) wide, the Norris Dam is an exemplar in the use of exposed *in situ* concrete. The texture of the sawn timber shuttering is fully expressed on the dam face and continued on the facades of the power station and support buildings, creating a crisp and purposeful aesthetic well suited to the progressive ethos of the TVA. The later Fontana Dam, 145 m (480 ft.) tall and 715 m (2345 ft.) wide, developed these themes further. The additional impetus of the war effort required the on-site workforce of more than 5000 to build in three continuous shifts. The Fontana Dam also demonstrated the practicality of the TVA's approach to construction: the shuttering for the concrete was provided from timber felled in the area that would then be covered by the new lake.

The second group of dams, those on the Tennessee River itself, are less dramatic structures in terms of their height. Their impact instead derives from the numerous flood-control devices and navigation passages that comprise much of their span across the river. Chikamagua Dam, near Chattanooga, completed in 1940, is a modest 40 m (130 ft.) in height but 1760 m (5775 ft.) in length, and continues to perform an

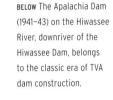

BELOW The Apalachia Dam (1941–43) on the Hiwassee River, downriver of the Hiwassee Dam, belongs to the classic era of TVA dam construction.

important role in flood prevention. As with the Norris Dam, its powerhouse is integrated into the front of the dam to form a unified composition.

As examples of architecture, engineering and industrial design that achieve a seamless unity, the dams, powerhouses and ancillary structures built by the TVA must rank as a considerable achievement in comparison to any others worldwide. More than six decades after their construction, they continue to impress with their sinewy robustness, striking use of materials and first-rate detailing. Even the smallest element of a great dam such as the Norris, the Fontana or the Hiwassee has been shaped with an eye to the complete, integrated whole, yet the design of each dam has retained its own distinctive personality.

The great social, regional and economic experiment that is the TVA has, from its earliest years, attracted international attention and, for the most part, admiration. Typical of the more thoughtful responses from overseas was presented by the distinguished British commentator Julian Huxley, in a 1943 book, following his fact-finding tour of the Tennessee Valley. To conclude his markedly upbeat analysis of the project he wrote: "In a way most significant of all, the TVA has succeeded in demonstrating that there is no antithesis between democracy and planning, and that planning can not only be reconciled with individual freedom and opportunity, but can be used to enhance and enlarge them."

TOP The Douglas Dam (1942) on the French Broad River was one of the many built by the TVA as part of the war effort, to boost electricity production.

ABOVE The Nickajack Dam (1964) on the Tennessee River was built to replace the Hale's Bar Dam of 1913. Its line of rotating barrier gates is clearly visible.

Key Facts

Structural engineer: André Coyne	
Height: 95 m (310 ft.)	
Length: 290 m (950 ft.)	
Thickness: 5.5 m to 47.5 m (top to base) (18 ft. to 156 ft.)	
Head of power generated: 170,000 kW	

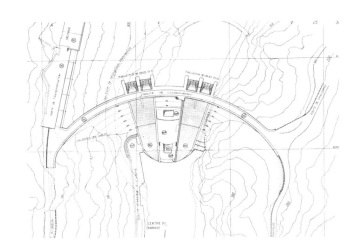

Aigle Dam
Dordogne, France, 1941–46

ABOVE LEFT Site plan showing how the dam fits the contours of the Dordogne Valley.

ABOVE RIGHT Construction view of the cills that deflect water at the base of each of the 'ski slope' spillways, the distinctive feature for which the Aigle Dam is famous.

Great dams do not always span mighty river gorges or retain wide expanses of lake. Some of the most physically dramatic are those associated with the steep valleys of the Massif Central region in France. There, a chain of dams was built from the 1930s to the 1950s, spanning the river valleys of the Dordogne, Vezère, Truyère and Cère, as part of a co-ordinated network generating hydroelectric power.

Following World War I, there was a growing interest in France in the potential of hydroelectric power. In 1920 Henri Queuille, the undersecretary of state, published his mission statement regarding the role of engineering in the creation of rural electricity distribution networks, with the aim of improving living standards and farming techniques. Following the formation of an electricity co-operative for the Diège area, the communes of the Haute-Corrèze were among the first rural areas in France to be supplied with electricity. The steep valleys and gorges that were characteristic of the upper reaches of the Dordogne river and its tributaries were of obvious interest in terms of their potential as sites for dams to generate power. In fact, the Dordogne hydroelectric dam system accounts for a quarter of France's national production of electricity – five billion kilowatt hours per year.

The design of all of the five dams of the Upper Dordogne – at Chastang, l'Aigle, Argentat, Marèges

and Bort-les-Orgues – bears the signature of chief engineer André Coyne, who had overseen the design competition and the construction of the Albert-Louppe Bridge (pages 72–73) at Plougastel under Eugène Freyssinet. When he came to design his first dams in the Dordogne he was aided, on such structures as the double-curved vault of Marèges Dam, by the architect Louis Brachet, but he would later develop his own distinctive design language. By any standards Coyne was a remarkable engineering designer, whom a contemporary critic described as conceiving dams as one would a cathedral, "those phantom vessels which carry in themselves the history of mankind and of civilization". From 1928 he was based in the Dordogne; many of his famous sequence of dams with design features in common, such as the location of the power plant at the base of the vault to form a unified, integrated composition of bold robustness.

The site of the Aigle Dam was chosen as it was the best for minimizing construction costs: the rocky sides of the valley were substantial enough to act as bearing points to support the flanks of the dam. Construction involved relocating the prehistoric site of Chambon to the level of the river. Two concrete batching plants, one on each bank, produced a total of 240,000 cubic metres (315,000 cubic yards) of concrete, which was then transported into position by hopper vessels suspended on cables between the plants.

The Aigle Dam is equipped with seven channels as sluices and for power production, with the ability to deliver a head of 170,000 kilowatts of power from the top of its 95 m (310 ft.) high paired 'ski-jump' spillways. The overflow water is propelled over these spillways out some distance from the dam face as a cataract into a settling pool below. The design of these and of other key elements of the dam was refined through the outdoor testing of scale models set in the run of a stream. Power is distributed from the transformer station at Breuil, which is sited high above the dam on the rocky hillside and is the focal point of thirteen power lines carrying 225,000 volts each, a charge boosted to 400,000 volts by two automatic transformers.

Other dams in the group include that of Bort-les-Orgues, known as the 'staircase of the Dordogne', 120 m (395 ft.) high and 80 m (265 ft.) wide at the base. It contains a reservoir of 477,000 cubic metres (625,000 cubic yards) of water and incorporates twenty-eight power generators. Its generating capacity is 350 million kilowatt hours per year, with a 200,000 volt distribution network. As at Aigle, a ski-jump chute provides for overspill of excess water.

BELOW The Aigle Dam is an exemplar of the refined and powerful forms in the work of André Coyne, who received the Prix d'Architecture in 1953.

Key Facts

Length:	3830 m (12,560 ft.)
Height:	111 m (365 ft.)
Length of reservoir (Lake Nasser):	480 km (300 miles)
Reservoir capacity:	169 billion m³ (221 billion cubic yards)
Annual generating capacity:	10 billion kWh
Cost:	US$1 billion

RIGHT The construction of four of the six hydraulic tunnels that form the foundation of the power plant.

FAR RIGHT AND BELOW Aerial view during construction (top), and the finished Aswan High Dam (below), showing the hydroelectric power station on the left with the inlet channel beyond.

Aswan High Dam
Egypt, 1960–71

Dams can sometimes be of qualified benefit to a nation. The gigantic enterprise of constructing the High Dam across the River Nile at Aswan, in southern Egypt, has been compared to the building of the Pyramids at Giza, and has produced impressive statistics in terms of its size and power generation since its completion in 1971. On the other hand, the project has its own raft of critics, at national and international levels, in a debate that still continues.

Since antiquity Egypt has owed its very existence to the presence of the River Nile, the longest in the world. It is reliant on the seasonal floodwaters that originate as late summer rains in the uplands of Ethiopia and then pass seawards, along the way irrigating and providing essential nutrients to the narrow strips of fertile land along the river banks. Approximately 95% of the country's population lives within 20 km (12 miles) of the Nile.

Since the volume of river water swells dramatically during the annual flood period, regulation of the flow by some form of dam was long contemplated as a means of providing stability to agricultural methods, and as a source of hydroelectric power to support the ever-increasing population of Egypt and the Sudan, as well as the region's nascent industry.

To these ends, the first Aswan Dam, the so-called 'Low' Dam, was built between 1899 and 1902. The dam was originally 1900 m (6200 ft.) long and 54 m

(180 ft.) high; it was heightened twice, but even this proved inadequate during peak flood conditions because there was simply not enough reservoir storage available, meaning that the sluices had to be opened in order to relieve pressure on the dam wall.

A structure on an altogether larger scale was clearly required, to be sited upriver towards the Sudan, and initial planning began. Yet if such a dam were to be built, the vast reservoir created would be bound to submerge innumerable historic artefacts and archaeological sites of world importance – a danger that prompted the United Nations Educational, Scientific and Cultural Organization (UNESCO) to initiate a worldwide appeal. International rescue operations began in 1960, and twenty-four monuments were successfully dismantled and relocated; these operations were supported by as many surveys and as much documentation as could be accomplished in the time available.

Initially intended to be part-financed by an American loan, and later it became the recipient of Soviet largesse, construction of the High Dam (as the project was known) began in 1960 and was completed just over a decade later. The reservoir was filled from 1964 until finally it reached capacity in 1976. Its construction is that of a conventional earthfill dam, with its body built of locally sourced granites and sands compacted by vibration. The total volume of material used (43,000,000 cubic metres; 56,000,000 cubic yards) is equivalent to seventeen times the volume of the Great Pyramid at Giza. A wall of impermeable clay was reinforced by a very extensive cut-off area in alluvial grouting soils in order to reduce water seepage from the reservoir. Known as Lake Nasser, it is 480 km (300 miles) long and 16 km (10 miles) at its widest point.

In terms of its overall impact on Egypt's national grid, the hydroelectricity produced by the twelve

175 megawatt generators of the High Dam, which first came on stream in 1967, once accounted for more than of half the nation's electricity requirements, although after twenty years this amount had fallen to 15%. Conditions for river navigation were improved and there have been periodic benefits such as protection against floods and its ability to alleviate the effects of drought, especially during the nine years of continuous drought from 1979 to 1988.

Yet critics of the High Dam point to the widespread environmental consequences of the changed hydraulic pattern of the Nile, in particular the loss of the rich fertilizing silt that is now retained by the dam, the increased salinity of farmland in the Nile Delta owing to reduced river flow, and the damage to the coastal ecosystem. To an extent, some of these effects can be mitigated, but others represent irreversible changes that – silting

apart – were not fully appreciated when the dam was first planned.

There will always be arguments on both sides when any engineering construction on the scale of the High Dam is contemplated. As with China's Three Gorges Dam (pages 114–17), the impact of such a project cannot but be national, long-term and decisive. Apart from electricity, there was political capital to be generated for the then president of Egypt, Gamal Abdel Nasser, as well as an instantly elevated status for the nation. Against present-day environmental assessment standards, however, the Aswan High Dam undoubtedly would have had little chance of passing the tests and being built. Nonetheless it will always remain a structure of world significance because it represents a very direct attempt to deal with a number of hugely important issues – flooding, drought and power generation.

Key Facts

Engineers: Changjiang Water Resources Commission/Huadong Investment & Design Institute/Zhongnam Investment & Design Institute

Length: 2000 m (6500 ft.)

Height: 180 m (600 ft.)

Reservoir capacity: 39.3 billion m³ (51.4 billion cubic yards)

Cost: US$25 billion

BELOW Aerial view of the dam from the reservoir, showing its mountainous setting and the scale of the future retained lake.

Power to the People?

Aside from the arguments for and against its construction from an environmental or social point of view, the Three Gorges Dam demonstrates the volatility of energy production economics: the cost of newer technology could challenge the project's aim of providing cheap hydroelectric power to the people of the Chinese interior.

Supporters of the dam point to a potential annual output of 85 billion kilowatt hours from its twenty-six (700 megawatt) generators, the equivalent production of eighteen nuclear power plants and cleaner than coal- or oil-fired equivalents. They cite China's per capita electricity consumption as only a third of the world average and the fact that 60% of the rural population currently lacks supply.

Critics voice two main concerns. First, the newly competitive electricity market will be faced with oversupply as more generating plants come on stream, and, secondly, hydroelectric power on this scale compares poorly with more sophisticated technologies, such as natural gas combined-cycle plants, which can decentralize supply and offer more local autonomy. As in the case of so many other aspects of the Three Gorges dam, the jury is still out.

Three Gorges Dam
Sandouping, Yichang, China, 1994–2009

More than any other civil-engineering project, great dams have tended to attract headlines and cause problems in direct proportion to their height and breadth – perhaps understandably, on account of their transforming impact on the valleys or the rivers in which they are built. Whole regional economies and ecologies are recast, a far-flung patchwork of villages is destroyed at a stroke, or a whole urban population is relocated as the waters rise. Requiring the flooding of 1300 villages and 140 townships, and the enforced migration of between one million and two million people, China's Three Gorges Dam on the Yangtze River (the third-longest river in the world) has proved a highly controversial undertaking.

The dam is welcomed by some for its capacity to protect the fifteen million inhabitants located downstream who are at risk from annual floods, which have claimed more than a million victims in the last century. Another of its alleged advantages is its potential to generate a tenth of China's electrical power requirements. On its projected completion in 2009, the dam will rank as the largest hydroelectric project in the world, producing energy equivalent to that generated by eighteen nuclear power stations or 40,000,000 tonnes of coal. Given that China's per capita energy consumption is only a third of the world average, and that the development of the nation's rural areas is stunted by the lack of cheap power, the dam has not lacked support from the highest levels of government. Also of benefit will be an improvement in the irrigation of farmland through flood control, as well as greater ease of navigation on the Yangtze River. A system of new locks forming part of the Three Gorges project will enable large ships to reach the hitherto isolated regions of central China; as a result a fivefold increase in the tonnage of shipping on the river, to upwards of 50,000,000 tonnes a year, is projected. The dam will be crossed by what will be the largest ship lift in the world, able to receive ocean-going vessels of up to 3000 tonnes.

Yet critics of the project – and there are many, internationally as well as in China – point to possible irreversible damage to the regional ecosystem, and also to the blow to the tourist industry resulting from the submersion of more than 1300 archaeological sites along the course of the 600 km (370 mile) retained lake, not to mention the partial destruction of the renowned landscape of the Three Gorges. Further concerns centre on the fact that the damming of the river is likely to set in motion a process of sediment deposit, because the silt that hitherto has been swept towards the sea, in the absence of the river's flushing action, is now likely to accrue in the lakebed. To some extent this problem may be resolved by the provision of twenty-three sluice gates at the base of the dam, which will be

ABOVE The main ship lock opened to river traffic in June 2003, allowing the passage of vessels through the five lock gates while dam construction continues.

OPPOSITE Water is released through the open sluice gates on the main dam section.

opened at the beginning of the flood season so that an artificial equivalent of the natural sluicing-out process can take place. The lake will then be allowed to fill afresh, boosted by the seasonal floods. Yet raw sewage and industrial waste would still be discharged into what will become a static body of water longer than Lake Superior in North America – potentially an open sewer in the making.

In construction and operational terms, the Three Gorges project exudes superlatives. The workforce numbers more than 28,000. It took four years to build the coffer dams in water as deep as 60 m (200 ft.) in order to divert the flow of the Yangtze River and allow the dam to be constructed. The crest length of the dam is 2 km (1.25 miles), compared to the mere 380 m (1250 ft.) of the Hoover (Boulder) Dam in Nevada. The power generation capacity of its two powerhouses, with their total of twenty-six turbine generators, is expected to be 50% higher than that achieved by the Brazil–Paraguay Itaipu Dam, currently the largest hydroelectric dam in the world. Estimates of the total cost of the enterprise

range from an official US$25 billion to an unofficial figure three times as high.

There can be no doubting the sheer scale of this enterprise, undertaken in some cases with outdated equipment and against a turbulent background of mismanagement and accusations of corruption, but it is now powering ahead towards completion before the end of the decade. The Three Gorges Dam is clearly as much a matter of national pride and prestige as a project determined solely by the economics of, or the need for, electrical power generation.

ABOVE Pedestrians and cyclists can cross the dam along a route atop the lock gates.

LEFT At its most intensive, construction on the dam proceeds on a twenty-four-hour basis and involves a peak workforce of 28,000.

Key Facts

Architects:	Wimmer Schwarz Hansjacob
Lead engineers:	Verbundplan
Annual generating capacity:	approx. 1,000,000 kWh
Maximum output:	172,000 kW
Water head:	6.8 m (22 ft.)

Austria's record of power generation using its abundant water resources is impressive. For example, 90% of the output of Verbund, the utility company that supplies approximately half of the country's electricity requirements, derives from hydroelectric power plants. The great majority of these are located on major rivers, including the Danube, the second-longest river in Europe.

The hydroelectric power station at Freudenau ranks as the world's first large-scale power station serving a city of one million or more people, and has the capacity to supply electricity to half the private households of Vienna. It is typical of 'run-of-the-river' designs, in which a flow of water is directed towards turbines set in the river. The effectiveness of such installations is dependent on a regular flow: here,

Freudenau Hydroelectric Power Station
Vienna, Austria, 1993–97

this is ensured by the head of water created between the higher, upstream section of the Danube towards Vienna and the lower, downstream section. The turbines in turn drive generator units producing electricity. At Freudenau each of the six generators is powered by a four-bladed Kaplan-bulb turbine driving a horizontal shaft, the diameter of the turbine runner being 7.5 m (25 ft.).

Water flow to the turbines is controlled by a system of four gates forming a weir. These remain closed when the Danube is flowing normally and the water is entering at the optimum rate of 3000 cubic metres (4000 cubic yards) per second. When the flow exceeds this level the gate blades rotate upwards from their concrete cills in the riverbed, forcing the surplus water over the weir. At their maximum vertical extension the gates allow the unimpeded passage of river water.

The River Danube, flowing through Budapest in Hungary and Belgrade in Serbia on its 2850 km (1770 mile) long route to the Black Sea, remains an important artery for the movement of goods and passengers. As a result it was necessary to provide substantial locks to permit the passage of boats from the higher, retained-water level upstream of the power station down to the lower, downstream section. Each of the two locks is 24 m (80 ft.) wide by 275 m (900 ft.) long, large enough to accommodate two boats, each up to the maximum size permitted on the Danube. A typical transit of the lock takes about twenty-five minutes. The passage of migrating river fish, the other travellers along the river, is provided for by a fish ladder. This is a chain of stepped pools that allows the fish to negotiate a 2 m (6.5 ft) difference in level, designed as a sinuous passage through the new landscape created on the right bank.

However, Freudenau is rather more than a power station with the environmentally conscious credentials of generating energy from a renewable source. It also serves as part of the flood-protection system for the city of Vienna, as well as helping to ensure that the Old Danube, the New Danube and the Prater rivers are supplied with clean water. Furthermore, it has gained an additional role as a recreational resource, its new landscaping forming part of a 13 km (8 mile) long promenade for walkers and cyclists along the riverbank. The part of the route crossing the river is an integral part of the power station structure: those who enter the visitor centre can enjoy spectacular views of the turbines in action.

Particularly effective as a sinewy sculptural composition are the precise outlines of the concrete structure and the sparkling lines of the steelwork which make the hydroelectric power station at Freudenau a model of purposeful design that holds its own against the scale of the river.

OPPOSITE TOP The two locks are sized to accommodate the largest craft that pass up the Danube.

LEFT The central section of the structure houses the turbine generators; a pedestrian and cycle route, part of the city-wide network, runs along the top.

ABOVE A view of the inside of the four-bladed Kaplan-bulb turbine that drives the generating units.

Key Facts

Designer: Félix Trombe/National Centre for Scientific Research, France

Surface area of each heliostat: 45 m² (485 sq. ft.)

Collective surface area of heliostats: 1800 m² (19,375 sq. ft.)

Dimensions of parabolic mirror: 40 m x 54 m (130 ft. x 180 ft.)

Highest temperature: 3400°C (6152°F)

Output: 1000 kW

Solar Furnaces

According to ancient Greek legend, one of the first practical applications of solar energy to create heat occurred during the Romans' siege of Syracuse in the third century BC, when Archimedes used a mirror to set on fire the sails of enemy ships. Among later experiments were those of the French natural scientist Georges-Louis Buffon, who, in 1747, constructed a mirror of 168 segments that could direct the energy of the sun to a single point. By varying the number of segments used, Buffon was able to set fire to an oak branch and to melt tin and gold.

Modern solar furnaces, including that at Odeillo, follow exactly the same principle: a heliostat tracks the path of the sun and reflects its rays on to a primary concentrator, such as a giant parabolic mirror, and then on to a secondary concentrator, an optical device that reflects or refracts the beam to increase its power ten- or twenty-fold.

Solar Furnace
Odeillo, France, 1963–70

Our periodic attempts to extract usable energy from the sun may have taken most of us no further than pyrotechnic experiments with a magnifying lens or a piece of glass in childhood, but this neglected energy source was set to become rather more than child's play in the wake of the two oil crises of 1973 and 1979. Several leading industrial nations, notably the United States, the Soviet Union, Spain, Italy and France, built prototype thermodynamic installations to convert solar energy into electric or mechanical power. In France, under the Electricité de France Themis project, experimental power stations were brought into service to test their efficiency and economic viability against those of more familiar energy sources. Despite the initial promise of the Themis programme, however, falling oil prices and the French government's decision to favour nuclear power generation above all else effectively put paid to the initiative and led to its closure in 1986.

Yet France's record of innovation in matters solar was more deeply rooted. From 1946 onwards, Félix Trombe and his team of researchers had laid the theoretical groundwork for the subsequent technology of capturing and concentrating the sun's energy through an array of flat reflectors, or heliostats, each of which could be angled to align the rays to form a parallel beam. This beam could then be directed on to a very large parabolic reflector, which

focused on a single point at which, theoretically, a temperature of 3800°C (6872°F) could be reached. By comparison, a very modest maximum of 100°C (212°F) is typically achievable using a flat reflector or collector alone, as in most domestic solar installations.

The theory was turned into triumphant practice with the completion of the solar furnace (*four solaire*) at Odeillo in the western Pyrenees, commissioned under the auspices of the Science and Engineering Institute for Materials and Processes (IMP), a satellite of France's National Centre for Scientific Research. In its elevated location (1500 m; 5000 ft. above sea level) in the mountain foothills, the largest facility of its kind in the world enjoys upwards of 3000 hours of sunshine a year, with very low humidity and a direct solar flux of between 800 and 1050 watts per square metre. This energy level is dramatically boosted to 1000 watts per square centimetre, equivalent to a maximum thermal power of 1000 kW, by the process of double reflection via the heliostats and then by the parabolic mirror.

The sixty-three heliostats are arranged on eight levels of a terraced slope. Each is designed to be moveable on two axes so that it can be aligned progressively to follow the movement of the sun; the collective surface area of 1800 square metres (19,375 sq. ft.) reflects the beam of sunlight parallel to the axis of symmetry of the parabolic mirror 40 m

ABOVE The sixty-three flat reflectors, or heliostats, on their terraced slope can be individually controlled to follow the direction of the sun. Each is moveable on two axes.

OPPOSITE TOP Seen in its rural setting, the giant parabolic mirror receives sunlight reflected to it by the heliostats.

OPPOSITE In the twilight the field of reflecting mirror plates takes on a dramatic, other-worldly aspect.

(130 ft.) high and 54 m (180 ft.) wide. A computer-controlled carriage to hold experiments at the focal point, 18 m (60 ft.) from the parabolic mirror, is housed within a 20 m (65 ft.) high laboratory building packed with instrumentation. At the focus, working temperatures approaching 3400°C (6152°F) can be attained.

The solar furnace at Odeillo has proved an invaluable research tool for IMP. Using its captive and pure heat source, ceramic materials can be tested without fear of chemical contamination or of background magnetic fields; various types of chemical atmospheres under different pressures can be substituted to gauge the effects of oxidization or inertness; and the properties, chemical composition and crystalline structures of materials can be examined or new methods of production refined. Since focusing its first solar beam, Odeillo has proved its worth in an array of experiments linked to space travel, such as that simulating the conditions to which a vehicle is subject when it passes through a planetary atmosphere, as well as less dramatic experiments linked to energy and environmental research. IMP's cadre of seventy site-based scientists and engineers has found that the furnace is an ideal site for fabricating wafer-thin slices of photovoltaic silicon, or for perfecting a type of glass used to package radioactive waste for safe storage.

"More powerful than 10,000 suns" runs the tourist publicity for Odeillo. At first sight, from the road or from the local narrow-gauge train, the mirror, as high as a ten-storey building, is breathtaking, its precise function initially mysterious. That it represents a significant part of the unfinished story of humanity's continuing, faltering attempts to harness the energy that nature offers us adds further to the visitor's sense of awe.

BELOW Building of the new breakwater at Malamocco will be followed by implementation of the navigation lock, which will be used by shipping during construction of the Mose System and when high-water defences are operating.

Key Facts

Total number of barrier gates: 78	
Inlet closure time: 4–5 hrs (including gate opening and closing)	
Maximum difference in level between sea and lagoon: 2 m (6.5 ft.)	
Breakwaters: 650 m to 1300 m (l) x 2.5 m to 4 m (h) (2130 ft. to 4265 ft. x 8 ft. to 13 ft.)	
Anticipated closures of the barriers: 3–5 times per year	

"**S**treets flooded. Please advise.": the reputed telegram from a Hollywood wit visiting Venice merely underlines a more serious, worldwide anxiety about the long-term health of La Serenissima. While its surrounding lagoon served the city-state well in the past, effectively stalling invasion by proving too shallow for the safe passage of foreign naval vessels, yet too deep for armies to cross, Venice remains arguably the most sensitive settlement on earth in its vulnerability to very minor changes in tidal rise.

The ever-increasing threats to the city derive from a range of phenomena, both natural and man-made, including the erosion of the thin, sandy spit separating the city from the Adriatic Sea; interventions to facilitate commercial port development over the last century that have adversely affected the morphology of the lagoon and reduced its buffering effect on storm tides; increased 'mining' of the city's groundwater supplies, which has

Venice Flood Defences
Venice, Italy, 2003–11

ABOVE The barrier gates, full of water, lie on concrete cills. In flood conditions, compressed air expels water from the gates, causing them to rise.

reduced the bearing capacity of the subsoil; and rising sea levels combined with a wider tidal range. The message is stark: engineering solutions must be found.

The need for protection is compelling. While there is a long history of catastrophic incursions of water, the city's worst-ever flood took place on 4 November 1966, when Piazza San Marco, the heart of Venice, was covered by 120 cm (47 in.) of water; another extreme flood occurred in 2002. Given the rises in sea level predicted for this century, in most years the piazza is likely to be under 30 cm (12 in.) of water for the whole of November, the period of greatest flood risk. The status of Venice as a UNESCO World Heritage Site, as well as an understandable reluctance on the part of the city authorities to contemplate obtrusive engineering structures such as canal-side walls or dykes, has severely constrained the construction of flood defences within the historic core of the city. Yet an extensive programme of piecemeal improvements continues, and most sections of the city centre have now received sufficient protection against the most frequent high tides (up to 110 cm, or 45 in., in tidal rise).

Wider solutions to meet the flood-protection brief – itself a matter of continuing debate – have come forward with some regularity over the past twenty years or so, each in turn falling foul of politics, funding or even their philosophy. The solution

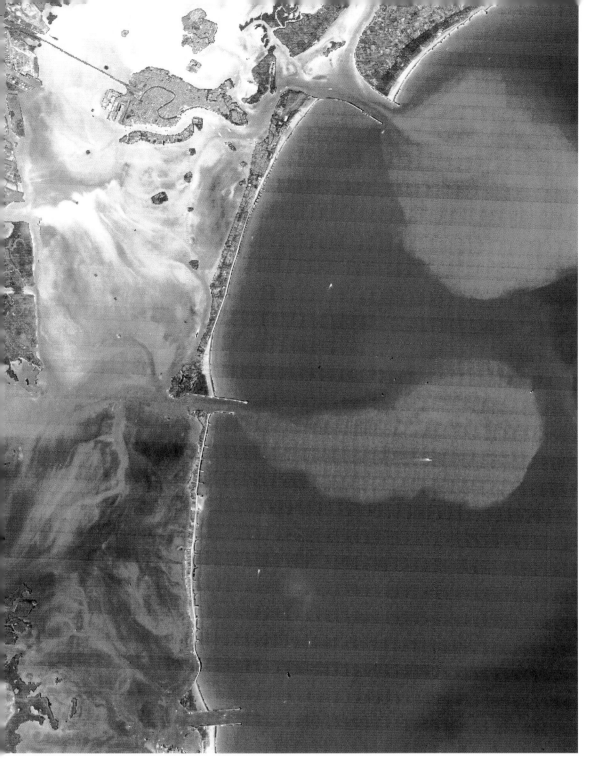

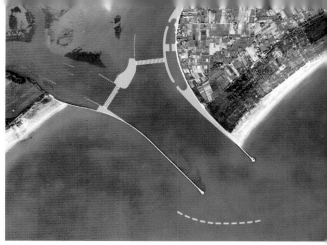

eventually chosen is an integrated system of works, including interventions for local defence of the lowest-lying urban areas, and mobile barriers to protect against exceptional high tides (called the Mose System) by temporarily closing the Lido, Malamocco and Chioggia inlets in the sand spit lying off Venice. At the time of writing, many local defence measures have been implemented, and more than 70 km (45 miles) of lagoon banks have been restructured and raised in Venice, Chioggia and other urban areas.

Any barrier cannot be allowed to degrade the water quality in the lagoon by impeding the process of exchange with the open sea, nor must it pose an unacceptable obstacle to navigation. Moreover, the prized visual qualities of the Venetian seascape must not be compromised. The Mose System meets these requirements by proposing barriers that remain out of sight underwater until brought into action as a flood defence. Each of the inlets will be closed by gates formed of parallelepiped caissons 20 m (65 ft.) wide, and varying in depth between 20 m (65 ft.) and

30 m (100 ft.) to correspond to the depth of the inlet in question. Bottom-hinged onto prefabricated concrete cills set in the seabed, the hollow boxes forming the barrier gates will be fabricated from sheet steel in dry docks on the mainland, internally braced, and then floated out to the site and positioned by crane. The two southerly inlets at Malamocco and Chioggia, each 400 m (1300 ft.) wide, will be closed by up to twenty gate modules, while the wider opening at the Lido will include an artificial island to reduce the run of gates required. Work has begun at Malamocco and Chioggia.

The ingenuity of the barrier design lies in the simple method of raising and lowering the barrier gates. In the closed, down position, lying in the cills on the seabed, they are full of water; this is driven out by compressed air when they are raised to an angle of between 40 and 50 degrees in high-water conditions, allowing for a differential in water level of up to 2 m (6.5 ft.) between sea and land sides. Each gate can move independently and bow to wave motion; it can even be removed and replaced, using a gantry crane, within eight hours.

ABOVE LEFT Aerial view of the Venice area and lagoon, with the main island of the city towards the top, showing the locations of the three inlets (from top, Lido, Malamocco and Chioggia) through which the tidal waters enter and leave the lagoon.

ABOVE The Mose System will be constructed at the (from top) Lido, Malamocco and Chioggia lagoon inlets. At each of the inlets, barrier gates and breakwaters will be inserted to strengthen the defences of the existing jetties. At Malamocco the new structure will include a navigation lock.

Key Facts

Client and Engineer: Rijkswaterstaat (Public Works Department)

Length of barrier: 6.8 km (4.2 miles)

Height: 53 m (175 ft.)

Number of piers: 65

Number of moveable gates: 62

Weight of each pier: 18,000 tonnes

Weight of each gate: 500 tonnes

RIGHT The huge barrier piers were precast on land and towed into position by floating heavy-lift cranes.

On the Rise

As the sea barrier demonstrates, the Dutch can boast great resolve and technical prowess in defending their land from the sea. But what might be the impact of the dramatic rises in sea level that may result from climate change, such as those caused by the melting of the polar ice-caps?

Researchers at the Institute for Environmental Studies in Amsterdam are taking a closer look at possible scenarios for The Netherlands. In theory about half the country would be submerged by a 6 m (20 ft.) rise in sea level caused by extreme climatic events, yet some raising of the dykes and strengthening of dunes might be technically feasible, and the Dutch record of water management would suggest that effective measures could be put in place. More problematic appears to be the severely reduced discharge capacity of the rivers Rhine and Meuse (Maas) as a result of sea-level rise.

The research embraces the many social, economic and political dimensions of such changes, developing proposals for how The Netherlands might respond. Thinking on this scale lies within the impressive tradition of Dutch regional planning, of which the sea barrier is one notable outcome.

Dutch Sea Barrier

Eastern Scheldt, The Netherlands, 1977–87

ivers break their banks, high tides driven by
insistent winds surge over sea defences, and
flood defences prove unable to contain rising waters.
The legacy of damage, death and disaster stemming
from great movements of water is a continuing
reminder of the destructive power of this element,
and the reason for such major works of engineering
as tidal barriers built to control the periodic surges,
or 'bores', on rivers. Such barriers often emerge as
dominant structures within the cityscape, for example
that guarding the city of Kingston-upon-Hull on the
east coast of England against the incursion of the
River Humber (pages 132–33); or, like the Thames
Barrier in London (pages 128–31), they can become
established visitor attractions. On a different scale,
sea defences can shape the form of coastal
settlements worldwide.

Nowhere is this more evident than in The
Netherlands, where over the centuries the Dutch have
learnt to engineer against the incursions of the North
Sea as well as to reclaim areas of land by means of
polders. This is an area of expertise for which they
have been much in demand throughout the world,
whether to help drain the Fens in eastern England or
the marshes of the Landes in France, but undoubtedly
their most challenging project to date has been the
Dutch Sea Barrier. This provides protection from high

tides driven by storms to the coastal perimeter little
short of 700 km (435 miles) long across the delta of
the Rhine, the Meuse (Maas) and the Scheldt rivers.

The original scheme to build a series of dams
across the tidal channels was given impetus by a
devastating flood in 1953, in which nearly 2000
people lost their lives and 250,000 hectares
(600,000 acres) of land were inundated. Yet a
problem arose from the fact that any fixed barrier
offering the necessary protection would have served
also to isolate the waters of the delta from the sea,
with a potentially serious impact on the balance of
the region's natural ecosystems.

The initial project begun in 1958 was curtailed
in 1977 in the face of environmental objections.
However, under the leadership of the a powerful
Rijkswaterstaat (Public Works Department), it
was eventually brought to fruition in 1987 with
the completion of the final and, in construction
terms, most challenging element of the chain of
dams and sluices − a barrier 6.8 km (4.3 miles)
long to close the mouth of the Eastern Scheldt.
Its innovative configuration comprised sixty-five
enormous concrete piers, each 18,000 tonnes in
weight, separated by sixty-two moveable steel gates
forming the protective barrier. These massive piers
were cast in three dry docks located on one of the
artificial islands already created in the earlier phase

ABOVE The main barrier
consists of three sections
with a total of sixty-two sluice
gates set between precast
concrete piers.

OPPOSITE Barrier sections link
a chain of artificial islands
protecting the Eastern Scheldt
to the right.

of barrier construction. They were then towed out from the flooded dock by a custom-designed vessel and lowered into place on to the seabed, which had been specially prepared.

Careful preparation of the seabed was needed partly because of the very considerable depth of water (some 40 m; 150 ft.) at the centre of the main channel, and also because the waterlogged sandy subsoil had to be transformed into a stable foundation for the piers: this was achieved by vibrating a grid of steel needles driven into the sand,

so that excess water was forced out and the seabed consolidated through compaction. On top of this compacted seabed was placed a layer of filter mattresses filled with graduated sand and gravel as protection against scouring by the powerful currents that run through the channels. The concrete piers were positioned and grouted to the mattresses and the assembly protected at its base by a skirt of graded rocks. The container thus formed was then backfilled with sand to increase its stability, before the piers were linked by concrete cills and by the

BELOW The tidal barrier is effectively a 'dyke with doors', allowing the tidal surges to be controlled and threats of flooding to be averted.

bridge structures that carry the roadway running the length of the barrier, connecting the artificial islands. This composite structure was then ready for the installation of the steel sluice gates, typically 5 m (16 ft.) thick and 40 m (152 ft.) wide, with the height of each doubling in sequence from a minimum of 6 m (20 ft.) as the channel deepens; each gate is almost 500 tonnes in weight.

In more than fifteen years of successful operation, the Eastern Scheldt barrier has not only provided reassurance and protection for a whole region, but in fact has also turned out to be an invaluable tool in the husbandry of environmental resources in the delta. In addition, its construction has resulted in a broader recreational use of the waters and shores of the delta. While similar elements of its design can be found in other tidal-surge barriers, there is currently no other barrier system on this scale anywhere in the world. The installation of even one single pair of piers and its corresponding gate would constitute a considerable project on its own in the context of a tidal river.

Key Facts

Architects: Greater London Council (GLC) Architects	
Engineers: Rendel Palmer & Tritton	
Construction workforce: 4000	
Weight of each gate assembly: 3200 tonnes	
Gate closure time: 9 minutes (each gate); 30 minutes (total barrier)	
Maximum head of water: 8.4 m (28 ft.)	

Thames Barrier
London, England, 1974–84

ABOVE Each gate is designed as a steel box girder, with the upstream water pressure resisted by the curved front face of the gate.

ABOVE RIGHT Aerial view of the barrier, showing the navigable passages between the piers.

OPPOSITE 1500-tonne hydraulic rams acting on a rocking beam raise and lower each gate.

Even in this age of more knowledge and greater power to control nature, the elemental threat posed by water to our urban settlements and to our countryside remains ever present. Indeed, with the seemingly irreversible melting of the polar ice-caps, coupled with increasing urbanization, the implications of rising sea levels are grave, especially where the settlement under threat has owed its existence to its proximity to navigable waterways. Such a problem writ large occurs with the River Thames, historically London's lifeline, where these external factors are critically reinforced by surge tides. These tides have their origin in the north Atlantic and can, on occasion, be forced by northerly winds down into the North Sea, causing huge volumes of water to be pushed up the Thames. Even without the surge tides, the high-water level at Tower Bridge is rising at the rate of 75 cm (30 in.) per century.

The implications of these tidal changes are very serious, with 1.25 million people at risk from flooding across an area of 115 square kilometres (45 square miles) – a danger brought home by the flood of 1953, when 300 people were drowned and large parts of Canvey Island at the mouth of the Thames were submerged. In response, various schemes for building a flood barrier across the river were brought forward, but they all foundered on the requirement of maintaining a clear opening of at least 450 m (1500

ft.) through which ships could pass en route to the London docks. However, once the new downstream port facilities at Tilbury, with their provision for the container trade, effectively made the historical docks redundant from the late 1960s, the way was clear to design a barrier with an opening closer in width to that of Tower Bridge itself, about 60 m (200 ft.). This barrier was intended to work in conjunction with the other primary means of flood defence, that of raising sections of the river-bank.

Raised river walls have several self-evident advantages, being straightforward to build, robust and secure from human operating error. Yet they have the disadvantage of blocking off views of the Thames, which are of great sentimental and touristic importance, and very much part of the attraction of this great river. In the event, new sections of flood-protection river wall and embankment – nearly 20 km (12 miles) in total – have been constructed and some existing sections raised; these defences work in conjunction with a new river barrier with rising gates built across the Thames on Woolwich Reach in south-east London. In building these extensive sections of embankment, full opportunity was taken to create new Thames-side walks, parks and belvederes.

Construction of the Thames Barrier began in 1974. It was formally opened by Queen Elizabeth II on 8 May 1984, although it had become operational at the end of 1982 and was first used for its intended purpose in February of the following year. In essence, the structure consists of nine concrete piers founded on solid chalk 50 m (154 ft.) below the riverbed, which is about 430 m (1400 ft.) wide at this point. Between these 65 m (215 ft.) long piers are set ten gates, with six forming navigable passages for shipping. The four largest gates are 60 m (200 ft.) wide and weigh more than 3700 tonnes each. Construction tolerances of plus/minus a mere 50 mm (2 in.) were met in the placement of the piers, a remarkable achievement given the exposed location.

Each of the six rising gates is fitted with counter-weighted, disc-shaped arms; in the open position the gate is full of water and sits in a concrete cill on the riverbed. When raised hydraulically as a flood defence, the downstream, curved face of the gate forms the barrier, backed by the upstream face, which is held vertical. This curved profile aids the distribution of loads caused by the difference between downstream and upstream water levels, which can be as high as 8 m (26 ft.), when the gates are closed and helps to retain the gate in the closed position without the need for undue locking force. There is no attempt to create a seal between the gate and the cill, as leakage is minimal and the water that does pass through serves a useful function in providing a high-pressure scouring action. The gates can also be raised clear of the water to be inspected and maintained.

When the threat looms of a dangerously high tidal surge, the rising gates are turned from their riverbed cills to the raised position and the four other openings are closed by falling radial gates, thus forming a continuous defensive wall of steel against the rising waters. It takes only a few minutes to close the barrier, but the process is slowed to reduce the chance of a reflective wave being created.

The barrier gate operating machinery is protected by laminated timber shells clad in stainless-steel panels, which also serve to enhance the visual impact of the structure.

Key Facts

Architects:	Shankland Ccx Partnership
Engineers:	Sir Murdoch MacDonald & Partners
Weight of steel barrier gate:	202 tonnes
Dimensions:	11 m (h) x 30 m (w) (36 ft. x 100 ft.)
Operation of barrier:	8 to 12 times per year
Cost:	UK£3,900,000

Tidal Surge Barrier
Kingston-upon-Hull, England, 1975–80

ABOVE The barrier was designed to be a major landmark, complementing a historic church tower in the city centre.

ABOVE RIGHT The triangular-sectioned footbridge links the tops of the two towers supporting the barrier gate.

Flood waters bring in their wake damage, despair, and even death, most notably urbanized areas are inundated. With much of its centre lying 2 m (6.5 ft.) below sea level, the historic city of Kingston-upon-Hull has proved vulnerable to flood waters propelled up the River Hull from the wider River Humber. Critical conditions occur when a high tide is amplified by a North Sea surge, producing a powerful funnelling effect in the southern waters of the Humber. This creates a surge wave that then enters the shallower River Hull. Surges of up to 2 m (6.5 ft.) passing up the river have been recorded, with dire consequences for the 10,000 urban properties alongside the river and ten times that number in the river's floodplain.

Since piecemeal raising of the riparian flood protection where the River Hull flows through the city centre would have proved expensive and impractical because of the many working industries that line the riverside, the regional water authority opted instead to build a barrier gate close to the meeting of the rivers Hull and Humber to protect the central area and the land upstream.

A gate that could be raised and then lowered back into the riverbed would have had a negligible visual impact in the preferred barrier site, which lies at the heart of the city close to the magnificent Cathedral of Holy Trinity and other valued parts of the historic urban fabric. However, it would always be prone to

impact damage and prove difficult to maintain without disrupting river traffic. The idea was also unpopular with the operators of river craft who tended to drag their anchors to keep clear of the river-banks. While the preferred alternative of a barrier that could be lifted clear out of the river avoided such problems of maintenance and navigation, the height at which the gate needed to be set so as to provide clearance for vessels would inevitably lead to a design that would rank as a prominent, landmark structure, comparable in its likely impact to London's Tower Bridge. Its functional parameters were simple enough: a water-way at least 25 m (82 ft.) wide and a shipping clearance of 26 m (85 ft.) above sea level, high enough for the passage of all tugs, barges and other craft that use the River Hull.

Starting from these raw functional parameters, the development of a structure worthy of its dramatic 'gateway' location required very close collaboration between the engineers and architects of the design team, aided by the use of sketch models and visualizations of this huge 'building' in its context. It was decided early on that the 202-tonne steel barrier gate, 11 m (36 ft.) high and 30 m (100 ft.) wide, was best 'parked' horizontally when in the raised position, thereby reducing wind loading and visual impact. When being raised or lowered, the gate turns through 90 degrees to or from the vertical position, running in guide channels set in the two support towers and coming to rest on a concrete cill set in the riverbed. The steel barrier gate was designed as four stiffened plate girders linked by diaphragms and covered with a skin of bolted steel plates. The construction began with the assembly of the two central beams on the river-bank, which were then craned into position to rest on temporary supports fixed to each tower. Outer beams were then lifted one by one and attached to the diaphragms, followed by the steel plates forming the face of the barrier, which were friction-bolted to the completed framework. Above the barrier gate, an enclosed walkway, triangular in cross-section to reduce its wind resistance, links the towers.

Triangles also occur as the plan form for the towers that support the barrier gate and for the escape stairs attached to them. Such a form helps to lend coherence to the overall design, as well as being an efficient structural shape. The towers were designed as rigid concrete tubes to resist wind loadings and to support the dead load of the gate itself, the counter-weights and the gear needed to lift it. Mass-concrete foundations, as deep as the towers are high, are set into the riverbed to support the whole structure. Particular care was taken with the board-marked *in-situ* concrete finish of the towers, exactly matching that chosen for the National Theatre in London, using white cement and a fine crushed-limestone aggregate. This finish has weathered well during the two decades of the barrier's operation and serves to emphasize the clean, robust lines of the structure.

Since its completion in 1980, the barrier has been lowered to protect the city on average about ten occasions a year. A refurbishment programme between 1996 and 2002 included replacement of the four 16-tonne chains that raise the gate.

Key Facts

Engineers: Team led by Sir Bruce White, Royal Engineers; (concept) Alan Beckett, Royal Engineers

Capacity (total throughput): 4,000,000 tonnes supplies, 12,000,000 personnel, 500,000 tanks

Weight of construction materials: (Phoenix caissons) 784,000 tonnes, 40,000 tonnes steel

Total length of floating roadway: 16 km (10 miles)

Total construction workforce: approx. 45,000

Mulberry Harbours
Arromanches, France, 1942–44

N o more poignant memorials to great engineering endeavour could be found than the stricken remnants of very large concrete structures beached at Shoeburyness in the Thames Estuary in England and at Arromanches on the French coast. These are two of the few surviving fragments of a construction programme that once employed a workforce of more than 45,000, and without which the Allied landings in Normandy (Operation Overlord) in 1944 could not have taken place. Following the pattern of many wartime innovations, the development of the 'Mulberry Harbours', as they were codenamed, involved a diverse group of individuals seconded to the project, which was being driven along by the authority of the British prime minister Winston Churchill. Many were peacetime sailing enthusiasts, others were recruited from civilian contractors, but all were galvanized by the pressing urgency of meeting that precious

window of favourable weather before the storms of autumn 1944 would take hold.

The idea of building artificial harbours to land men and *matériel* (materials and equipment) on the Normandy coast, on the assumption that the existing ports would be heavily defended or sabotaged beyond use, crystallized in Churchill's famous memo of 30 May 1942 to (Lord) Louis Mountbatten: "Piers for use on beaches. They must float up and down with the tide. The anchor problem must be mastered. Let me have the best solution worked out. Don't argue the matter. The difficulties will argue for themselves." But the prime minister's directness and brevity belied the true task ahead. Partial solutions were soon rejected. Artificial breakwaters alone could protect ships and barges while *matériel* was transferred on to landing craft or rafts, but beaching them involved a twelve-hour delay, as well as double-handling. Some form of pierhead, on the other hand, would allow unloading direct on to road transport, whatever the tides and sea conditions.

Nothing short of an independent harbour, with pierheads on which the incoming ships could be unloaded and roadsteads on which vehicles could move ashore, would do the job. The pierheads needed to be adjustable to suit tidal conditions, as Churchill correctly surmised, because a rigid pierhead grounded on the seabed would have been

TOP The remains of one of the Phoenix caissons at Arromanches today.

ABOVE The line of Phoenix caissons and block-ships that formed the breakwater of the Arromanches Mulberry B Harbour.

RIGHT Aerial view of the Mulberry B Harbour in operation at Arromanches.

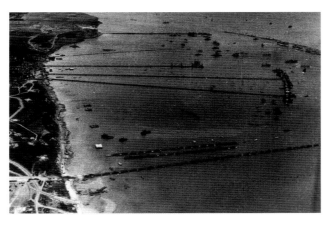

more than 6 m (20 ft.) above the level of a ship's deck at low tide, hence out of reach of the on-board cargo derricks and difficult to access using the then scarce mobile cranes. It was also impractical to link a rigid pierhead to the floating roadway needed to land *matériel* onshore. The solution adopted was a pierhead on which the platform would rise or fall in step with the tides, based on the design of a dredger that had been seen in action in a South American harbour. This was achieved by setting a 'Spud', or leg, 1.2 m (4 ft.) square and 27 m (90 ft.) long, on each of the four corners of the 'Whale', the pierhead platform, 60 m (195 ft.) long and 18 m (60 ft.) wide, which was fabricated from welded steel and concrete infill. Electric winches with reduction gearing raised or lowered the pierhead. The roadsteads to shore were supported on float units codenamed 'Beetles'. Surrounding the harbour was a permanent break-water formed by 'Phoenixes' – huge concrete caissons 18 m (60 ft.) high, 60 m (195 ft.) long and 15 m (50 ft.) wide, which were towed into position and then sunk – and supplemented by sunken ships.

Two separate Mulberry Harbours were towed by tugs across the English Channel at the modest pace of 5 km/h (3 mph): Mulberry A, to support the American forces landing at 'Omaha' Beach, and Mulberry B, for the British landing-point at Arromanches. After only four days in use the former was largely destroyed in the severe storm that raged from 19 to 23 June. Mulberry B, however, proved a success, with more than 326,000 troops, 54,000 vehicles and 100,000 tonnes of supplies being landed during its first six days of operation. This process continued at the rate of 9000 tonnes a day until the end of August 1944, when the ports of Antwerp and Cherbourg had been secured by Allied forces.

As an example of creative engineering, leadership and ingenuity, the Mulberry Harbours were an undoubted triumph. Equally impressive in retrospect was the total secrecy maintained throughout the construction period as to the final destination and purpose of the huge components being cast at special building sites around the south of England. The bigger picture only became clear to the many builders of Mulberry with the first BBC radio despatches from the Normandy beachhead. As an eminent structural engineer later wrote: "The audacity of Mulberry lay in its magnitude, the complexity of the means needed to fulfill its functions, the vagueness with which, of necessity, the site was known and the phenomenal speed with which the component parts had to be constructed in the UK and assembled on the far shore."

BELOW A Phoenix caisson ready for towing across to Arromanches. In total, about 50 Phoenixes were built by contractors across the south of England.

Energy and Natural Forces

135

Sea Defences

136 Discovery and Exploration

Structures designed to enable or support exploration and discovery are very much free of 'packaging' and applied design, and often all the more eloquent for that. Many are part of the private domain of the research campus and have no public presence; others, such as the great telescopes, are memorable and familiar in form, coming to stand as symbols for the science that they serve. Yet all these structures somehow carry the promise of new knowledge.

Situated on mountain tops in favoured regions of clear skies, terrestrial telescopes have continued to develop in size and power, from the classic large reflectors such as that on Mount Wilson, California, with which the American astronomer Edwin Hubble studied galaxies, or the Hale Telescope on Mount Palomar, also in California, with its 5 m (16 ft.) single mirror representing until recently the practical limit to the size of a mirror. While the basic form of telescopes has remained remarkably constant, modern innovations have included computer-aided tracking of celestial objects, the replacement of photographic film with more efficient electronic detectors, and the use of fibre optics to capture multiple objects. The popular image of the lone observer at an eyepiece or exposing a photographic plate now belongs to the past.

From its *ad hoc* beginnings on the back of World War II technology, the science of radio astronomy has evolved its own distinct family of structures, which have achieved ever-greater levels of penetration and

RIGHT Rolled out of the Vehicle Assembly Building at the Kennedy Space Center the previous night, Space Shuttle *Columbia* arrives at Pad 39B in the early morning in preparation for launching.

BELOW Apollo 14 lunar module *Antares* reflects a circular flare created by the sun. The lower slope of the moon's Cone Crater is visible at the extreme left.

precision in the information they cull from space. The great dish aerials of the Lovell Radio Telescope (Jodrell Bank) in the UK (pages 140–141) and its many worldwide successors – some examples aligned as a group of synchronized dishes – are perhaps the best-known and most prominent form of receiver. Other installations may involve arrays of smaller aerials or optical devices set out as a regular grid, their signals being blended by computer to achieve the effect of a far greater focal length than is possible with a single instrument, through a technique known as aperture synthesis. The scale of these radio telescopes is such that they become major interventions in the landscape, with their aerial arrays extending into the distance. In one case the natural landform has been co-opted to turn a dish-shaped depression into a giant receiver.

Quite apart from the research vehicles themselves – shuttles, space stations and telescopes, all remarkable examples of engineering in their own right – the physical exploration of space has called for launch complexes of a scale that belies its origins in the tarpaper-covered huts of the earliest rocket pioneers. Whereas the launch of a V2-derived rocket was a simple, if often hazardous, operation, as the size of launch vehicle increased to that of the Saturn V rocket needed for the American Apollo programme, structures of an entirely new order of magnitude were needed in order to assemble, test and launch the rockets. This is most evident in the Kennedy Space Center's Vehicle Assembly Building (pages 156–57), the largest building in the world and a vertical structure whose only antecedents might be found (horizontally) in the great airship hangars.

As the extreme limits of physics are approached –

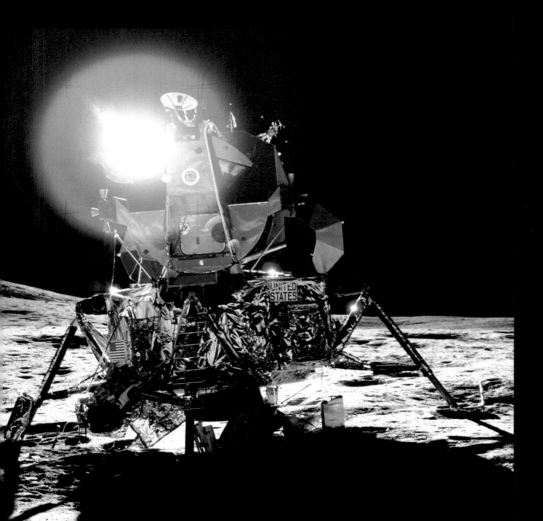

towards minimum temperatures or in the realm of subatomic particles – the size and complexity of the research equipment needed for experiments appear to increase almost exponentially. Whereas the realm of theory can often be successfully advanced on blackboards or notepads, experimentation and observation increasingly demand structures that are not only enormous in their dimensions but also house equipment that needs to be installed and operated at very demanding levels of precision. For example, CERN – the European Nuclear Research Institute in Geneva – combines great size, in the form of its 27 km (17 mile) underground ring tunnel, and the need for great accuracy in the equipment aligning the beams of particles that circulate within (pages 154–55). To build such a setting for experiments calls for civil and mechanical engineering of the highest order.

Wind tunnels are arguably the group of structures that best exemplifies the evolution of a very specific research tool through a series of progressive improvements in technology, instrumentation and

scale, as designers have developed installations that can more closely reflect real-life conditions for the objects under test. Although such wind tunnels as the pioneering group at Langley, Virginia (pages 148–51), constructed from the early 1930s onwards, are of epic dimensions and undoubted grandeur, they have certainly not been shaped by self-conscious aesthetics – the performance of the tunnels has always mattered more than their appearance. Untouched by the visual refinements that would be applied to a large dam structure or other more visible artefact, they have simply done their job, whether the data they yield is to refine the profile of a supersonic aircraft or to improve the aerodynamics of a mass-production car.

These superstructures impress precisely because they have not been designed to impress. Their forms have evolved directly from the functions they need to perform, without the need for applied styling or visual enhancement. Knowing that they are the tools of discovery is also part of their attraction.

BELOW Project Mercury astronauts trained in MASTIF – the Multiple Axis Space Test Inertia Facility – to gain control of a spacecraft that could move or tumble, in unexpected ways through space.

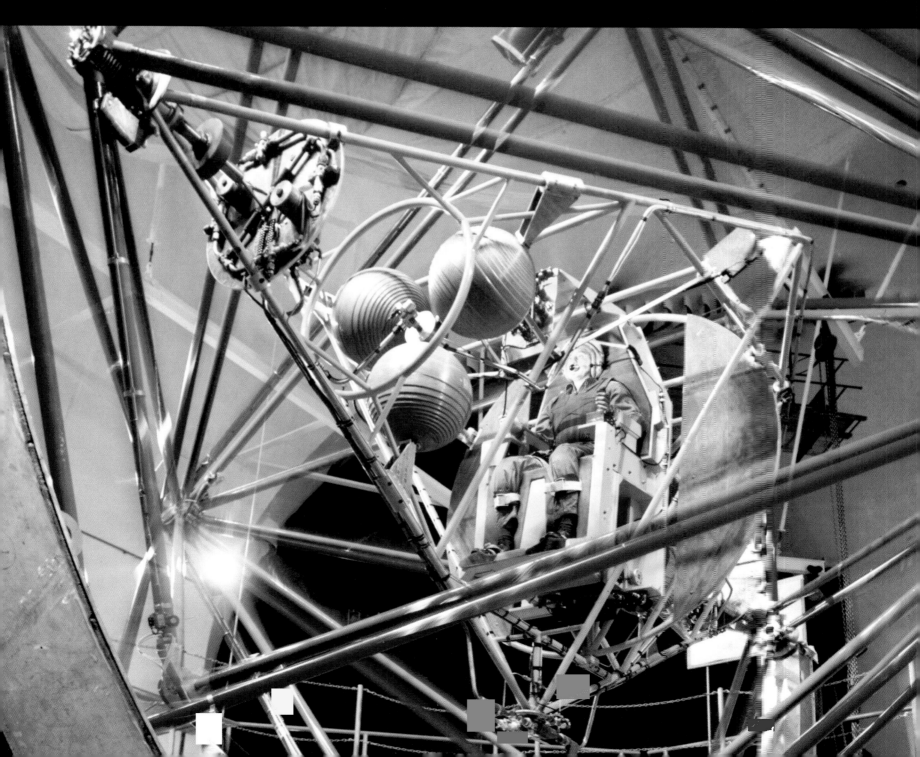

RIGHT Inspecting the steel-plated surface of the bowl: some idea of its immense size can be gained from this photograph.

FAR RIGHT The second-largest fully steerable radio telescope in the world, the Lovell Telescope turns on a reused railway track.

Lovell Radio Telescope

Jodrell Bank, Manchester, England, 1955–57

More often than not, first ideas turn out to be the best ones. Such was certainly the case when World War II radar specialist Dr (later Sir) Bernard Lovell returned to Manchester University in 1945, intent on continuing his earlier research into cosmic rays with the aid of an army-surplus radar transmitter. In search of a suitable location without the radio interference to which his work would have been subject in the city, he was directed to the university's Botanic Garden at Jodrell Bank, on the Cheshire Plain, 32 km (20 miles) south of Manchester. Instead of cosmic rays, Lovell's research soon turned to meteors, and important discoveries were made, aided from 1947 onwards by a large aerial array built from scaffolding poles and a great quantity of steel wire. Lovell's team began to explore the mysterious radio waves emanating from the depths of the universe, notably those from the Andromeda Galaxy.

Fleshed out in sketches prepared by the Sheffield structural engineer Charles Husband, a buildable design for a fully steerable radio telescope at Jodrell Bank, 76 m (250 ft.) in diameter, emerged. The bowl would be lined with steel sheets, thus equipping it to deal with radio frequencies far shorter than the 1 m (3 ft.) wavelength possible with a lining of steel mesh, as had first been intended. This last-minute decision to upgrade the dish surface was prompted by the discovery in 1951 that the hydrogen atom had an

emission wavelength of 21 cm (8.3 in.): with a solid dish surface, radio exploration of the Milky Way and distant stars would be within the grasp, uniquely at the time, of Jodrell Bank. Even as the contractors were mobilizing on site, a bold choice was made in favour of a dish surface formed of 7100 welded steel panels each 2 mm (0.08 in.) thick, fixed to a totally upgraded support structure.

By a quirk of fate, international fame followed swiftly on the telescope's completion in the summer of 1957, when its powerful radar proved to be the only instrument available in the West that was capable of tracking the carrier rocket of the Soviet satellite Sputnik I. The telescope was subsequently used to transmit commands to Pioneer 5, America's first successful probe into deep space, as well as to help to track Russia's unmanned space missions to the moon and to Venus. It proved invaluable in receiving and processing the telemetry from many Russian and American satellites as they voyaged into the heart of the solar system.

Huge bearings atop a pair of towers support the telescope dish, which is rotated horizontally around a circular track by two electric motors around a central bearing. Raising or lowering the dish is achieved through gear racks within each tower, so that the telescope can follow a radio wave source across the sky; all motors are controlled by an electromechanical analog computer. Growing demand for more precise tracking, as observers work with ever-shorter radio wavelengths, has led to an ongoing upgrade of the telescope. In 1987 it was renamed the Lovell Radio Telescope to honour the astronomer. The old steel reflector, damaged by rust after thirty years' continuous service, has been replaced by a surface of galvanized-steel plates five times smoother than the previous one. A holographic profiling technique was used to set each panel into the parabolic dish with great precision, thereby ensuring that the accuracy of the whole dish when all panels are in place is very close to that achieved for each individual panel.

Not surprisingly, since 1957, when the Lovell Telescope came into service, the title of the world's largest radio telescope has passed to younger claimants. Since 1972, the 100 m (330 ft.) radio telescope at Effelsberg near Bonn, Germany, operated by the Max Planck Institute of Radioastronomy, has ranked as the world's largest fully steerable dish. The 100 m (330 ft.) dish at Green Bank, West Virginia, the brainchild of the US National Radio Astronomy Observatory, which became operational in 2000, has achieved pre-eminence as the most sensitive such instrument in the world, able to work at wavelengths as short as 6 mm (0.24 in.). If size alone is the criterion, the largest single-dish radio telescope is Cornell University's fixed 305 m (1000 ft.) dish at Arecibo in Puerto Rico, which lies in a hollow in the hills and is able to survey only a limited sector of the heavens.

To a degree, size matters, in radio telescopes as in much else, but perhaps only a British team could have obtained the 18-inch (45 cm) gear racks from the redundant battleships HMS *Royal Sovereign* and HMS *Revenge* to provide the mechanism to elevate their telescope at Jodrell Bank. Clearly something of the Meccano spirit lives on, a lively *bricolage* of scientific possibilities and handy hardware.

BELOW Jodrell Bank's Mark II telescope in front of the Lovell Telescope. The Mark II is part of the Multi-Element Radio Linked Interferometer Network (MERLIN) group of radio telescopes across Britain controlled from Jodrell Bank.

Key Facts

Site area: 10 ha (25 acres)	
Number of telescopes: 14	
Ryle Telescope: eight 13 m (43 ft.) diameter dishes in 8 km (5 mile) line	
One Mile Telescope: three 18 m (60 ft.) diameter dishes in 1.6 km (1 mile) line	
Area of original pulsar aerial array: 1.8 ha (4.5 acres)	
Telescope control: by computer from the Cavendish Laboratory, Cambridge University	

Mullard Radio Astronomy Observatory
Cambridge, England, 1957–

TOP LEFT Two pioneering telescopes: two of three dishes of the One Mile Telescope (1962–64), seen through the 4C Aerial Array (1957).

TOP RIGHT The One Mile Telescope achieved a world first in the use of aperture-synthesis techniques.

Cambridge, with its ancient university and its research institutes, would seem to be exactly the right place in which to advance theories of the cosmos, and in fact is one of the world's greatest centres for innovation in astronomical theory and practice. Its forte has long been radio astronomy, pioneered by the Cavendish Laboratory from 1945 under Professor Sir Martin Ryle. Now known as the Mullard Radio Astronomy Observatory (MRAO), the centre is currently located at Lord's Bridge, 8 km (5 miles) outside the city, and has become the site of world-class research, as recognized by the Nobel Prize awarded to professors Ryle and Hewish in 1974.

The MRAO has pioneered interferometry: the technology of combining signals from an array of separate telescopes to produce the same quality of image as would be possible using a single dish with a diameter as large as the greatest separation distance between the individual telescopes. Since the size of the telescope in relation to the radio wavelength determines the level of detail that can be observed, this method, also known as aperture synthesis, can help to maximize image quality. Pioneered for meas-urements of radio wavelengths, aperture-synthesis techniques have been transposed to far shorter – and, in terms of the precision of equipment required, more demanding – optical wavelengths, thanks to advances in electro-optics, computing and laser metrology.

The most visible and familiar evidence of interferometry and aperture synthesis at Lord's Bridge is the series of eight dish aerials forming the Ryle Telescope, each 13 m (43 ft.) in diameter with Cassegrain mountings (in which the signal collected by the main dish is reflected back to the receiver by a smaller secondary reflector). Four mobile aerials are mounted on a 1.2 km (0.75 mile) long rail track and, for low-brightness astronomy, are brought together within a 100 m (330 ft.) baseline; the other four are mounted at fixed 1.2 km intervals, yielding a maximum baseline of 4.8 km (3 miles), which is used when high-resolution images are required.

An important part of the observatory's work is the mapping of cosmic microwave radiation that reaches back to the very origins of the universe, when it was a mere 300,000 years old. This background radiation has since cooled to the point at which it can be detected only at radio wavelengths. Mapping the way in which the radiation varies in intensity across the sky helps astronomers to understand the formation of galaxies as well as the first moments of the universe, but because such variation is so small, highly sensitive custom-built telescopes are required: the one at Lord's Bridge, the Cosmic Anistropy Telescope (CAT), which uses three receiving horns as aerials.

Radio astronomy can prove of great assistance in boosting the effectiveness of optical telescopes, which, apart from Hubble (pages 146–47), are earthbound, and images from which improve in detail as the size of the instrument increases. Aperture-synthesis techniques have made it possible to combine the light from four small separated telescopes and to synthesize images in which can be seen detail a thousand times finer than that obtainable with individual optical instruments. The Cambridge Optical Aperture Synthesis Telescope (COAST) is used to study the surfaces of individual stars and the interaction between stars close to one another. Developed in the mid-1990s, this was the world's first separated-element optical/infrared aperture-synthesis telescope.

Larger in scope than COAST, but building on the same Cambridge innovations in optical/infrared technology, an ambitious project involving collaboration between the university's Astrophysics Group and teams from New Mexico and the Naval Research Laboratory in Washington, DC, is under way

at the Magdalena Ridge Observatory in New Mexico. This will create an array of telescopes that will be optically linked to form a single great instrument the size of a football field. It will consist of eight to ten telescopes, each 1.4 m (4.6 ft.) in diameter, at a distance of up to 400 m (1300 ft.) apart. Signals from these telescopes will be blended to produce an image as if from a telescope with a primary mirror 400 m (1300 ft.) in diameter, compared to Hubble's 2.4 m (8 ft.) The telescopes will be able to produce images of complex objects in space far more quickly than competing arrays. This huge collaborative project is moving towards becoming available for observational use at the end of 2007.

Through such ventures, the work and influence of MRAO extend far beyond the boundaries of Lord's Bridge. The dishes that form such a familiar feature of the Cambridge skyline are only a very small part of the picture of cosmology.

BELOW Five of the eight dishes that together form the Ryle Telescope (1968–71). Four are fixed and the others can be moved along a baseline track to provide the desired configuration.

Key Facts

Telescope planned by: Staff of the Royal Observatory, Greenwich

Diameter of primary mirror: 4.2 m (13.8 ft.)

Weight of telescope assembly: 210 tonnes

Internal diameter of dome: 21 m (70 ft.)

Cost: UK£15,000,000

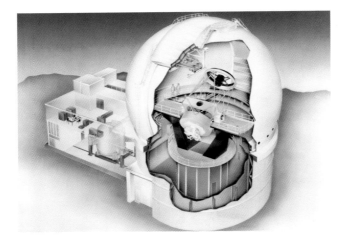

Sir William Herschel

The most famous member of a family of British astronomers, Sir William Herschel (1738–1822) combined expertise in astronomical observation with innovation in the field of telescope-making. It was Herschel who confirmed the existence of the planet Uranus in 1781. He designed and built by far the largest telescopes of his day, up to 12.2 m (40 ft.) in length with mirrors as large as 1.2 m (4 ft.) in diameter, but it was his systematic and methodical approach to observation that proved so productive. Aided by his sister Caroline, who herself discovered eight comets and several nebulae, Herschel identified the satellites of Uranus and of Saturn, then proceeded to make an extensive catalogue of the stars, in which he recorded more than 1500 galaxies. Through his observations he concluded that our galaxy is a disc-shaped arrangement of stars.

William Herschel Telescope
La Palma, Canary Islands, 1985–87

ABOVE Cut-away section, showing the telescope enclosure rotating above the base of the instrument and the service rooms.

OPPOSITE TOP The 4.2 m (13.8 ft.) primary mirror is tested prior to installation.

OPPOSITE CENTRE Sections of the prefabricated cladding for the telescope dome are manoeuvred into place.

OPPOSITE Disturbance to the telescope chamber is minimized by the location of support activities in the concrete structure below and to one side.

Named in honour of Sir William Herschel, one of the greatest astronomers of all time and a pioneer of observational astrophysics, the third-largest single-mirror telescope in the world, at its opening in 1987, crowns a ridge on the island of La Palma in the Canaries. With the land dropping away to the Atlantic to the north and sheer cliffs descending to the pine-clad slopes of the island's interior, a more perfect site and sight, both astronomically and scenically, would be hard to find. The William Herschel Telescope is the largest in Western Europe and the brainchild of the Royal Observatory, Greenwich, London. It represents the final development in a line of post-war Greenwich-designed telescopes that began with the Isaac Newton Telescope (mirror diameter 2.5 m; 8.2 ft.), which served at the Herstmonceux Observatory in Britain from 1967 and in La Palma from 1984, and continued with the Anglo-Australian Telescope (3.9 m; 12.8 ft.) at Siding Springs Observatory in New South Wales (1974). Specifically designed as an all-purpose instrument, the Herschel Telescope is kept open to requests from astronomers for observation time and facilities.

Bringing together on the top of a mountain ridge the component parts of a telescope weighing more than 210 tonnes called for some ingenious solutions to logistical problems. First shipped from Britain in

the autumn of 1985 were the telescope's azimuth bearings and the hydraulic system to support its primary mirror, both components requiring extremes of accuracy in their installation. The following spring the main parts – the drive system, the mirrors and the plant needed for the periodic re-coating of the primary mirror – arrived at La Palma and were transported to the site overland. This was no small feat considering that some pieces were as large as 6 m x 8 m (20 ft. x 26 ft.), weighed up to 30 tonnes and had to be moved along the tight bends and steep gradients of the mountain roads. The whole haulage process took a full four weeks, but installation of the components made rapid progress, and the level of stability required of the structure by the design team in Greenwich was soon achieved.

At the heart of the telescope lies the 4.2 m (13.8 ft.) diameter clear-aperture paraboloidal primary mirror, with a focal length of 10.5 m (35 ft.), cast in a glass-ceramic material (Cervit) that benefits from an infinitesimal coefficient of expansion at the telescope's normal operating temperatures. With a diameter-to-thickness ratio of eight to one, the mirror was relatively thin at the time of manufacture, but it was – and remains – one of the most accurate ever made. The mirror's surface is covered with aluminium, which, when the coating is fresh, reflects up to 85% of the light falling on it. Exposure to ambient dust, pollen and humidity reduces the mirror's efficiency, however, meaning that an annual resurfacing operation is required: this involves the removal of the mirror module, giving it a good scrub with caustic soda, and re-aluminizing it in a vacuum tank – no mean task when the whole mirror weighs 16.5 tonnes.

All telescope mirrors on this scale are subject to deflection owing to their weight alone, which, if unchecked, would render them useless because they would bend and deform many thousands of times more than the optical tolerances required for successful observations would permit. As the mirror size increases, the problem becomes exponentially worse. In this respect, a 4.2 m (13.8 ft.) diameter telescope becomes three times more difficult to build than a 2.5 m (8.2 ft.) one. Providing the necessary, variable support for the primary mirror in the Herschel Telescope called for sophisticated mechanical-engineering design: the mirror in effect 'floats' on an array of sixty pneumatic cylinders arranged in rings on the floor of the mirror cell and divided into three 120-degree sectors. Each cylinder is individually controlled to admit pressurized nitrogen from a reservoir or to flush it into a vacuum tank, so that the loading exerted by the mirror at any point when the telescope is tracking – and thus its

deformation – can be maintained within prescribed limits. When the pneumatic system is not pressurized, the mirror rests on a system of spring-loaded rubber pads.

Protecting the telescope and its drive mechanisms, a 320-tonne onion dome sits on top of a concrete cylinder that is open to ground level, setting the centre of rotation of the telescope about 13 m (45 ft.) above the lowest floor level. This whole volume is kept free of secondary activity, so as to minimize thermal disturbance of the air around the telescope, and thus to achieve optimum observational conditions. The steel framework of the dome, including the ring girder that carries the telescope's transport system and the arch girder that supports the opening shutter and wind shield, were fabricated in Vancouver, demounted and then shipped from Canada to La Palma. Once assembled, the dome framework was covered with steel plates and the shutter and wind shield fabricated from aluminium.

William Herschel, together with his sister Caroline, who shared in his observations and discoveries, would surely have welcomed an instrument that echoes an earlier link between Britain and Spain – the altazimuth reflector telescope he delivered to the Madrid Observatory in 1802.

BELOW A view of the Hubble Telescope with the earth below. The photograph was taken from the Space Shuttle after the successful servicing mission in 1997. The telescope's open aperture door can be seen.

Key Facts

Orbit: 630 km (380 miles) from earth

Velocity: 8km (5 miles) per second

Servicing missions: December 1993, February 1997, December 1999

Distance travelled by images from Hubble to receiving centre: 150,000 km (90,000 miles)

Images collected by the telescope: approx. 10,000 per year

Edwin Hubble

Considered as one of the founding fathers of American astronomy, Edwin Hubble (1889–1953) pioneered observation of the composition of galaxies, proving the existence of separate galaxies in space where previously there had been no definite proof of any outside our own. He also made the discovery that the universe is expanding.

Working with the 2.5 m (100 in.) Mount Wilson telescope in 1924, Hubble took many thousands of photographs of the so-called Andromeda Nebula and discovered that it was actually a distinct galaxy of stars. He was able to confirm this theory by identifying changes in luminosity of certain points of light between a series of photographic plates, typical of very bright and unstable stars called cepheides.

Hubble made further observations that identified other, more distant, galaxies and discovered that they were receding from one another, which suggested that the universe is continually expanding; 'Hubble's Law' states that the further away a galaxy is, the faster it seems to be moving.

Hubble Space Telescope
1977–86; in orbit, 1990–

The swirling mixture of gases and dust particles that is the earth's atmosphere forms a barrier to astronomical observations, by impeding or blocking light at infrared and ultraviolet wavelengths, and by making it harder to observe very distant stars (it is also responsible for the twinkling effect of stars). Earth-based telescopes, even with the most advanced technology, cannot wholly overcome these constraints. The world's great optical telescopes will continue to evolve, but can never achieve the unfettered clarity promised by an instrument located in space.

In the early 1960s the United State's National Aeronautics and Space Administration (NASA) launched two Orbital Astronomical Observatories. The concept of an orbiting instrument matured into the idea of the Large Space Telescope (LST), and by the mid-1970s the LST project had evolved into that of an orbiting telescope platform that would be able to return to earth for servicing and would carry an array of interchangeable instruments. In 1975 the European Space Agency joined the project, and in 1977 NASA was given the official go-ahead by Congress.

The core group of instruments, selected on the basis of scientific consensus, comprised five primary devices: the Faint Object Camera, Wide Field/ Planetary Camera, Faint Object Spectrograph, High Resolution Spectrograph and High Speed Photometer. The design and construction of the telescope-housing

and instruments involved contractors, consultants and scientists from twenty-one US states and twelve countries; the project's complexity caused the launch date to be put back from 1983 to 1986 to allow further refinement of key devices. Thanks to the concurrent development of the Space Shuttle, NASA decided that the telescope would be maintained and updated in space, an innovative concept made possible by the orbiting platform's modular nature. But in 1986 the *Challenger* disaster caused the Shuttle programme to be set back, and with it the launch of the newly named Hubble Space Telescope. Finally, on 24 April 1990, the telescope was propelled into space aboard the Shuttle *Discovery* and placed in orbit.

Proof that the Hubble was robust and the logistics of maintenance using the Space Shuttle workable was provided early on. Initial images from the telescope were fuzzy and indistinct, caused by the outer edge of its primary mirror having been ground too flat (by only a fiftieth of the thickness of a human hair), a phenomenon known as spherical aberration. As part of the first servicing mission in December 1993, the engineering team devised a corrective package dubbed COSTAR (Corrective Optics Space Telescope Axial Replacement), the size of a telephone box, which located five pairs of corrective mirrors in front of the main camera and the two spectrographs, dramatically improving image quality. The pragmatic

ingenuity of Hubble's engineering team is also seen
in its solution to the problem of reviving an infrared
camera and spectrometer that had become inactive
through depletion of the cooling system. They devised
a mechanical cooling system based on high-speed
microturbines, the fastest spinning at 200,000 rpm,
fifty times the speed of a car engine.

Hubble's longevity and status as an observational
resource, more powerful today than at its launch,
owe much to its robust underlying concept – the
modularity that allowed astronauts on regular Shuttle
missions to repair or replace individual instruments.
Through these upgrades, the platform has been
refreshed to the point of becoming virtually a new
observational facility. Hubble continues to beam
back images of breathtaking quality, as well as, for
example, providing confirmation of the existence
of supermassive black holes, and revealing the
origins of gamma rays and quasars.

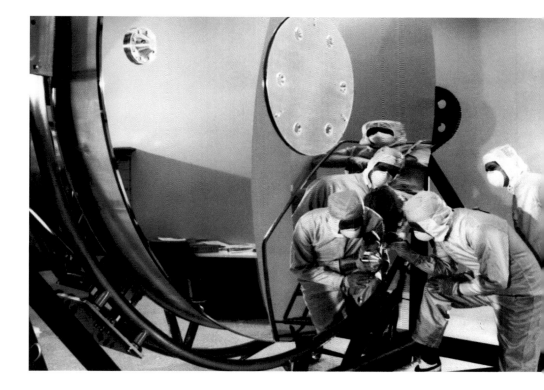

ABOVE Technicians inspect the
primary mirror of the Hubble
Telescope at the Marshall
Space Flight Center in 1982.

LEFT A view of the Hubble
Telescope as it is berthed
and lifted up by a robot
arm during a Space Shuttle
servicing mission.

Key Facts

Wind speed: 195km/h (120 mph)	
Power: 2984 kW (2 x 4000 bhp)	
Overall dimensions of the test tunnel: 9 m (h) x 18 m (w) x 17 m (l) (30 ft. x 60 ft. x 56 ft.)	
Propeller dimensions: 10.7 m (35 ft.)	

RIGHT The Eight Foot [2.4 m] High-Speed Wind Tunnel, at Langley, which became operational in 1936.

Wind Tunnel Evolution

Between 1909 and 1912, Gustave Eiffel, in Paris, made the first significant use of simple wind tunnels of his own design to test the aerodynamics of structures. But the important design innovation was the invention in 1908 by the German Ludwig Prandtl of a return-air wind tunnel that recirculated the airflow to produce a highly efficient mechanism.

Many wind tunnels were constructed subsequently: it is estimated that by 1941 there were at least 135 worldwide, and three or four times that many have since been built. The impressive series of wind tunnels built at the Langley Research Center constitutes perhaps the world's most famous group. They have helped to shape the development of aircraft and other modes of transport, including trains, ships and cars, and without them many developments in modern aerodynamics would have been impossible.

Despite the advent of increasingly sophisticated computer programs over the last two decades, the future of the wind tunnel as a research tool seems assured. While forms may evolve further and instrumentation may become more precise, the basic operating principles will remain the same.

Full-Scale Wind Tunnel
Langley Research Center, Hampton, Virginia, USA, 1929–31

Although they are sometimes obliged to serve gamely as backdrops for group photographs of participants at aeronautical conferences, wind tunnels have been built for a far more serious and valuable purpose. It is true to say that no modern aircraft, spacecraft or launch vehicle has gone forward to production or into use without first being tested and refined in some form of wind tunnel. In this field, the United States' National Aeronautics and Space Administration (NASA) can lay claim to pre-eminence, with its total of forty-two operational wind tunnels ranging in scale from those able to test a full-sized aeroplane to others a few centimetres in width for assessment of matchstick-sized models. This number can be compared with Britain's twenty-seven, France's eighteen, Japan's sixteen, Germany's eleven, Canada's five, and the four of The Netherlands.

Essentially, wind tunnels anywhere in the world, however epic their dimensions, are tube-like structures in which wind is generated by a large fan to flow over various test objects – such as aircraft, engines, wings, control surfaces, rockets, spacecraft, cars or models of any of these. The test object is held in a stationary position in the tunnel, and is monitored by instrumentation that records airflow around it and the aerodynamic forces acting upon it. Wind-tunnel design aims to create high-speed, low-turbulence airflow through the test section so as to allow measurements to be taken of the resulting forces on the object under test. Most tunnels comprise five basic components: a settling chamber, which ensures the air is flowing in one direction; the contraction cone, where a large volume of air at low velocity is reduced to a small volume of air at high velocity, but without creating turbulence; the test section, where the test object and the sensors are located; the diffuser, which slows down the airflow; and the drive section, which provides the force to propel air through the tunnel. Wind tunnels can be configured as either an open-circuit or a closed-circuit design, depending on whether the air is recirculated or not.

NASA's wind tunnels are located at two main sites: the Langley Research Center at Hampton, Virginia, which comprises twenty-three major wind tunnels; and the Ames Research Center in Mountain View, California, which hosts a further twelve, including the largest wind tunnel in the world, the National Full-Scale Aerodynamics Complex; its test section measures a formidable 24 m x 31 m (80 ft. x 100 ft.).

LMAL
34590

TOP The Full-Scale Wind Tunnel proved its worth in the development and testing of high-performance combat aircraft during World War II.

BOTTOM Not all of the models or prototypes tested in the FST were taken through to full production. The craft seen here was not built to be flown, but had an electric motor to drive the propeller as part of the study of its aerodynamics.

It is Langley, however, that is the site of what was the largest wind tunnel in the world until 1945. Completed in 1931, this is the Full-Scale Wind Tunnel (FST), designated a US National Landmark on its official decommissioning in 1985. Design of the FST began in 1929, under a team led by Smith J. DeFrance, and benefited during the Depression from cheap materials and engineers glad of the work.

The FST marked the first time that a complete aeroplane, full wingspan and all, could be tested in a wind tunnel, and in the course of its sixty-four-year working life everything from biplanes to a Mercury space capsule, as well as helicopters, submarines and motor cars, was evaluated in the tunnel. As a result of its size and configuration, potential distortion of results through scale factors was minimized, and test findings could be extrapolated for other speeds with confidence.

Power to create the airstream through the central test section 9 m (30 ft.) high, 18 m (60 ft.) wide and 17 m (56 ft.) long was provided by the FST's twin 10.7 m (35 ft.) four-bladed wooden propellers, each powered by a 4000 horsepower electric motor. Upwards of 160 tonnes of air were circulated around the 255 m (835 ft.) closed circuit, producing wind speeds of up to 195 km/h (120 mph). The whole installation rises to a height of more than 29 m (95 ft.), and is 131 m (430 ft.) long and 67 m (220 ft.) wide. Endowed with proportions of such grandeur, the FST proved a flexible and robust design tool, especially for aircraft, from basic aerodynamic testing during the 1930s, to the fine-tuning of full-size prototypes in World War II, and free-flight testing of vertical take-off and landing aircraft in the following decade. Even a submarine, the US Navy *Albacore*, the world's fastest in 1950, took its place in the FST.

The tunnel's flexibility was further proved following renovations carried out during the 1960s and 1970s, when the FST was equipped for free-flight dynamic model testing – a technique unique to the facility – which made use of 1:10 or 1:5 scale models that were controlled by remotely located pilots. Once again, the FST proved that, in this field at least, size (and power) does matter.

Key Facts

Wind speed: 180 km/h (110 mph)

Length of tunnel complex: 100 m (330 ft.)

Dimensions of wind tunnel: 27 m (l) x 14 m (w) x 30 m (h) (90 ft. x 45 ft. x 100 ft.)

Length of experimental chamber: 16 m (53 ft.)

RIGHT Air is drawn into the test chamber by the six huge fans, each more than 10 m (33 ft.) in diameter.

FAR RIGHT A model of Concorde being tested in the wind tunnel. More humble test objects have included the Citroën 2CV.

OPPOSITE TOP The oval test chamber can be used to evaluate the aerodynamic qualities of objects as large as airliners.

OPPOSITE Aerial view of the tunnel facility, showing the test chamber in the middle and extract fans to the top of the picture.

ONERA Wind Tunnel
Chalais-Meudon, Paris, France, 1932–34

Such are the visual assets of this famous wind tunnel that the creator of the *Tintin* comics, Georges Rémi (Hergé), could not resist including it in one of his drawings as the background for one of Tintin's aeronautical adventures, three years after it opened in 1934. Since then, what was until World War II one of the world's largest wind tunnels has contained for aerodynamic testing some famous objects, notably the Mirage III fighter, the Caravelle airliner, and Concorde, not forgetting the Citroën 2CV. The French ski team has also used the tunnel to work out their optimum posture for descent of the slopes. It stands half hidden at the end of a wooded valley, in the park-like setting of Chalais-Meudon in an outer suburb of Paris, one of the earliest components of a research facility developed by Office Nationale d'Etudes et de Recherches Aérospatiales (ONERA) – France's national aerospace establishment. This wind tunnel was the most impressive addition to a long line of notable French structures of this type, which included engineer Gustav Eiffel's own installation in the offices of his practice in Paris.

Chalais-Meudon, which could already boast a long pedigree of achievement as a centre for France's aerial activities, was an entirely appropriate site for the tunnel. Here, from 1793 onwards, was located the nation's first manufactory of observation balloons; in 1877 the site became a military aviation establishment,

and during World War I more than 300 observation balloons a month were produced there. Today ONERA continues to make active use of the site, in particular for world-class aeronautical research, and Chalais-Meudon has official recognition and support as a showcase for France's technical innovation in the air.

The tunnel, a concrete classic, defies strict categorization as a building type. Its nearest close relative might be the Full-Scale Wind Tunnel (FST), completed in 1931, at Langley, Virginia, in the United States (pages 148–51), which could produce wind speeds of up to 195 km/h (120 mph) compared to ONERA's 180 km/h (110 mph) and hosted an equally impressive range of test objects during its lifetime. But the American example cannot compare with the French in terms of inherent style. The grand scale of the structure is set by the huge oval entrance opening, through which filtered air is drawn across the test object in the central chamber by the six extract fans in the rear wall, each more than 10 m (33 ft.) in diameter. These circular openings are strengthened by radiating concrete fins in the manner of a rose window in a French Gothic cathedral. Also cathedral-like in spirit are the external flying buttresses that resist the outwards thrust created by the fast-moving airstream.

At 100 m (330 ft.) in total length, the tunnel is an essay in the art of directness when it comes to the

detailing of *in situ* concrete: the board marks left by
the timber shuttering are proudly expressed, but lack
the studied preciousness of meaningless decoration
that the architects of the Modern Movement swore to
abolish. Design of glazing is also direct and unself-
conscious, with necessary openings simply subdivided,
in the tradition of the best lean and sinewy industrial
and engineering structures that are the glory of the
inter-war decades in France. In the mid-1920s the
great Swiss-born French architect Le Corbusier
searched for examples of monumental industrial
structures to contrast favourably with the excesses of
Beaux Arts architecture: in the following decade, the
ONERA tunnel would have provided excellent material.

Established in 1946, ONERA combines a national
status and purpose – it falls under the administration
of the French Ministry of Defence – with a commercial
orientation, hence its mixed workload of military
and civilian projects. ONERA has pioneered research
techniques and equipment for the aircraft and
aerospace industries, often on a pan-European basis,
but also with NASA, with the US Air Force and with
Soviet, and later Russian, counterpart organizations.
Its European achievements include contributions to
the development programmes of Concorde and
Mirage, and also of Airbus, Ariane and the Rafale
fighter. Besides these, the establishment has
collaborated on more than a hundred EU-funded
research projects, including studies of reducing
aircraft noise, of minimizing drag through techniques
of laminar flow, and, not surprisingly, into the
improved design and calibration of wind tunnels.

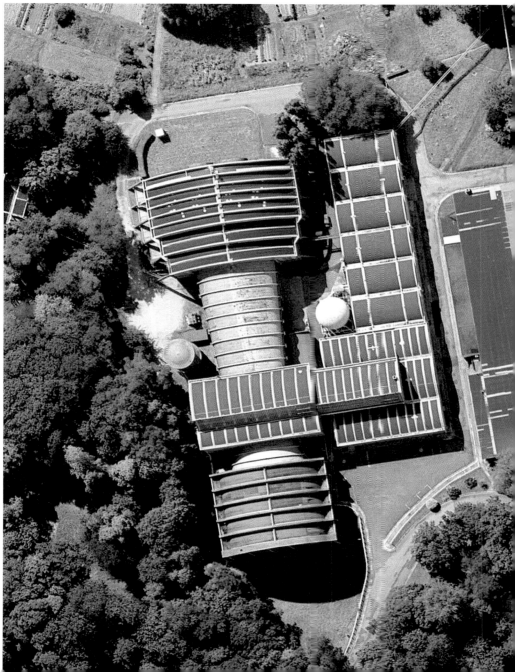

Key Facts

Engineers: Electricité de France/Knight Piésold/Gibb/Geoconsult/SGI/Brown and Root/Intecsa/Hydrotecnica Portuguesa

Length of ring tunnel: 27 km (17 miles)

Size of largest cavern: 42 m (h) x 82 m (l) x 35 m (w) (138 ft. x 270 ft. x 115 ft.)

Depth of cavern below surface: 60–100 m (200–330 ft.)

Cost: (civil engineering) US$197,000,000; (committed investment) US$1.7 billion

CERN Large Hadron Collider
Geneva, Switzerland, 1997–2006

ABOVE CERN's 27 km (17 mile) ring tunnel lies beneath both France and Switzerland. Subatomic particles are accelerated around the tunnel 11,000 times a second, at a speed approaching that of light.

ABOVE RIGHT AND OPPOSITE
The vast scale of the equipment has determined the size of the huge underground chambers, currently under construction and due for completion in 2006.

Much of the fascination of structures located largely underground is that their full extent – and the engineering achievement they represent – can never be properly appreciated at ground level. Huge quantities of steel and concrete can be poured into the ground or great chambers excavated with little visible result on the surface. Probably no better example of buried marvels can be found than the underground caverns and great ring tunnel of the Conseil Européen pour la Recherche Nucléaire (CERN), near Geneva, Switzerland. This remarkable international and egalitarian organization, which recently celebrated its fiftieth birthday, can trace its origin to initiatives by leading scientists in the 1940s to ensure that Europe had access to a world-class physics research facility and, at the same time, to resist the post-war 'brain drain' to the United States. Today the very opposite is true, with more American physicists working at CERN than Europeans in US particle physics laboratories. An incidental but widespread by-product of CERN's activities was its promotion of the World Wide Web, which was initially conceived as a means for researchers worldwide to pool information but is now a valued tool in daily life.

CERN exists to probe many of the really big questions of physics. For example, why do particles have mass? What might the universe have been like in the first fraction of a second of its existence? To aid their investigations into the composition of matter and the forces that bind matter together, the researchers at CERN have furnished themselves with some remarkable pieces of equipment. Perhaps most notable are the huge supercollider machines, or accelerators, that hurl subatomic particles such as electrons, protons, neutrinos and positrons towards one another at velocities close to the speed of light, in the process replicating conditions that have not existed since the Big Bang itself. Particles circle CERN's 27 km (17 mile) ring tunnel, which runs underground beneath this corner of both France and Switzerland, more than 11,000 times a second.

By mutual agreement between the twenty member states of CERN, this equipment is progressively updated to reflect evolving research requirements. The latest and most dramatic development in CERN's recent history was the decision to retire its Large Electron Positron Collider (LEPC) and replace it with the Large Hadron Collider (LHC), inside which protons and other nuclei will crash head on, Big-Bang style. Including the recording devices needed to capture these particle collisions, the LHC will rank as the most complex scientific instrument ever built: it is on target for completion in 2006, partly aided by the fact that the superconducting magnets that accelerate and direct the particles around the ring can be installed within the existing tunnels.

More challenging proved to be the search for space underground to accommodate the detectors and related computer installations needed for the LHC, which were far larger than the now obsolete LEPC support equipment. New underground chambers up to 82 m (270 ft.) long, 35 m (115 ft.) wide and 42m (138 ft.) high are needed, but the geological conditions prevailing at the locations favoured by researchers are far from ideal, especially given the additional stresses likely to be created in the weak rock layers as the excavation of these chambers proceeds. The only excavations of comparable proportions were carried out to create an underground ice-hockey venue from solid rock in Lillehammer, Norway, and in the crossover chamber for the Channel Tunnel (see pages 64–67), which involves a much shorter span. Casting the roof vault for each chamber once the enclosing walls of the chamber were complete has required a complex process of hanging the vault from a network of ground anchors installed above the chamber roof, through galleries excavated from the main vertical-access shafts.

There are further parameters of the LHC that have complicated the construction process – for example, in places the mass-concrete walls are up to 2 m (6.5 ft.) thick to protect researchers from radiation; the computer chambers needed to be at least 100 m (330 ft.) below ground level to achieve adequate clearances; and access shafts to this same depth were required to deliver components of the huge detector machines and pieces of superconductor magnet. All this is a far cry from the facilities available to CERN's earliest researchers in the 1950s, which tended to be constructed by shallow cut-and-cover methods without the need to optimize geological conditions.

Extensive computer modelling has supported the planning of the underground excavation process as well as the building-out of the equipment chambers, enabling relative risks to be assessed and alternatives evaluated, but ultimately the construction process remains as open-ended as the work of CERN's own researchers, with neither on a modest scale. Far beneath this benign landscape where France meets Switzerland further secrets of the universe are giving themselves up.

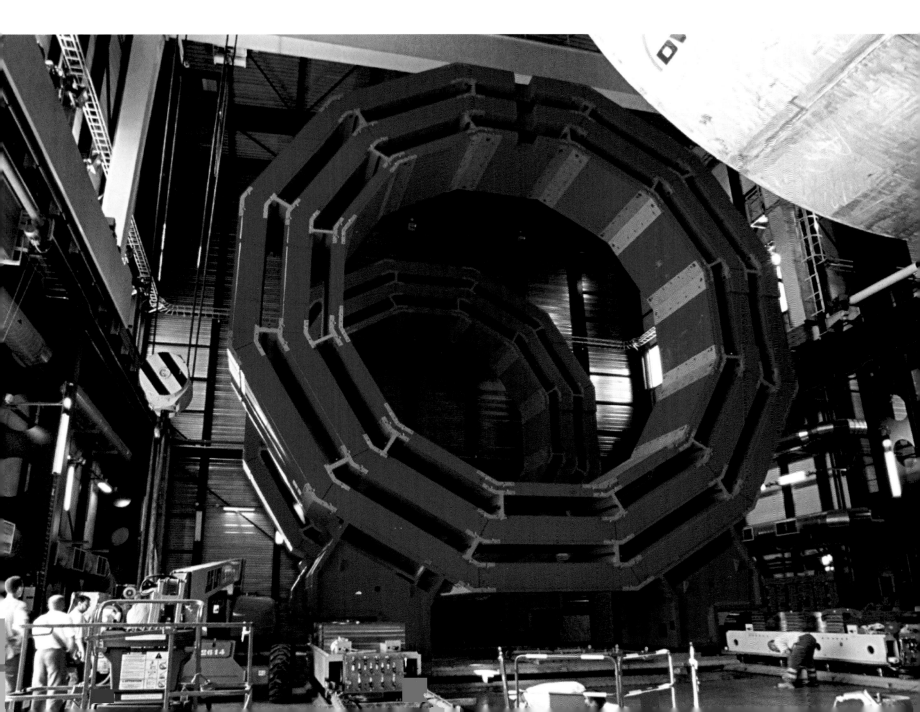

Key Facts

Site area (Cape Canaveral): 57,000 ha (140,000 acres)

Volume of the VAB: 3,700,000 m³ (4, 00,000 cubic yards)

Area of the VAB: 3.2 ha (8 acres)

Dimensions of the Apollo/Saturn rockets: 110 m (h) x 10 m (circumference) (360 ft. x 33 ft.)

Cost of an average Shuttle mission: US$450,000,000

The Apollo Missions

From Kennedy Space Center were flown the missions that made up the Apollo programme (1963–72), designed to land astronauts on the moon and return them to earth. Powered by the very large and reliable Saturn rocket, a series of exploratory missions to test systems took place, including the first orbit of the moon in December 1968 by the Apollo 8 mission. The culmination was the launch on 16 July 1969 of Apollo 11: a Saturn V rocket carrying the three astronauts, the command and service module *Columbia* and the lunar module *Eagle*.

On 20 July astronauts Neil Armstrong and Edwin 'Buzz' Aldrin landed the lunar module in the Sea of Tranquility, where it spent more than twenty-one hours. Armstrong and Aldrin walked on the moon, established a small scientific base, evaluated surface conditions and then lifted off to rendezvous with *Columbia*, which was piloted by Michael Collins. Later Apollo missions saw extended stays and explorations, so that by the end of the sixth, and last, mission in 1972, twelve astronauts had travelled more than 97 km (60 miles) on the surface of the moon.

Vehicle Assembly Building

John F. Kennedy Space Center, Cape Canaveral, Florida, USA, 1962–68

ABOVE Moveable platforms in front of the Vehicle Assembly Building (seen here under construction) transport rockets to the launch site.

To the US Army engineers starting out on the programme that was ultimately to lead to landing a man on the moon, Florida's Cape Canaveral Air Force Station (now the John F. Kennedy Space Center) could hardly have been bettered as a site for the test firing of their rockets: the landtake offered them was very large (57,000 hectares; 140,000 acres), flat and virtually empty of settlements. Theirs were modest beginnings: for their first launch in July 1952 of a Bumper 8 rocket, in effect a modified V2, the engineers co-opted a painters' scaffold to prepare the rocket for launching and used a converted tarpaper-covered bathhouse as a control centre. In the ensuing half-century, things happened on a rather larger scale.

NASA's Apollo/Saturn programme of the late 1960s envisaged by far the largest space vehicle the world had ever seen, calling for one of the largest hangar spaces ever built. The Vehicle Assembly Building (VAB) would house four of these rockets at one time, in its original form with a volume of 3,700,000 cubic metres (4,800,000 cubic yards) and a footprint of 3.2 hectares (8 acres). These epic dimensions directly reflect the scale of the contents: each rocket stood 110 m (360 ft.) high and had a maximum girth of

10 m (33 ft.). In planning the VAB, various options were studied by NASA's engineering team. Originally conceived on plan as a cruciform, then as an in-line, arrangement that would have yielded a long, narrow slab of a building, the structure finally emerged as a back-to-back plan form with a central aisle between the two rows of assembly bays. The resulting rectangular box had the merit of being the least expensive structure to build, as well as being the strongest, able to resist hurricane winds.

Internally, the VAB was divided into two sections. The high-bay section contained four bays, each large enough to receive a mobile launcher carrying a fully assembled Apollo/Saturn rocket and five pairs of extensible work platforms. The low-bay section took the form of a steel framework supporting work platforms that hinged open to receive the rocket stage (section) and then closed around it, enabling the engineers to simulate the operation of each stage and monitor its electronic and mechanical systems. Three out of the four high bays were customized for Apollo/Saturn vehicles, with the fourth bay being held ready for any other rockets capable of fitting through the gigantic T-shaped doors that formed the outer walls of the high bays. Higher than St Peter's Basilica in Rome and New York's Statue of Liberty, these doors, comprising four lower horizontal-sliding sections and seven door leaves that open vertically above them, each take forty-five minutes to open fully.

But NASA first had to build the site. Because the existing terrain lay barely above sea level, the land was raised more than 2 m (6.5 ft.) by using a total of some 1,150,000 cubic metres (1,500,000 cubic yards) of consolidated silt dredged from the bottom of the nearby Banana River. In the process, an access channel was dredged, along which the rocket stages could be transported to the VAB by barge. Yet even in its consolidated state, the site still posed problems for foundation design, when the trial borings revealed layers of silt and petrified wood above the bedrock that lay 50 m (165 ft.) below the surface. To found the steel frame of the VAB, more than 4000 steel-pipe piles, each 40 cm (16 in.) in diameter, were driven down to the limestone bedrock and backfilled with sand; each pile cluster was then capped with concrete. In all, more than 200 km (125 miles) of pipe were needed, and the whole process took six months to complete. On top of these pile clusters, a ground slab containing 23,000 cubic metres (30,000 cubic yards) of concrete was cast.

Nearly 90,000 tonnes of steel were needed to build the VAB, comprising 45,000 separate pieces weighing up to 33,000 kg (72,750 lb) each, secured in place by more than a million bolts. Such huge quantities are explained by the sheer size of the completed building, one of the largest in the world: 218 m (715 ft.) in length – twice that of an American football field – 158 m (518 ft.) in width and 160 m (525 ft.) in height.

Yet the VAB is only part, if the most celebrated, of what is known as NASA's Launch Complex 39. Originally tailored for the assembly, testing and launching of the Apollo vehicles – it was here that the Apollo 11 craft were built and lifted off, carrying the first men to land on the moon – Launch Complex 39 was still used, with some modification, for Space Shuttle operations. The complex includes giant mobile launcher platforms, on which the rockets can be assembled inside the VAB, transported to the launch pad and then dispatched into space; a carrying system (the crawler-transporter) for moving the immensely heavy rockets and their launchers to the launch pad; a moveable servicing gantry more than forty-five storeys tall, from which the final preparation of the rocket can take place when at the launch pad; and a control centre from which the whole launch operation can be masterminded.

RIGHT An aerial view of the VAB, showing how its massive form stands out in the flat landscape. The rest of Launch Complex 39 stretches away to the right.

ABOVE RIGHT An Apollo/Saturn vehicle in preparation inside one of the huge bays.

158 Leisure

oing out, viewing what the world has to offer, or attending an exhibition, sports event or public display are consistently popular pastimes the world over, and have generated distinctive groups of sites and buildings, including the remarkable structures that are described in this section.

The parade of international exhibitions and world's fairs towards the end of the nineteenth century, including five held in Paris, was a blend of education and entertainment attracting a huge following, showcasing emerging technology and demonstrating a new scale of building. By their nature as temporary structures (although many survive to this day), the most advanced and best remembered buildings of these exhibitions were able to break free of the conservative conventions of the 'permanent' architecture of their day.

In the twentieth century, international exhibitions continued to display innovative structures. The 1958 International Exhibition in Brussels offered Le Corbusier's hyperbolic–pyramidal sail forms in concrete in the Philips Pavilion, as well as the steel and cable structure of the French Pavilion. Montreal's Expo '67 featured engineer–inventor Richard Buckminster Fuller's huge dome for the United States' Pavilion and engineer Frei Otto's tensile roof structure for that of West Germany, both demonstrating the potential of their respective space-enclosing systems.

Stadiums for spectator sports have proved to be an important building type, with their own functional demands; they offer designers the opportunity to create atmosphere and a sense of occasion for the events hosted. All such structures need to address such familiar design issues as sheer scale and the flexibility to accommodate different events, viewing conditions, spectator movement and changes in the weather. They can also provide the opportunity for innovative structural design.

Post-World War II development focused initially on the design of enclosed stadiums that offered flexible, unimpeded space, exemplified by the Palazzetto dello Sport in Rome (pages 172–73), modestly sized but immensely pleasing in its design, and by the Raleigh Arena in North Carolina (1953), with its dramatic roof structure of interlocking inclined parabolic arches. But the need for greater capacity and improved conditions for broadcasting led to the rise of the 'superstadium', such as the now-defunct Houston Astrodome in Texas (1965), with a seated capacity of 65,000, and the New Orleans Superdome (1975), the largest clear-span structure in the world, which can seat 87,500 for concerts.

More recently, innovation has reappeared in the design of large stadiums to improve viewing conditions for spectators, either by bold steep raking of the terraces as in the Bari Football Stadium (1980) in southern Italy, or by more critical review of sightline sections and plan configuration through computer modelling. The way in which stadiums are roofed has also evolved. While Munich's Olympic Stadium (pages 174–77) provided all-weather protection through the installation of a tensile tent over the sports areas, Sydney's Telstra Stadium (pages 178–79) and London's new Wembley Stadium

RIGHT Richard Buckminster Fuller's geodesic dome served as the United States Pavilion at Expo '67 in Montreal.

OPPOSITE The British Airways London Eye, as the giant wheel by the River Thames is called, was intended to occupy its site for five years. Its tenancy may yet be extended owing to its great popularity.

(pages 180–81) offer their own, different solutions to problems of spectator – and pitch – protection. Partly moveable roofs offering varying degrees of enclosure have become a practical option, and are often hung from great supporting arches or trusses that in themselves are an effective landmark, as the Wembley arch will be for London. At their best, stadiums are emerging as leaner, tauter, more elegant structures, while very consciously striving to recreate the all-important sense of occasion of an earlier generation of venues.

Parks or gardens are an alternative destination for public pleasure and diversion, and have often had as their focus a giant Ferris, or viewing, wheel, that allows people to look down on a city from on high – a perennial human delight. Vienna's *Riesenrad* (pages 162–63) and the Thames-side London Eye are both structures that, in their design and erection, are examples of technical innovation in the service of pleasurable pastimes.

In a different way, gardens and parks have, perhaps unexpectedly, given rise to other structures of boldness and daring. Historical precedents for large climate-controlled enclosures for the nurture and display of plants are to be found from Joseph Paxton's greenhouse at Chatsworth, England (1836–40), onwards. They have been reinterpreted in more recent structures, most radically in those associated with the thinking of Buckminster Fuller, including the St Louis Climatron (1954). This modestly sized geodesic dome pioneered a successful use of solar energy and convection cooling, which influenced later dome design. At the largest scale, the enclosure of a natural environment using a geodesic structure has been triumphantly achieved in the form of the Eden Project in the south-west of England (pages 166–69), where former quarry workings have been transformed into the largest plant enclosure in the world.

Elsewhere, natural materials have been put to new uses in structures where visitors can appreciate spaces that are unfamiliar yet in harmony with the activities they shelter. In the timber gridshell roof (pages 170–71) that covers the Conservation Workshop at the Weald and Downland Open Air Museum in the south of England, five layers of oak laths are combined to form an undulating volume that is easier to experience than to describe, and is a far cry from the orthodoxies of orthogonal space.

From giant stadiums to the Downland Gridshell, the best buildings for leisure and public pleasure display an extrovert confidence in which the structural engineer has played a full part.

Key Facts

Engineers: (concept) Walter B. Bassett, (structure) Feilendorf & Hitchins	
Height above ground: 65 m (21 ft.)	
Diameter of the wheel: 61 m (200 ft.)	
Speed of rotation: 0.75 m/sec (720 rpm)	
Original number of cabins: 30	
Number of wheel spokes: 120	

LEFT The wheel was erected with the aid of two steam cranes supported on temporary timber towers.

The London Eye

Although intended for the same purpose – that of observation from on high – as Vienna's Ferris Wheel, the British Airways London Eye, opened to the public in 2000, includes two important innovations in its design that do not appear in the configuration of the standard Ferris wheel. First, the fact that the wheel is supported from the land side only, leaving the Thames-side face unimpeded by structure, maximizes visibility for passengers. Secondly, instead of being suspended from above as in a ski lift, the passenger capsules are fixed on the rim of the wheel by special bearings with a stabilizing mechanism.

The London Eye is the largest public observation wheel in the world, reaching a height of 135 m (445 ft.) above ground, with a capacity of 800 passengers for each thirty-minute circuit. Compared to the Vienna wheel, the Eye is a sleek and elegant structure, but it remains in debt to its Viennese ancestor.

Giant Ferris Wheel
Vienna, Austria, 1896–97

RIGHT One of the two tripods supporting the central axle, at the beginning of construction.

Even without its celebrity as a scene-stealer in Carol Reed's classic film *The Third Man* (1949), Vienna's Ferris Wheel, the *Wiener Riesenrad*, would surely have retained pride of place in the affections of those citizens and visitors who have ridden on it during an almost unbroken century of service. In the film, when Harry Lime (Orson Welles) invited his companion on the wheel to contemplate the "little people" as insignificant specks on the ground below, he was merely adding a macabre gloss to humankind's continuing fascination with being able to look down upon a great city from a high place.

Over the years, since its opening on 25 June 1897, the *Riesenrad*, built as part of the Golden Jubilee celebrations for Emperor Franz Josef in Vienna's Prater district, has outlived Ferris wheels in Paris, London, Blackpool and Chicago, all long departed, and has provided the inspiration for the London Eye, itself a latter-day crowd-pleaser. Vienna's wheel was designed by Walter B. Bassett, a Royal Navy lieutenant and engineer, supported by structural engineers Feilendorf & Hitchins; their work has matched with the commercial expertise of local entertainments promoter Gabor Steiner. The wheel's steelwork and fabrication were entrusted to the renowned Glasgow firm of W. Beardmore & Co., who pushed the project through to completion in just over six months.

As a generic structural type, all Ferris wheels – named after the American engineer G.W.G. Ferris who built the first of the line for Chicago's 1893 Universal Exhibition – can be described as a 'bridge' consisting of two identical semicircles, supported by a central spindle or axle (10.9 m; 36 ft. long, 0.5 m; 1.8 ft. in diameter, and weighing 16.3 tonnes in the case of the *Riesenrad*) and by flexible spokes; 120 of the are used in the Vienna wheel. As the wheel rotates, only those spokes that are approaching or leaving the downward

vertical plane at the crown of the 'bridge' actually bear the compressive load, on the same principle (though inverted) as that of a bicycle wheel. In Vienna, taking the combined weight of the wheel and its fifteen (originally thirty) cabins, the spindle is cradled by two open pivot blocks, each supported by a pair of latticework pylons braced together, carrying loads down to eight foundation points. More recent Ferris wheels, such as the London Eye, follow exactly the same structural principle, although the Eye is more than twice the size of its Viennese cousin, rising to a height of 135m (443 ft.) above ground, compared to the *Riesenrad*'s 65 m (213 ft.).

Any giant wheel is at its most vulnerable at the time of erection. At Vienna, no scaffolding as such was used to erect the pylons and the wheel. Instead, the contractors built two timber towers, which were raised progressively to their final height of 70 m (230 ft.). On each tower was placed a steam crane with a 17 m (56 ft.) jib length with which to lift the spindle up to its mounting height of 35 m (115 ft.). But before this could be done, the spindle needed to be brought from the railhead on a transporter pulled by sixteen horses. This duly sank in the soft Prater mud and had to be retrieved using lifting gear. Pulled by steam cranes rather than by horses, the spindle then completed its journey on a new loadbearing track, and up the sloping legs of the pylons to its final resting place on the two pivots.

Assembly of the wheel itself then proceeded in segments: one segment was hung by spokes from the spindle hub, and further segments were attached to both ends of the first and fastened back to the hub with spokes, hence the emerging structure was self-supporting throughout. This process was inherently simpler than that used to build the London Eye, which was assembled horizontally as a complete wheel on the River Thames and then pulled up to the vertical by a giant crane on a lifting barge. The outer rim of the Vienna wheel is connected to the inner by radial latticed members and diagonal tie rods; the rims are some 6 m (20 ft.) apart. To improve resistance to wind loading, half the wheel spokes, which are formed from 10 mm (0.4 in.) diameter wire cables with lugs at each end, are set at right angles to the spindle, while the remainder are set diagonally. Two traction cables powered by a pair of slip-ring motors on a common axle drive the wheel at 720 rpm through friction shoes bearing upon the outer faces of the rims.

When Lady Horace Rumbold, wife of the British Ambassador, knocked the final bolt into place, enabling Vienna's Great Wheel to rotate for the first time, few of those present could have guessed that this 'temporary' structure was to become a permanent feature of the Vienna skyline, in much the same way as the Eye is fast becoming an essential part of London's landscape.

BOTTOM LEFT The wheel itself was assembled progressively upwards in sections, each segment being hung off the central axle then linked back by spokes.

BELOW The Vienna Ferris Wheel's cabins are top-hung. In 1947 they were halved in number from the original thirty.

Key Facts

Design and manufacture:	Intamin AG (Switzerland)
Length of track:	850 m (2800 ft.)
Lift height:	128 m (420 ft.)
Angle of descent:	90 degrees
Vertical drop:	120 m (400 ft.)
Cost:	US$25,000,000

Top Thrill Dragster

Cedar Point Resort, Ohio, USA, 2002–03

ABOVE LEFT Rising high above the peninsula of Cedar Point, the Top Thrill Dragster is a landmark visible from a long-distance.

ABOVE RIGHT The ride twists through 270 degrees as it falls vertically from the summit of what is the highest roller-coaster in the world.

Even in this age of electronic entertainments, there remains a great deal of life and invention left in more traditional diversions, in which patrons can subject themselves to thrills and apparent dangers, secure in the knowledge that they will come to no real harm. The roller-coaster ride is one such diversion, a core attraction and landmark of amusement parks worldwide and seemingly as popular today in its latest incarnations as it ever was in the heyday of New York's Coney Island resort in the early twentieth century. It is also the subject of fierce competition between rival sites, as each strives to offer rides that rise higher, fall faster or include new gyrations.

However large and impressive, all roller-coasters work on the same simple principle – that of building up a reservoir of potential energy by being pulled or propelled up to the top of the first incline, known as the lift hill. As the coaster descends on the other side this potential energy is converted into the energy of motion – kinetic energy – which carries the coaster up the second incline, where it gathers fresh potential energy. The forward motion continues, with the force of gravity slowing the vehicle on an upward slope and accelerating it on a downslope. Because some energy is lost through friction between the coaster and the track and through air resistance, the reservoir of energy becomes steadily depleted in the course of the ride.

The history of roller-coasters represents a fascinating instance of a product's evolving by progressive, competitive innovations, with each new development prompting a response from rival ride-builders. Much effort and ingenuity have been spent in devising new motions through which the customers can be transported, including loops and corkscrews – these became commonplace after the safety problems that had bedevilled loops when they first appeared in the early 1900s had been solved.

Tracks formed by a pair of steel tubes, first introduced in the 1950s, enabled rides to weave their way in smooth curves above the heads of spectators with a minimum of support, compared to the dense framework that is required for wooden roller-coasters. In fact, the structural problem is straightforward enough – the need to support a track more than 120 m (400 ft.) above the ground, in the case of the roller-coaster pictured here, and to resist the changing forces caused by the coaster car and its passengers in motion.

All such elements are on show at the Ohio resort of Cedar Point, to many the epicentre of the coaster world because it offers the public no fewer than sixteen different rides. Its latest, the Top Thrill Dragster, claims to be the tallest and fastest roller-coaster in the world. Cedar Point's otherwise flat peninsular site has been transformed by a cluster of metal mountains and the sinuous looping profiles of the highest rides.

To brand each roller-coaster at Cedar Point, the designers select a theme that identifies the ride and determines the style of the hardware. In the case of the Top Thrill Dragster, the ride was intended to capture the energy, excitement and dramatic velocities of a drag-racing circuit. Hence the six nine-passenger cars built in fibreglass and steel are styled as drag-racers and are launched from a 'pit stop' that echoes those of the real sport. Even the sides of the overhead track are decorated in racing chequer-boards. The track on which the coaster cars run is built from steel tubes welded together to form truss sections supported at intervals on columns, or acting as the vertical faces of the 128 m (420 ft.) high tower up which the coaster rises from the pit stop and down which it falls at the record speed of 192 km/h (120 mph).

In addition to those along the top of the tubular-steel track, wheels run below the track and along its sides, so that the car is securely anchored to the track as it twists and turns. Such a multiple wheel arrangement is an essential feature of all tubular-steel roller-coaster designs. The hydraulic system that launches the cars forward to the record velocity in four seconds was developed by ride's builders, the Swiss company Intamin, through computer modelling. A full-scale mock-up of the launch section was then built in a field in Switzerland to establish that the system actually propelled the cars high enough to reach the first bend of the Top Thrill Dragster. Bringing cars to a halt after the run is achieved by a magnetic system that uses the principle of linear induction between the coaster and the track.

The Top Thrill Dragster is a relatively straight-forward, if challenging attraction, relying on speed, height and acceleration to provide a memorable experience for its riders. What makes it so dramatic as a structure is its sheer height, towering as it does above the already remarkable rides of Cedar Point. These include Millennium Force, at 95 m (310 ft.) high and Magnum XL-200, at 62 m (205 ft.) high, both previous holders of the title of the world's tallest roller-coaster. But past evidence would suggest that even the Dragster's record is under threat. Somewhere, structures of tubular steel are being shaped to rise and ride higher.

ABOVE RIGHT AND RIGHT A giant tubular-steel framework supports the vertical loop of track. The track sections are formed as sectional steel trusses. Three sets of wheels on the roller-coaster grip each rail of the tubular-steel track.

Key Facts

Architects:	Nicholas Grimshaw & Partners
Structural engineers:	Anthony Hunt Associates
Area of site:	18 ha (45 acres)
Area occupied by biomes:	2.2 ha (5.4 acres)
Maximum size of biomes:	240 (l) x 110 (w) x 55 m (h) (790 x 360 x 180 ft.)
Diameter of hexagonal geodesic modules:	5–11 m (16.5–36 ft.)
Cost:	UK£86,000,000

BELOW The Biome link, containing visitor facilities, leads to the Warm Temperate Biome beyond.

Richard Buckminster Fuller

The American engineer–inventor Richard Buckminster Fuller (1895–1983) was one of the most influential designers of his generation. Besides being the acknowledged father of the geodesic dome, he produced a whole series of designs springing from his Dymaxion theories, which advocated maximum efficiency in materials with least waste and reaping the full benefits of industrialization. His Dymaxion House (1928) was a remarkable example, as suitable for mass production as a motor car.

In 1954 Fuller patented a system of lightweight components to construct geodesic domes, which enable a large space to be enclosed with great efficiency; reputedly more than 300,000 were built by his followers world-wide in the next three decades. The largest for which Fuller was responsible was that of the Union Tank Car Company at Baton Rouge, Louisiana, with a diameter of 118 m (595 ft.). He is better known for his dome, with a diameter of 76 m (250 ft.), for the United States Pavilion at the Montreal Expo '67. It is impossible to overestimate Fuller's continuing influence on many of our leading structural designers.

Eden Project

Cornwall, England, 1995–2001

Britain's 'millennium projects' – a diverse collection of publicly funded buildings and landscaping projects celebrating the beginning of the new century – have attracted praise and criticism in equal measure, but the scheme has delivered some undoubted winners, of which the £86,000,000 Eden Project, near St Austell in Cornwall, is incontestably one. This dramatic transformation of the 18 hectare (45 acre) site, formerly the Boldeva china-clay quarry, into a complex presenting the plant life of two climate zones – humid tropics and warm temperate – has become hugely popular since it opened in 2001, yet at its heart the project retains a powerful educational and research agenda. With hindsight, it can be seen that Eden's historical precedents are to be found in sources other than mainstream architecture: in the great gardens of Versailles in France and Kew in England, in the St Louis Climatron (designed by architects Murphy & Mackey) in the United States, and, most notably, in the pioneering structures of the American architect-engineer Buckminster Fuller, who proposed cover Manhattan with a giant geodesic dome, on the model of his (built) domes to protect rolling stock of the Union Tank Car Company or the US Marines.

Creating the largest plant enclosure in the world against the south-facing slope of the quarry present-ed a formidable challenge. The initial structural concept, amounting to a giant lean-to greenhouse

that would have echoed the ridge-and-furrow roof structure invented by Joseph Paxton for his Crystal Palace (1851) in London, and would have been support-ed on arched trusses springing from the quarry rim, had to be abandoned because the very complex and ever-changing landform profile made precise sizing impossible and it was not feasible to reshape the quarry pit to allow the use of uniform truss spans.

Having abandoned this approach, the design team achieved a breakthrough in conceiving the enclosure as a series of eight interlocking geodesic 'biomes' of varying diameter, arranged in a sequence that snakes around 2.2 hectares (5.4 acres) of the site, much as soap bubbles join up with one another. The hexagonal format of the dome modules readily adapts to changing ground contours and offers a geometry that is easily resolvable by computer modelling. They also provide a highly efficient means of creating the large unimpeded enclosures required: the tropical biome, for example, ranges up to 110 m (360 ft.) in width, 55 m (180 ft.) in height and 240 m (790 ft.) in length.

From this basic concept, the structure as built was evolved as a two-layer space frame, the outer layer being formed as an icosahedral geodesic skin composed of hexagonal modules with diameters between 5 m and 11 m (16.5 ft. and 36 ft.), each fabricated from six galvanized-steel tubes acting in compression. These components were small and easy

OPPOSITE Aerial view of the Eden Project in its setting of a former quarry. Arriving at the entrance and reception (centre left), visitors pass through the terraced garden landscapes to access the Warm Temperate Biome (left) and the Humid Tropics Biome (right).

ABOVE Visitors move through the biome at different levels, often coming close to the hexagonal roof structure.

OPPOSITE TOP Inside the Humid Tropics Biome, showing the junction between the dome and the quarry face behind.

OPPOSITE BOTTOM Computer-generated visualization showing how the biomes interlock to form a sinuous chain of volumes.

to handle, making it feasible for the hexagons to be assembled on the ground, then craned into position and bolted to one another through a cast-steel node. From the nodes run hollow circular members linking back to a level of triangular space trusses. Structural stability is created by the effect of the intersecting shells acting together, with resultant loads taken down to reinforced-concrete strip foundations around the perimeter of the biomes.

In the search for maximum transparency in the external skin of the geodesic domes, glass was ruled out on the grounds of weight alone. Instead, a system of 'pillows' was devised to fill the hexagons, pentagons and triangles comprising the outer layer of the structure, with the cross dimension of the largest 'pillow' approaching 11 m (36 ft.). Multiple layers of ethyltetrafluoroethylene (ETFE) foil formed the skin, which was held in extruded aluminium frames bolted to the primary structure. ETFE is a remarkable material – only 1% of the dead weight of

a comparable glass skin, highly transparent to a wide spectrum of light and, in the triple-layered form chosen, capable of allowing heat to be retained. To cap these desirable properties, ETFE presents a self-cleaning surface that, Teflon-like, is impervious to pollution, weathering or UV light, with a thermal insulation performance better than that of double glazing and a predicted life of at least forty years. Full-size mock-ups of the hexagonal modules were used to help determine the optimum camber of the 'pillows', which varied up to a maximum of 10% of the span for the outer ETFE layer and 15% for the inner.

The biomes form a lofty carapace whose appearance changes with the weather, by turns misty and mysterious with condensation on humid, wet mornings, becoming more transparent as the level of humidity falls. The whole Eden complex is evolving day by day: new specimens are introduced, a third 'arid lands' biome is in prospect, and the plants flourish in their geodesic bubbles.

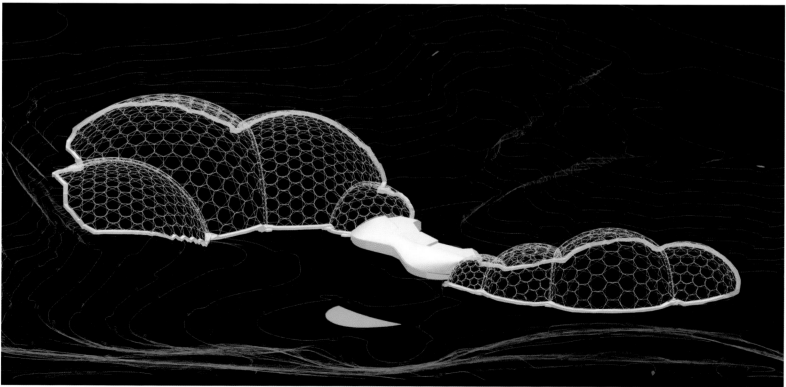

Key Facts

Architects: Edward Cullinan Architects

Structural engineers: Buro Happold

Number of timber scarf joints: 6000

Floor area: 500m² (5400 sq. ft.)

Cost: UK£1,300,000

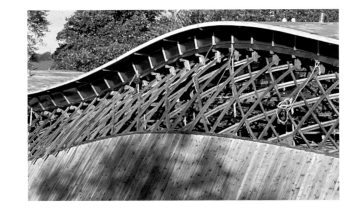

Downland Gridshell

West Sussex, England, 1997–2002

The description 'barn-like' brings to mind images of amplitude, generosity and grand dimensions – useful attributes when the search is on for a large volume uncluttered by intermediate supports.

Such was the case at the Weald and Downland Open Air Museum, a working village settlement in West Sussex that attracts more than 140,000 visitors a year. They are drawn by its collections of more than 10,000 rural artefacts and, particularly, by its cluster of around fifty farmhouses and other structures from the south of England, all now relocated on a wooded chalk slope of the Weald. An important strand of the museum's activities centres on its acknowledged expertise in the conservation of historic vernacular buildings such as those on display.

The museum had initially contemplated a standard off-the-shelf building to house the conservation studio workshop where its carpenters would be based, set over a base or podium containing the archival material and administration offices. Whatever its form, a sustainable, economical and sympathetic structure was required, and one that might at the same time express the essence and ethos of the Downland Museum. On top of a conventional concrete box to house the artefacts collection, a latter-day 'barn' was proposed as the enclosure for the conservation studio, which would take the form of a timber gridshell structure, such as had been pioneered in Germany and Japan. Timber gridshell construction requires very high standards of craftsmanship, as well as complex computing programmes to determine the form.

In essence, a gridshell resembles a double-curvature shell, with a combined shape and strength, but composed as a grid and not as a continuous surface. The grid can be formed of any suitable structural material – steel, aluminium, even cardboard tubes, or, as here, of oak laths. These last are capable of assuming the bent profile of the roof and are combined as a double layer of two laths in each direction to achieve the necessary strength in cross-section while retaining flexibility. The construction process began with the selection of suitable oak trees in Normandy, from which the random lengths of timber were rough-sawn and then transported by container to Newcastle for fine planing. All visible defects were cut out of the planed lengths and standard laths 35 mm x 50 mm (1.4 in. x 2 in.) and 6 m (20 ft.) long were prepared by finger-jointing. Six laths were then scarf-jointed with high-strength timber adhesive to form a single 36 m (118 ft.) piece, of which 1500 were needed to form the gridshell.

Assembly of the gridshell began with the laying out of the lath bundles as a diagonal grid on a flat supporting scaffold, the laths being held together at their nodes by purpose-made bolted cramps. The edges of the grid were then lowered very gradually by adjusting the supporting scaffolding until the curved vault of the gridshell assumed its ultimate shape, as predicted by computer modelling. Once the final cross-sections were achieved and the loads distributed throughout the structure, the ends of the lath bundles were rigidly secured to the timber floorplate that had been attached to the roof of the concrete box below. In settling to the vault profile, the laths betrayed their natural origins by flexing, creaking and (very occasionally) breaking. A further, fifth, layer of laths was then fixed on top to provide triangulated stiffening for the grid. The resultant roof encloses a rectangular plan area 50 m (165 ft.) long, 12 m (40 ft.) high and 10 m (35 ft.) wide.

Clad in locally farmed cedar boards, the Downland Gridshell has already proved a notable asset and popular events venue for the museum.

ABOVE The gridshell assuming its final profile prior to cladding. The end of the lath bundles were later clamped to the edge of the concrete floor slab.

OPPOSITE TOP LEFT Sections of the gridshell are glazed to allow light into the interior.

OPPOSITE TOP RIGHT The open interior of the gridshell is large enough for reassembling full-size exhibit buildings.

OPPOSITE BOTTOM View of the entrance, showing external cladding of locally cut cedar boards.

Key Facts

Engineers/architects:	Pier Luigi Nervi and Annibale Vitellozzi
Diameter of dome:	60 m (200 ft.)
Rise of dome:	21 m (67 ft.)
Seating capacity:	5000

Pier Luigi Nervi

A great innovator in the design of concrete structures, Pier Luigi Nervi (1891–1979) combined the roles of architect, engineer and contractor to create buildings that appear to be the products of successful intuition rather than of calculation, although in his writings he saw no conflict between the two. Besides his advances in the technology and aesthetics of precast concrete, notably in the process of site assembly, Nervi pioneered a form of construction that he called *ferro-cemento*, in which cement mortar is sprayed on to preformed reinforcement to form shells of extreme thinness and economy.

Structures to span and enclose large volumes formed an important part of his work, as demonstrated by his two sports arenas in Rome and by his exhibition hall in Turin – a space of monumental proportions. Nervi also enjoyed successful collaborations with leading architects such as Giò Ponti, on the Pirelli Tower in Milan; Marcel Breuer and Bernard Zehrfuss, on the UNESCO building in Paris; and the Australian architect Harry Siedler, on an elegant office tower in Sydney.

RIGHT The cast roof elements create an elegant geometric pattern on the underside of the dome, which appears to float effortlessly above the band of glazing.

Palazzetto dello Sport
Rome, Italy, 1956–58

In contrast to the current crop of mega-stadiums and auditoriums that can tend to overwhelm by their enormous dimensions, it is timely to recall others in which the sheer quality and panache of design ensure them a permanent place among the world's most notable structures. Rome's Palazzetto dello Sport is an undisputed member of this latter group. Built for the seventeenth Olympic Games in 1960, the structure achieves an elegance and an effortless grace that still impress. It also exemplifies the clarity of line possible within the disciplines of design in precast concrete.

Designed as an indoor venue to house the smaller Olympic events, the stadium represents a further evolution of one of the Italian engineer–constructor Pier Luigi Nervi's favoured structural forms, that of the cupola or flat dome, often following a curved profile. In collaboration with architect Annibale Vitellozzi, Nervi devised a curved roof form circular on plan, covered by 1620 reinforced-concrete elements, each a mere 25 mm (1 in.) in thickness. These were precast on site using brick moulds lined with cement mortar, and positioned on to a supporting framework of steel scaffolding by a tower crane operating at the centre of the dome. At the outside edge they form the distinctive 'piecrust' profile that undulates between the supporting structures below. Erection of the dome took a mere thirty days.

This carapace of a dome is supported at its perimeter by a ring of thirty-six Y-shaped buttresses, each leaning at the tangential direction of downward thrust, towards the foundations so as to avoid bending stresses, and bearing on to a prestressed reinforced-concrete ring beam 2.5 m (8 ft.) in thickness and 81.5 m (267 ft.) in diameter. These buttresses take an equal share of the total load through triads of fan-shaped precast elements, which work through to bearings at the intersection of the ring beam that forms the edge of the dome. The roof elements are supported and separated by gently curving concrete ribs, creating a coffered effect that also resolves itself visually into a set of what appear to be annular rings, with an echo of natural forms that is characteristic of the work of this designer.

This structural system allowed the designers to achieve a very shallow and elegant dome, less than a third as high as it is wide, with a diameter of almost 60 m (200 ft.) above the bearing points. At the apex of the dome a ring beam receives the ends of the ribs and forms part of the structure of the central rooflight element, which brings daylight down to arena level and further reinforces the lines of the ceiling ribs. This central corona also acts as a housing for lighting, extract fans, public address systems and other services.

The most remarkable achievement of the design is the sense of lightness, almost uplift, achieved with the dome itself, so that it appears to float rather like a parachute above the tall band of clear glazing that rises above the banks of spectator seating and forms an encircling gallery. The floating effect is further reinforced by strong daylight catching the sides of the ceiling coffers and by the slenderness of the supporting buttresses when viewed from within. Since the size and usual impact of the bearings at the head of the Y buttresses are also minimized, the cleanness and clarity of the designer's lightly set roof lid are maintained.

The clarity of the design is also safeguarded by the housing of all the services and support functions for the stadium as a ring in the undercroft of the terraced seating, which mirrors in counterform the profile of the dome above. The stadium allows a capacity of 4000 spectators for tennis, basketball and gymnastics, a number rising by 1000 for boxing or wrestling contests. One of Nervi's most enduringly satisfying works, the Palazzetto has proved itself flexible enough to accommodate all manner of events under its serene and light dome. Its continuing attraction lies in the dynamism of its supporting structure set against a dome that has something of the calm and repose of Antique architecture.

BELOW The dome is supported by a ring of thirty-six Y-shaped buttresses, which follow the line of the downward forces.

Key Facts

Architects: Behnisch & Partner

Engineers: Frei Otto, Leonhardt Andrä & Partners

Covered area: 74,000 m² (800,000 sq. ft.)

Height of tallest mast: 80 m (265 ft.)

Number of masts: 12

Length of tensile cables: 210 km (130 miles)

Acrylic roof panels: 2.9 m x 2.9 m x 4 mm (9.5 ft. x 9.5 ft. x 0.16 in.)

Frei Otto

As a singular influence on numerous designers worldwide, this former stonemason's apprentice, born in 1925, ranks as a founding father in the development of tent-like structures. Trained as an architect, he established in 1957 the Institute for Lightweight Structures in Berlin, later transferred to Stuttgart. At the institute he and his colleagues used scale models to explore and test the possibilities of lightweight tensile roof structures and later pioneered computer programs to calculate the complex forms involved.

The first major structure resulting from these experiments was the German Pavilion for the 1967 Montreal Expo, designed with Rolf Gutbrod; this was followed by the Munich Olympic Stadium. Several of Otto's most notable designs are located in arid zones, including the Intercontinental Hotel and *Haj* tents for pilgrims in Mecca, Saudi Arabia.

Otto has continued to develop his interest in natural forms and, more recently, in the potential of gridshell structures and pneumatically supported enclosures.

Olympic Stadium

Munich, Germany, 1969–72

ABOVE The cable net form proved versatile enough to cover a variety of different sporting events. In the case of the swimming pool and the athletics arena, the roof incorporates an additional insulating layer.

OPPOSITE View of the Olympic complex, with swimming pool in the foreground, athletics arena to the right, and stadium beyond. The concept as built differed from the competition entry in that the masts were placed beyond the extent of the cable net structure to provide the maximum unimpeded clear space within.

Tensile structures have often proved attractive to designers charged with the enclosure and protection of complex public spaces such as sports stadiums, where the forms they adopt can echo the dynamism of the events taking place. In the case of the 1972 Olympic Games at Munich, the concept was especially bold: a tent structure to cover a whole landscape of sports sites, including the swimming pool, the stadium and an athletics arena. Such structures, using a minimum of material, can offer great efficiency where wide spans are needed.

Many of the pioneering initiatives in the field of designing roof structures of this kind were centred on the research and built projects of Stuttgart's Institute for Lightweight Structures, under the leadership of Frei Otto. The Munich project followed directly in the line of development of tensile fabric structures by Otto from the 1950s onwards; these included the German Pavilion for the 1967 Montreal Expo, which coincidentally re-emerged as home for the Institute after being transported back to Germany.

The initial competition-winning concept for the 1972 Olympic Games by the architect Gunter Behnisch and his team was for a continuous 'tent' roof to cover a number of venues and supported by masts rising through the surface. This configuration resulted in many parts of the roof being too flat, and therefore likely to deform under prestressing of the net and

under wind and snow loads, greater curvatures being more efficient and stable. Adding more masts to achieve greater curvature of the net threatened to compromise the flexibility of the interior spaces and dilute the clarity of the overall concept. In the design as executed, the three sites are roofed as independent structures covering a total area of 74,000 square metres (800,000 sq. ft.).

A more promising solution created sufficient curvatures in the roof surface by supporting it with guyed masts, set at a number of points beyond its edge, and by dividing the whole roof surface into many smaller sections coupled together. Rather than having the roof surface propped up high as by a tent pole, a more efficient proposal proved to be to suspend it from a separate system of cables hung from tall masts, thus freeing the internal spaces from obtrusive structure.

The design of the Olympic Stadium roofs began before the widespread availability of the now-commonplace computing techniques for such calculations, although the techniques used proved advanced enough to help work out the geometry of the athletics stadium roof under prestressing of the net. Otherwise, the process began with simple physical models, using polyester mesh fibre for the roof membrane, wires to form the nets and steel bars for the masts, which helped to establish preliminary

calculations and dimensions. The next stage of measuring the mechanical performance of the roof net was the building of a set of 1:125 scale models in the Institute on a test bench, encircled by a battery of Linhof cameras to record relative movements in three dimensions when loads were applied. Photogrammetric measurements were later used to refine the shape of the roof of the swimming pool without recourse to scale models.

These models needed to be exactly proportional in their geometry and elasticity to the structural prototype, because they helped to size each of its structural members when it was prefabricated. The difficulties of modelling were compounded by the fact that final geometry of the structural members and the structural force acting on them were not yet known. Absolute accuracy was not to be expected from hand-made soldered models, and the penalties for errors in calculating the length of components of cable net structures were severe in terms of extra stresses created.

But in practice, turning the rough models into a buildable project proved to be akin to bespoke tailoring. A total of 3800 square metres (41,000 sq. ft.) of pattern plans – scale drawings of the net surface – were drawn out at 1:10 scale. These defined the exact dimensions of all cables, fittings and intersection points for manufacture and assembly.

The Munich cable net comprises a square mesh on a 75 cm (30 in.) grid, and 210 km (130 miles) of cable in all, made up of nineteen heavily galvanized wires, secured by aluminium cramps at their intersections. The net forms an accurately sized and a stable material to drape over the double-curved roof surfaces, which are supported from masts and external guys. Panels of acrylic plastic sheet are fixed above the net surface to provide weather protection.

The nets were assembled on the ground before being lifted into position, followed by the suspension cables, and the stresses checked within the whole system, with adjustments made at the end of the net cables or at the anchorages of the suspension cables.

Munich proved to be a turning-point from which laborious, experimental methods of resolving the design of tensile structures began to be replaced by evolving computing techniques. However, the largely intuitive approach of the Stuttgart Institute, translated through physical models, had already delivered real innovations in the field.

Key Facts

Architects: Bligh Lobb, a joint venture of Bligh Voller Nield

Engineers: Sinclair Knight Merz; Modus Group

Area of site: 16 ha (38 acre)

Seating capacity: 120,000 (Olympics) 80,000 (post-Olympics)

Span and height of arch: 295 x 70 m (970 x 230 ft.)

Cost: AUS$600,000,000

RIGHT The stadium under construction with the two giant structural arches clearly visible.

BELOW Night view across water terraces, at the front edge of the stadium's entrance plaza.

Bligh Voller Nield

One of Australia's most potent architectural forces, Bligh Voller Nield Architects was formed by the merger of four firms – Bligh Voller, Lawrence Nield & Partners Australia, Grose Bradley, and Pels Innes Neilson & Kossloff. Their combined portfolio includes universities (University of the Sunshine Coast); airports (Brisbane Terminals); medical, research and corporate buildings; and the design of the Cook and Phillip Park in Sydney. Their work is known for its creativity and its powerfully modelled forms.

The practice has a considerable record in the masterplanning of sports venues and campuses, including that of the 2000 Olympics in Sydney and the Hellinikon Masterplan for the 2004 Olympics in Athens, as well as in the design of award-winning sports buildings such as the Sydney International Tennis Centre.

Telstra Stadium

Sydney, New South Wales, Australia, 1996–99

The centrepiece of the 2000 Olympic Games in Sydney, Telstra Stadium (formerly Stadium Australia) can lay claim to being the largest and best equipped of its breed ever built. With a seating capacity of 120,000 during the Olympics or 80,000 as currently used, and a scale that can be judged from the fact that four Boeing 747 aircraft could fit side-by-side under the span of its main arch, this facility is also notable for its in-built flexibility. It is capable of being changed from being a Rugby League venue on one day to a cricket or Australian Rules football arena on the next. From its pre-Olympic opening in March 1999 and even after the Games, Telstra Stadium has achieved benchmark status as a world-class venue, yet one with a distinct nod towards the nation's climate and sporting heritage.

The 16 hectare (38 acre) stadium site is ringed by its own green belt of 440 hectares (1060 acres) of 'Millennium Parkland' and is supported by 10,000 parking spaces near by, as well as by rail, bus and ferry services. Half a million cubic metres (654,000 cubic yards) of soil – a total of 90,000 lorry-loads – were moved to cut and fill the site; five drilling rigs sunk to the shale bedrock the 1800 piles needed to support the stadium, with a further 800 beneath the temporary end stands. On top of these piles, concrete footings and thrust blocks up to 2 m (6.5 ft.) thick form the building's foundations. The four thrust blocks receiving loads from the 300 m (990 ft.) main arches that support the roof canopy are six storeys high, weigh more than 140 tonnes each and are, not surprisingly, heavily reinforced.

Telstra Stadium's most visible important innovation lies in the design of its roof. Although there are contemporary examples worldwide that employ a similar parabolic roof form, such as the 80,000-seater Stade de France (1998) in Paris, the Sydney facility needs to provide shade from the harsh sun while minimizing sharp contrasts and shadows on the pitch, and achieving the most favourable conditions for television broadcasting. Its 3 hectares (7 acres) of roof are shaped as a curvilinear, hyperbolic paraboloid shape, pitched up in the form of two white shells with echoes of Sydney Opera House or, as some have put it, of the Australian slouch hat. The roof covering is formed by 10 m x 10 m (33 ft. x 33 ft.) polycarbonate tiles of varying opacity separated by a grid of stainless-steel drainage gutters, supported by a sub-framework flexible enough to allow for thermal changes. The translucency of the roof suits Australian conditions by maximizing daylight while providing effective protection from the sun and rain to more than 80% of the spectators. In this respect, the stadium manages to avoid the claustrophobic atmosphere so often associated with closed-roof

venues, which can also suffer from the further disadvantage of unsatisfactory turf growth.

Following its use at maximum capacity for the Olympics in 2000, the stadium was reconfigured to its current all-seated layout by removing the two upper stands at either end of the ground; the playing area can be changed between oval and rectangular, and the seating moved by means of hydraulic rams to suit the particular sporting event ahead. Spectator dynamics played their part in the design process, resulting in such bold, direct solutions as the four giant ramps; these not only provide visual anchorage to the oversailing roof but also serve as a highly efficient means of evacuating spectators rapidly down to ground level in the event of fire and of accessing the upper levels by service vehicle. Further innovations include the use of light voids that push daylight down into the innards of the stadium and thus reduce the energy burden of artificial lighting.

In the evening, dramatic lighting comes into its own, notably from the Olympic Plaza pylons: nineteen steel lighting columns each named after an Olympic city and topped by 'flying saucer' luminaires. These support solar panel arrays to power the lights that illuminate the plaza by night: a particularly pleasing example of low-key sustainable energy use amid the superlatives of the stadium.

BELOW An evening fixture in progress at Telstra Stadium, with a full-capacity crowd.

Key Facts

Architects: Foster & Partners with HOK Sports

Structural engineers: Connell Mott MacDonald

Contractors: Multiplex

Height and span of arch: 133 m x 315 m (435 ft. x 1035 ft.)

Circumference of stadium: 1000 m (3280 ft.)

Capacity of stadium: 90,000

Cost of stadium, site and development: UK£757,000,000 (stadium UK£353,000,000)

Foster & Partners

A truly international practice in scope, reputation and buildings, Foster & Partners has become synonymous with the ability to design and deliver projects at scales varying from city masterplans to a range of door furniture. Their work is characterized by the confident use of a design language that has been refined through three decades of high-profile buildings.

The work of the practice has combined corporate architecture, such as the headquarters for the HSBC Bank in Hong Kong and London and for the Commerzbank in Frankfurt, with major public buildings and spaces including the new German Parliament in Berlin, and in London the Great Court of the British Museum and the recent recasting of Trafalgar Square. The Metro in Bilbao in Spain and Chek Lap Kok Airport in Hong Kong (see pages 42–45) are examples of the practice's involvement in the area of transport and communications.

Wembley National Stadium
London, England, 1996–2006

ABOVE The great arch is intended to be a new landmark; as this visualization shows it will be visible from many miles away.

BELOW Sectional views of the stadium showing the dish-shaped arena bowl (left) and the clear-span arch supporting the suspended roof structure (right).

"The church of football" was how Pelé, one of the world's greatest footballers, described London's Wembley Stadium: "the capital of football and the heart of football". Once forming part of the British Empire Exhibition of 1924, designed by Sir John Simpson and Maxwell Ayerton, with Sir Owen Williams as structural engineer, the stadium had acquired a patina of reverence and respect not accorded to other notable buildings on the exhibition site. Wembley was the venue of choice for international footballing contests such as the 1966 World Cup, the

1968 European Cup Final and the European Championships of 1996. Its atmosphere was also legendary – the famous 'Wembley roar' – and its twin towers a landmark on the north London skyline.

But in the company of such shiny new sports venues as the Stade de France in Paris or Sydney's Telstra Stadium (pages 178–79), Wembley could never offer sports and music fans a competitive array of on-site facilities. Today, in particular for income-generating corporate sponsors, these need to include banqueting halls, pre-function gathering spaces and

state-of-the-art provision for media coverage. Such facilities formed part of the brief for the new Wembley National Stadium, designed as the largest all-seated football and rugby stadium in the world to offer a roof over *all* its 90,000 seats; in addition, it had to be able to host major athletics events with a capacity of up to 75,000 spectators, equal to that of the Stade de France and marginally greater than that of the Athens Olympics 2004 Stadium. As with any multi-function brief of this kind, a balance needed to be struck to maximize spectator sightlines for each different sport; but to include provision for occasional major athletics events at the National Stadium made better economic sense than building an additional permanent facility near by. To host athletics events, a heavy-duty temporary platform structure will be built using a prefabricated steel 'kit of parts', as typically deployed for Formula One motor racing circuits, although with platform erection likely to take up to ten weeks, such switching of sports is not contemplated casually.

Wembley Stadium, although much-loved, was also cramped and spartan. By comparison, the National Stadium will offer each spectator almost a third more personal space, with wider seats and greater legroom; more than 2000 toilets; 300 dedicated viewing positions for the mobility-impaired; and escalators to speed spectators to the upper levels. A giant concourse encircling the building will provide catering for up to 40,000 people at any one time. Yet the most notable improvements relate to spectator enjoyment – steep raking of the seats and a tuning of plan geometry ensure that everyone will enjoy an unobstructed view of events below; bringing seats as close to the pitch as possible will heighten the sense of involvement and help to reinforce the 'Wembley roar', as predicted by acoustic modelling tests.

Aside from the drama of the circulation areas, the visible architecture of the National Stadium will focus on the scale and sweep of its partially retractable

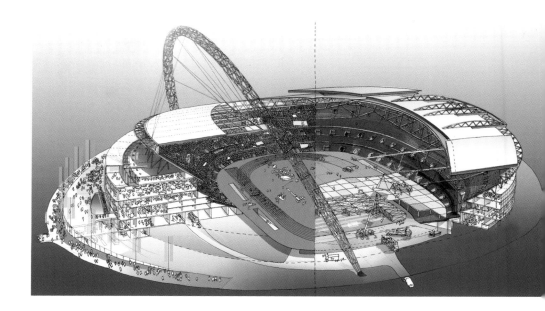

roof. When fully opened, it will allow sunlight to fall on the sacred turf of Wembley, but when the weather turns it will take a mere fifteen minutes to close the roof and cover all the spectator seats. Hung from a steel arch spanning 315 m (1030 ft.) and rising almost 135 m (440 ft.) above pitch level, the roof forms the world's largest clear-span structure for a stadium, yet uses only two-thirds the weight of steel required for a conventional trussed girder. The arch serves a further vital purpose, that of providing a replacement for the iconic twin towers of Wembley, loved by generations of spectators but impossible to retain in a meaningful way as part of the new stadium, despite a vigorous grass-roots campaign. Visible from central London and dramatically lit, the arch certainly has landmark potential by virtue of its rainbow-shaped profile, rather more so than the flatter arch structure used to support the roof of Sydney's Telstra Stadium. Above all, the Wembley arch stands for a new century in which national pride is signalled on giant electronic screens rather than raised on a flagpole above each of the twin towers. When the National Stadium opens for business in early 2006, a new Wembley tradition will begin with that unmistakable roar.

ABOVE Cut-away view of the stadium with the roof in the open position.

SuperStructures of Tomorrow

When science-fiction writers or film directors contemplated the future of urban life, they tended to do so in familiar images of multilevel intersections, airspace filled with personal 'autogiros' and 'stratoliners', and clusters of streamlined structures. Comics of the 1930s onwards presented an insistent, clamorous and mechanistic modernity to their readers, in which imaginary superstructures played a central role. The future was seen as an airbrushed and heightened version of the present, only larger.

Speculating today on what might lie ahead in the world of superstructures is a rather more complex matter, not only because we now have the technology to build almost anything from the pages of a comic that we might wish to, but also because we are rediscovering the art of urbanism, which should ultimately determine the way in which many potential superstructures respond to their settings. Is the next generation of structures likely to follow the patterns already established or are there developments ahead at which we can only guess? In reviewing the possibilities, we can first look again at some aspects of innovation in structural engineering during the twentieth and twenty-first centuries.

Alongside the practicalities of getting structures built, the discipline of structural engineering has always fostered imaginative schemes that stretch a particular hypothesis to its limit and yet also offer a version that can be realized. Richard Buckminster Fuller's geodesic domes came in several sizes, in theory; the largest proposed would have been able to enclose Lower Manhattan in New York, but the design embodied the same principles as those of the smaller domes actually built. Combining small repetitive structural units to enclose large volumes, as geodesic domes do, has generated one group of structures; spacedecks (three-dimensional structures used to cover large areas, theoretically unlimited in possible extent) are another, and potentially form a group of superstructures in their own right.

A further active strand of speculation that could generate its own family of superstructures is that explored by designers through the use of models – built for testing ideas rather than practical elements. Akin to a form of three-dimensional sketching, the miniature models made by such designers as the architect–engineer Santiago Calatrava explore the essence

LEFT NASA's nuclear-powered 'Prometheus' project, the Jupiter Icy Moons Orbiter, stands for a new generation of spacecraft that will be superstructures in their own right.

of potential structures and can later shape
the design of a great canopy roof or a bridge.
Model studies of junctions between materials, of
details, and of forms, have all sparked concepts
for full-size structures and will continue to do so
as each idea or hypothesis is tested.

Material World

Most of the materials used in structures are
familiar and well understood. Innovative designs
can be created by making better and more subtle
use of the materials we have to hand. High-yield
steel, lighter or better-performing concretes,
improved alloys and new composites are all
available to build structures that use material
more efficiently and can help promote more
elegant solutions, combining rigidity and
lightness. There are certainly challenges on offer
for the materials engineer, from improving the
strength of glass, through the wider application
of composite materials to the possibility of using
living plant species as building fabric.

Promising lines of development in materials
science are already in place; some are driven by
advances in such fields as aviation, where the
use of composites is becoming routine. These –
and other – possibilities are persuasively
presented by Adriaan Beukers of the Technical
University of Delft in the Netherlands in his
remarkable book *Lightness*, subtitled 'The
inevitable renaissance of minimum energy
structures'. Drawing upon the work of the
university's Faculty of Aerospace Engineering,
Beukers sets out the case for making use of such
materials as carbon-fibre-reinforced polymers,
which can outperform steel and have the
potential to allow the central span of a suspension
bridge to be dramatically increased, perhaps by
two or three times. In his account he describes
other new materials that can enclose space,
protect fragile contents or provide environmental
control. Their application at the scale of a major
structure is an exciting, open-ended prospect.

Evolving Prospects

Will a new breed of previously unheralded
superstructures emerge from the building types
we already know? A glance at the structures

presented in the Communications chapter of this book would suggest that such developments are likely to evolve. Airports, for example, are already facing the problems of great size, with ever larger aircraft in prospect and passenger orientation a real issue. We shall certainly see more designs that use some form of all-encompassing, oversailing roof to unify the passenger concourse, the best and boldest of which may well qualify as superstructures. In railway stations, likewise, concourses and platform halls present comparable opportunities for grand, sweeping enclosures that celebrate travel. Great stadiums and arenas will also evolve further as potential superstructures, driven by Beijing (2008) and succeeding Olympiads.

Great bridges will always lay claim for consideration as superstructures, since they are prominent, stand-alone designs for which the main structural options are well understood but where advances continue to be made. Distances spanned will increase still further, bridge profiles be lightened and structural design assumptions further refined. As British engineer Matthew Wells concludes his review of notable bridges, "[Bridge] structures will take on a level of attenuation and efficiency not seen previously." While the extent of these future innovations remains unknown, there are already bridges that indicate promising future directions, for example in large-scale cable-stayed designs, including the Millau Viaduct in France (pages 94–95) and Stonecutters Bridge in Hong Kong.

Rise of the SuperTower

Could the business buildings of the future become superstructures? Arguably not, in the most obvious sense of displaying their structure as a feature in its own right, as did Chicago's finest towers of the 1970s – the John Hancock and the Sears. More recent high-rise designs have hidden their frames behind cladding that has become either a smooth skin or a layered façade to mediate between inside and out. There is simply less scale-giving structure to be seen.

Of far greater interest as candidates for superstructures are those high-rise buildings that seek to reinvent the tower by enriching

TOP A rendering of Ove Arup & Partners' Stonecutters Bridge in Hong Kong indicates how effective this cable-stayed design will be in forming a harbour 'gateway' and responding to the scale of the seaway beyond. As well as designing the bridge, the practice is also contracted as the engineers responsible for the supervision of construction.

BOTTOM LEFT Australia's Enviromission Solar Tower project would be the world's first solar-powered conventional electricity generating station, drawing in warm air at the base of a huge chimney to drive its 32 turbines. It will generate enough electricity to power 200,000 homes.

BOTTOM RIGHt With its integrated landscape, mixed uses and distinctive profile, Ken Yeang's Nara Tower in Malaysia exemplifies the architect's innovative approach to the design of sustainable high-rise structures.

its content and form, on the model of Ken Yeang's 'bioclimatic' skyscrapers in Malaysia or Frankfurt's Commerzbank Headquarters by Foster & Partners. There is undoubtedly real promise in designs such as these, which incorporate great garden atriums or landscape platforms.

In structural terms there are no immediate limits on building higher than, for example, the 508 m (1,667 ft.) of Taiwan's Taipei 101 Tower, 2004, apart from the logistics of managing what is a vertical city in its own right, but urban high-rise superstructures of the future will need to provide fresh and convincing solutions to the problem of how they meet the city at their base. The likely impacts of these structures on microclimate, transport systems and the life of the street are still not fully understood. Resolving such questions will generate a whole range of design solutions in which the form of the tower will be enriched, its content more varied, and its profile as distinctive as those of the leading entries in the recent competition for the World Trade Center site ('Ground Zero') or as intriguing as the sketches of a future downtown Philadelphia made by the great American architect Louis Kahn in the late 1960s.

In these studies Kahn developed generic forms for his towers that broke away from familiar orthogonal geometry to embrace the alternative possibilities of isosceles triangles, creating a family of high-rise buildings that rose as cranked platforms instead of smooth shafts. While these were only concepts without real-life clients, they did point out a direction that the urban tower might take in the future. There are even echoes of these possibilities among the World Trade Center site competition entries.

Whatever the particular outcome for Ground Zero, we can be confident that there remains vigorous life in the concept of the high-rise building, and that such imperatives as the need to protect structures of this magnitude against terrorist threat, to ease vertical circulation and to provide the appropriate treatment of the ground level will be resolved. It is a certainty that high-rise superstructures will continue to be mooted and that their appeal will remain

TOP A whole neighbourhood being built offshore, Dubai's Palm Island project shows how civil engineering can help to realize the most imaginative of designs.

CENTRE Santiago Calatrava's concept for the Transport Hub at the World Trade Center makes use of wing-like structural forms to give greater scale and presence.

BOTTOM With its many segmented mirrors forming a huge reflecting surface, the Overwhelmingly Large Telescope, as the biggest terrestrial telescope in the world, promises to deliver unprecedented images of the cosmos.

undimmed by counterarguments of practicality and economics. The relevant technology to support the high-rise is already in place – sophisticated damping mechanisms can reduce sway at their summits, building management systems can allow more personal control of the working environment and energy consumption can be further lowered. What we now await is a radical reinvention of the form of the tower.

Beyond Buildings

Our presentation of superstructures has included those that do not fall within the usual definitions of civil engineering or architecture. It is in such works, perhaps, that a crop of new superstructures can be expected, because their scale can be readily increased to that of the landscape. While not a single structure in any conventional sense, Dubai's Palm Island project now under construction involves the development of a new residential district more than 5 km (3 miles) in diameter, built in the waters of the Gulf, and large enough, it is claimed, to be visible from space.

Ever larger radio telescopes, great wind farms and banks of solar arrays are planned or in progress. In Australia a giant solar generator more than 915 m (3000 ft.) high, designed by Jörg Schlaich of Schlaich, Bergmann & Partners, is proposed, while the Overwhelmingly Large Telescope (OWL), 100 m (330 ft.) in diameter, for the European Southern Observatory, is planned to enter service in 2015. These will undoubtedly rank as superstructures in the future.

In celebrating the size, complexity and history of our superstructures and of the teams that designed and engineered them we should also salute engineering achievement at the micro scale, because innovation here can deliver dramatic benefits for many. The design of a successful low-cost unit that could at a stroke simplify the workings of a sites-and-services housing project, for example, or a new construction system entirely sourced from locally available materials, might equally qualify as superstructures. Structures at both scales embody the essence of engineering – a creative response to a real-world problem.

Further reading

Listed below are books and some journal articles in which you will find further information about the superstructures explored in this book. For ease of reference, this list of further reading (which is not intended to be comprehensive) is organized by superstructure. Some of the super-structures in this book are not included below, simply because there is little in print about them, but you will find information about these and all the others featured by searching on the Internet.

188

Waterloo International Terminal, London, England
pp. 18–19
Angus J. MacDonald, *Anthony Hunt*, London (Thomas Telford) 2000
Rowan Moore (ed.), *Structure, Space and Skin: The Work of Nicholas Grimshaw & Partners*, London (Phaidon) 1993

Oriente Station, Lisbon, Portugal
pp. 20–23
Martha Thorne (ed.), *Modern Trains and Splendid Stations: Architecture, Design, and Rail Travel for the Twenty-first Century*, London (Merrell) 2001
Anthony Tischhauser and Stanislaus von Moos (eds.), *Calatrava: Public Buildings*, Basel, Berlin and Boston (Birkhäuser) 1998
Alexander Tzonis, *Santiago Calatrava: The Poetics of Movement*, London (Thames & Hudson) 1999

Lehrter Station, Berlin, Germany
pp. 24–27
Anthony Holgate, *The Art of Structural Engineering: The Work of Jörg Schlaich and His Team*, Stuttgart (Axel Menges) 1998
Duane Phillips and Alexandra Geyer, *Berlin: A Guide to Recent Architecture*, London (Batsford) 2003
Martha Thorne (ed.), *Modern Trains and Splendid Stations: Architecture, Design, and Rail Travel for the Twenty-first Century*, London (Merrell) 2001
John Zukowsky, *The Architecture of Von Gerkan, Marg and Partners*, Munich, London and New York (Prestel) 1997

Jubilee Line Extension, London, England
pp. 28–31
Colin Davies, *The Work of Michael Hopkins and Partners, Volume 2*, London (Phaidon) 2001
Foster: Catalogue 2001, Munich, London and New York (Prestel) 2001
Richard MacCormac, *MacCormac Jamieson Pritchard – Architectural Monograph*, London (John Wiley & Sons) 2004
Kenneth Powell, *The Jubilee Line Extension*, London (Laurence King) 2000
Kenneth Powell, *New London Architecture*, London (Merrell) 2001

TWA Flight Center, JFK International Airport, New York, USA
pp. 36–39
Antonio Román, *Eero Saarinen: An Architecture of Multiplicity*, New York (Princeton Architectural Press) and London (Laurence King) 2002
Rupert Spade, *Eero Saarinen*, London (Thames & Hudson) 1971
The TWA Terminal: Photographs by Ezra Stoller, intro. by Mark Lamster, New York (Princeton Architectural Press) 1999

Haj Terminal, Jeddah, Saudi Arabia
pp. 40–41
Skidmore, Owings & Merrill: Architecture and Urbanism 1973–1983, intro. by Albert Bush-Brown, London (Thames & Hudson) 1984

Hong Kong International Airport, Chek Lap Kok, Hong Kong
pp. 42–45
Foster: Catalogue 2001, Munich, London and New York (Prestel) 2001
David Jenkins (ed.), *On Foster ... Foster On*, intro. by Deyan Sudjic, Munich, London and New York (Prestel) 2000

New Area Terminal, Barajas International Airport, Madrid, Spain
pp. 46–49
Kenneth Powell, *Richard Rogers: Complete Works, Volume Three*, London (Phaidon) forthcoming

Cardington Hangars, Bedfordshire, England
pp. 50–51
Nikolaus Pevsner, *Bedfordshire and the County of Huntingdon and Peterborough*, The Buildings of England, London (Penguin) 1968

CargoLifter Airship Hangar, Brand, Germany
pp. 52–53
Sara Hart, 'Buckminster Fuller's dreams of spanning great distances are being realized in big projects', *Architectural Record*, vol. 190, no. 5, May 2002, pp. 267–76
Michele Janner et al., 'The CargoLifter Hangar in Brand, Germany', *Arup Journal*, vol. 36, no. 2 (millennium issue 6), 2001, pp. 24–31
Andy Pearson, 'Shed Zeppelin', *Building*, vol. 265, no. 8145 (28), 14 July 2000, pp. 48–50

Yokohama Port Terminal, Yokohama, Japan
pp. 56–59
Simon Alford, 'Ticket to Ride', *Architects' Journal*, vol. 9, no. 216, 12 September 2002, pp. 24–31
Foreign Office Architects, *The Yokohama Project*, Barcelona (Actar) 2002

Falkirk Wheel, Falkirk, Scotland
pp. 60–63
Marcus Fairs, 'Falkirk's Millennium Wheel Starts to Roll', *Building*, vol. 265, no. 8156 (40), 6 October 2000, pp. 18–19
'The Falkirk Wheel: A Rotating Boatlift', *Structural Engineer*, vol. 80, no. 1, 2 January 2002, pp. 11–12
Victoria Madine, 'You say you want a revolution', *Building*, vol. 267, no. 8229 (14), 12 April 2002, pp. 20–23

The Channel Tunnel, Folkestone, UK–Calais, France
pp. 64–67
Graham Anderson and Ben Rostrow, *The Channel Tunnel Story*, London (Spon) 1994
Colin J. Kirkland (ed.), *Engineering the Channel Tunnel*, London (Spon) 1995

Bridges:
Transporter Bridge, Middlesbrough, England
pp. 70–71
Albert-Louppe Bridge, Plougastel, France
pp. 72–73
Sydney Harbour Bridge, Sydney, New South Wales, Australia
pp. 74–75
Salginatobel and Schwandbach Bridges, Switzerland
pp. 76–77
Bailey Bridges, worldwide
pp. 78–79
Ganter Bridge, Eisten, Valais, Switzerland
pp. 80–81
Alamillo Bridge, Seville, Spain
pp. 82–83
Pont de Normandie, Honfleur–Le Havre, France
pp. 84–87
Erasmus Bridge, Rotterdam, The Netherlands
pp. 88–89
Øresund Link, Copenhagen, Denmark–Malmö, Sweden
pp. 90–93
Millau Motorway Viaduct, Tarn Valley, France
pp. 94–95

David Bennett, *The Creation of Bridges*, London (Aurum) 1999
David P. Billington, *Robert Maillart's Bridges: The Art of Engineering*, Princeton NJ (Princeton University Press) 1979
David J. Brown, *Bridges: Three Thousand Years of Defying Nature*, London (Mitchell Beazley) 1993
Bernhard Graf, *Bridges that Changed the World*, Munich, London and New York (Prestel) 2002
Bernard Marrey, *Les Ponts modernes: 20e siècle*, Paris (Picard Éditeur) 1995
Alexander Tzonis, *Santiago Calatrava: The Poetics of Movement*, London (Thames & Hudson) 1999
Matthew Wells, *30 Bridges*, intro. by Hugh Pearman, London (Laurence King) 2002

Chain Home Radar Towers, England
pp. 96–97
Robert Buderi, *The Invention that Changed the World: How
    a Small Group of RADAR Pioneers won the Second World
    War and Launched a Technological Revolution*, New York
    (Touchstone Books) 1997

Torre de Collserola, Barcelona, Spain
pp. 98–99
Kenneth Powell, *Telecommunications Tower, Barcelona.
    Architect: Sir Norman Foster and Partners*, trans.
    Carmen Hernandez, Blueprint Extra 06, London
    (AA Publications) 1992

Dams of the TVA, Tennessee, USA
pp. 104–07
*Built for the People of the United States: Fifty Years of TVA
    Architecture*, exhib. cat., ed. Marian Moffett and
    Lawrence Wodehouse, Knoxville, Art and Architecture
    Gallery, University of Tennessee, 1983
Walter L. Creese, *TVA's Public Planning: The Vision, the
    Reality*, Knoxville (University of Tennessee Press) 1990
Julian Huxley, *TVA: The Adventure in Planning*, Cheam
    (Architectural Press) 1943

Dams:
Aigle Dam, Dordogne, France
pp. 108–09
Aswan High Dam, Egypt
pp. 110–13
Three Gorges Dam, Sandouping, Yichang, China
pp. 114–17

Dams, London (Thomas Telford) 2000
Tom Little, *High Dam at Aswan: The Subjugation of the
    Nile*, London (Methuen) 1965
Dai Quing, *The River Dragon Has Come!: Three Gorges Dam
    and the Fate of China's Yangtze River and Its People*, ed.
    John G. Thibodeau and Philip Williams, trans. by Ming Yi,
    (M.E. Sharpe; East Gate Books) 1998

Freudenau Hydroelectric Power Station, Vienna, Austria
pp. 118–19
Perpectiven (special issue: *Kraftwerk Freudenau –
    Energieversorgung*, articles by Knut Leitner *et al.*), no. 1,
    1997, pp. 8–64, 68–72

Venice Flood Defences, Venice, Italy
pp. 122–23
Austin Williams, 'Making Waves', *Architects' Journal*,
    vol. 217, no. 13, 3 April 2003, pp. 38–40

Dutch Sea Barrier, Eastern Scheldt, The Netherlands
pp. 124–27
John B. Herbich, *Handbook of Coastal Engineering*, New
    York (McGraw-Hill) 2000

Thames Barrier, London, England
pp. 128–31
Stuart Gilbert and Ray Horner, *The Thames Barrier*,
    London (Thomas Telford) 1984
Elizabeth Williamson and Nikolaus Pevsner with
    Malcolm Tucker, *London: Docklands*, The Buildings of
    England, London (Penguin) 1998

Mulberry Harbours, Arromanches, France
pp. 134–35
Bertrand Lemoine, *Birkhäuser Architectural Guide:
    France: 20th Century*, Basel, Berlin and Boston
    (Birkhäuser) 2000

Lovell Radio Telescope, Jodrell Bank, Manchester,
England
pp. 140–41
Bernard Lovell, *Voice of the Universe: Building the Jodrell
    Bank Telescope*, New York (Praeger) 1987

Hubble Space Telescope, in orbit
pp. 146–47
Robin Kerrod, *Hubble: The Mirror on the Universe*, Toronto
    (Firefly Books) 2000

Full-Scale Wind Tunnel, Langley Research Center,
Hampton, Virginia, USA
pp. 148–51
James R. Hanson, *Engineer in Charge: A History of the
    Langley Aeronautical Laboratory*, Washington, DC,
    (Government Printing Office) 1987
Anthony M. Springer (ed.), *Aerospace Design: Aircraft,
    Spacecraft, and the Art of Modern Flight*, London
    (Merrell) 2003

Eden Project, St Austell, Cornwall, England
pp. 166–69
Hugh Pearman and Andrew Whalley, *The Architecture
    of Eden*, London (Transworld) 2003
Hugh Pearman, *Equilibrium: The Work of Nicholas
    Grimshaw & Partners*, London (Phaidon) 2000
Kenneth Powell, *New Architecture in Britain*, London
    (Merrell) 2003
Tim Smit, *Eden*, London (Bantam Press) 2001

Downland Gridshell, West Sussex, England
pp. 170–71
Kenneth Powell, *New Architecture in Britain*, London
    (Merrell) 2003
Derek Walker and Bill Addis (eds.), *Happold: The Confidence
    to Build*, London (Spon) 1998

Palazzetto dello Sport, Rome, Italy
pp. 172–73
Pier Luigi Nervi, *New Structures*, London (Architectural
    Press) 1963
Agnoldomenico Pica, *Pier Luigi Nervi*, Rome (Editalia) 1969

Olympic Stadium, Munich, Germany
pp. 174–77
Behnisch & Partner: Bauten und Entwürfe 1952–1974,
    Stuttgart (Verlag Gerd Hatje) 1983
Peter Blundell-Jones, *Günter Behnisch*, Basel, Berlin and
    Boston (Birkhäuser) 2000
Dominique Gauzin-Müller, *Behnisch & Partners: 50 Years
    of Architecture*, London (Academy Editions) 1997

Wembley National Stadium, London, England
pp. 180–81
Kenneth Powell, *New London Architecture*, London
    (Merrell) 2001

189

Glossary

arris A term usually referring to the edge formed by the meeting of two surfaces, often of different structural members. In the case of welded steel components, the sharp arris is sometimes ground down to produce a smooth, rounded edge.

best practice In the construction industry – as in many other fields of activity – a body of experience and precedents that form a set of working practices that are commonly accepted as sound, efficient and sustainable.

coffer dam A watertight shield used to create a dry working area in wet conditions within which a bridge pier can be cast or a retaining wall built.

cut-and-cover method A simple and economical technique of excavating a trough and then decking it over to form a shallow tunnel, often with a roadway at ground level. Many of the first underground railway lines, notably those following the alignment of major boulevards, were built by using this method.

concrete A hard, stone-like building mixture formed by adding water to cement, sand and aggregates (stones) and then allowing it to 'cure' (set). Concrete is a primary structural material of immense importance. It is used in many forms and finishes, notably:

    mass concrete A form of concrete, defined by its high curing temperature, that is ideal for use in high-load foundations, since it can support the weight of a structure without breaking, in compression, and is readily cast as a monolithic (one-piece) foundation.

    reinforced concrete While mass concrete is an ideal material where it is used in compression, it is weak under tension. One solution is to embed metal reinforcement bars or mesh into the concrete, which bond together to act as a single structural element. Fortuitously both the steel and the concrete expand at the same rate as the temperature rises during the curing process.

    prestressed concrete A further refinement of reinforced-concrete construction is to pre-tension the cables that are cast into the concrete or run within a structural beam, thereby building in resistance to the loads to be carried.

    in-situ **and precast concrete** *In-situ* concrete structures are cast in their final position. The concrete is poured into a mould (known as formwork or shuttering) and set in place. Precast concrete elements are made off-site, usually in factories, and transported into their final position.

    fair-faced concrete Unfinished, raw concrete, straight from the mould, which can have a strong aesthetic appeal. A great variety of effects can be achieved, depending on the surface finish of the formwork or shuttering, as well as on the aggregates of the concrete mix.

diaphragm Bridges and other concrete structures will often incorporate diaphragm walls as vertical elements that separate the bridge deck from the arch. Hence they act in compression, taking the load downward. Examples of use include the Westminster Jubilee line station (pp. 29–30) and the Albert-Louppe Bridge (pp. 72–73).

falsework A temporary structure, which is subsequently removed, supporting the formwork or shuttering required to cast the concrete in major structures such as bridges.

finger-joint When two pieces of timber need to be joined together to form a single length, each end can be machined to form finger-like prongs that interlock to form a joint of great strength when they are glued together. This technique is exemplified in the construction of the Downland Gridshell (pp. 170–71).

Hilti rivet A proprietary fixing system to join metal components, using a high-pressure gun and a patented design of rivet.

lugs A bracket attached to a (usually) metal structure to provide a fixing point for cables and other components. Bailey bridges (pp. 78–79) include many lug fixing points to enable sections to be manoeuvred or fixed together.

parallelepiped Sea defences often include breakwaters and walls faced with precast-concrete components shaped as parallelepipeds – six-faced solids with each face in the form of a parallelogram – that form a wave-breaking wall; four-armed components known as tetrapods may also be used. Parallelepipeds are being used in the sea defences of the Venice Lagoon (pp. 122–23).

pin-joint Joints between elements forming a structural framework can be either rigid (fixed in place) or pin-jointed (allowed to rotate). A simple example, the three-pinned arch, has pin-joints at the base and at the centre of the arch, but rigid joints at the elbows. An elegant use of this form is found in the Waterloo International Terminal (pp. 18–19), where pin-jointed roof trusses are boldly expressed.

purlin Most conventional roof structures are formed with rafters, members following the direction of the roof slope, and purlins, which run horizontally to provide intermediate support for the rafters, thus reducing the distance the rafters need to span and their overall dimensions.

scarf-joint A larger-scale variant of the finger-joint, in which the ends of the timbers are notched then glued, bolted or strapped together. This process was used to join together the finger-jointed timbers of the Downland Gridshell (pp. 170–71) to form long, continuous laths.

shutters or shuttering The mould into which concrete is poured until it sets or 'cures'. The shutter can be formed from a variety of materials – timber, steel and fibreglass among them – and, depending on its surface finish, can create different textural effects in the concrete surface. Careful planning of works can allow shuttering to be reused, most notably in the casting of bridge piers; those of the Øresund Link (pp. 90–93) were cast as a series of vertical 'lifts', with the steel shutters moving upwards for each. Undoubtedly the grandest use of shuttering ever was that of Eugène Freyssinet's huge timber shutter, floated out on barges, to cast each of the three arches of his Albert-Louppe Bridge (pp. 72–73).

soffit The underside of a bridge deck, floor or beam. In the case of a bridge, it can be a highly visible element that contributes to the aesthetics of the whole structure. This is especially when it can be seen from ground level, as in the Millau Viaduct (pp. 94–95).

stringer A long horizontal structural member, often part of a bridge, such as those forming part of the sections of a Bailey bridge (pp. 78–79).

thrust block At the points where great arches meet the ground, huge forces are created that are resisted by special foundations, or thrust blocks, which can absorb the loading. The thrust blocks are sized and shaped according to the loading involved. Their typical scale can be gauged from those supporting the twin arches of Sydney's Telstra Stadium (pp. 178–79).

transfer structure Building complexes often involve a vertical mix of functions, each of which has its own preferred structural module, varying from cellular rooms to concourses that need to be free of obstructive supports. Transfer structures are used to make such stacking possible, as is the case in the Westminster Jubilee line station (pp. 29–30), in which the cellular office building is set above the open box enclosing the station concourse.

triangulation Structures become particularly robust if they are 'triangulated' with diagonal structural members. The triangulated frames are more rigid, and 'lock' together as a set, redirecting the forces acting on the structure.

truss Open frameworks made up of relatively slender sections, often combined with cables in tension, to form a structure composed of triangles. They are typically used to support a roof or to provide rigidity for a glazed façade, and are usually fabricated in metal. Many of the structures presented in this book include some form of truss, examples being:

    bow-string truss Seen at Waterloo International Terminal (pp. 18–19), this type of truss takes a curved profile implied by the name.

    kipper truss Found in the New Area Terminal of Madrid Airport (pp. 46–49), this form of truss has a V-form profile and reinforces the glazed façades of the terminal piers.

Vierendeel structure or truss A large-scale beam, with no diagonal members, used to resist lateral as well as axial forces, and often used where large openings are required.

Index